Crucible of
Reconstruction

Crucible of Reconstruction

*War, Radicalism
and Race
in Louisiana*

1862–1877

Ted Tunnell

Louisiana State University Press
Baton Rouge and London

Designer: Albert Crochet
Typeface: Linotron Bembo
Typesetter: G & S Typesetters, Inc.
Publication of this book has been assisted by
a grant from the Andrew W. Mellon Foundation.

LIBRARY OF CONGRESS CATALOGING IN PUBLICATION DATA

Tunnell, Ted.
  Crucible of reconstruction.

  Bibliography: p.
  Includes index.
    1. Reconstruction—Louisiana.   2. Louisiana—Politics
and government—Civil War, 1861–1865.   3. Louisiana—
Politics and government—1865–1950.   4. Louisiana—Race
relations.   5. Afro-Americans—Louisiana—History—19th
century.   I. Title.
F375.T86   1984   976.3'061   84-7843
ISBN 0-8071-1181-3

For Peter and James

Contents

Maps

Acknowledgments

No scholar writes a book without the help of others. My greatest debt is to Leon F. Litwack. His guidance and support were of inestimable value in the course of research, writing, and revision. I am grateful to Letitia Lane for the maps as well as for proofreading the manuscript. Kenneth M. Stampp, Eric Foner, and Lawrence N. Powell read most of the chapters and the book is much the better for their comments. Clarence L. Mohr helped with the final revisions. Grace O'Connell proved a fine critic as well as an accurate typist. *Southern Studies* graciously permitted me to reprint my article "Free Negroes and the Freedmen: Black Politics in New Orleans During the Civil War," XIX (Spring, 1980). Libraries all over the country rendered valuable assistance, especially the Department of Archives, Troy H. Middleton Library, Louisiana State University, and the interlibrary loan staff of Southwest Texas State University Library in San Marcos. My editors at LSU Press proved unsparing in their assistance. Finally, I wish to acknowledge my debt to Laura and Marshall Coleman Twitchell, R. M. Twitchell, Bert Holland, and Clark Holland for their help with the section on Marshall Harvey Twitchell. Such mistakes as remain are, of course, my responsibility.

Part I

Wartime
Reconstruction

1862–1865

Prologue

Viewed from six miles above the earth in a modern jetliner, the Red River winds its way across north central Louisiana like a giant anaconda. Now are visible the meanders, islands, and cutoffs hidden from the motorist by the levees that line the river's shores. The town of Colfax reposes on the high east bank, about twenty-five miles above Alexandria. Founded right after the Civil War, it remains a quiet farm community with the ambiance of an earlier era. The business district, a row of storefronts opposite the railroad, calls to mind a turn-of-the-century photograph. Half a mile from the center of town near the grassy levee, across the street from the antique premises of the Colfax *Chronicle*, stands the Grant Parish courthouse. Its vaguely Mediterranean-modern lines and expensive-looking veneer seem more appropriate to Southern California than to this shady village setting. The visitor's eye quickly finds the historical marker near the corner of the building, easily readable from the road: "On this site occurred the Colfax Riot in which three white men and 150 negroes were slain. This event on April 13, 1873 marked the end of carpetbag misrule in the South." Actually, about 105 blacks died on that terrible Easter Sunday, and Reconstruction of course ended in 1877, not 1873. But these are mere quibbles; in the larger sense that matters the marker is true to history: Such were the means by which Louisiana whites overturned Reconstruction. Fifty miles up the Red River Valley, in the small town of Coushatta, another historical marker describes the 1874 execution-slaying of six white Republicans and the lynching of two Negroes in the parish jail.

Downtown New Orleans boasts the most imposing reminder of the "Tragic Era." In the center of a traffic island at the foot of Canal Street, directly in front of the ferry terminal, a white obelisk points skyward. Erected in 1891, it commemorates the Battle of Canal Street, renamed

I

the Battle of Liberty Place after Reconstruction. On September 14, 1874, on this very river front, the White League routed the Metropolitan Police and Radical governor William Pitt Kellogg's black militia. Inscribed on the memorial are the names of the White League captains and their comrades-in-arms who fell in the fight. A plaque in the ground, of recent date, assures the visitor that the triumph of white supremacy celebrated by this phallic stone is not the philosophy of modern-day New Orleans. Three hundred yards up Canal Street, plainly visible from the White League monument, the gray granite United States Custom House presides over the southwest corner of the French Quarter. Work began on this ponderous structure, which covers an entire city block, over a decade before the Civil War and remained uncompleted until after Reconstruction. This "unfinished shell, temporarily covered with a worthless roof," as a government architect put it, was the nerve center of Republican Louisiana and the scene of many a party intrigue. The Metropolitan Police made their last stand against the White League on the street out front and afterwards found refuge in the cavernous interior.[1] No historical markers grace this site.

Louisiana probably has the most intricate history of any Reconstruction state. At times the tale grows more tangled than the region's labyrinth of swamps and bayous. The North reconstructed Louisiana not once, or twice, but three times: wartime Reconstruction under Lincoln, from 1862 to 1865; presidential Reconstruction under Andrew Johnson, from 1865 to 1867; and Congressional or Radical Reconstruction, from 1867 to 1877. To some extent, Arkansas and Florida underwent similar trials, but nowhere did the length and complexity of events surpass the Louisiana experience.

Each shift of policy on the Potomac brought new actors center stage in New Orleans. General Nathaniel P. Banks, Thomas J. Durant, and Michael Hahn, the main figures during the war, either left the state after Appomattox or assumed lesser roles. The Unionist James Madison Wells ruled Louisiana in the Johnsonian phase but vanished into

---

1. Stuart Omer Landry, *The Battle of Liberty Place: The Overthrow of Carpet-Bag Rule in New Orleans, September 14, 1874* (New Orleans, 1955), 96–101, 228–30; *Senate Executive Documents*, 41st Cong., 2d Sess., No. 73, pp. 1–2.

near obscurity with the Reconstruction Acts. Carpetbaggers like Henry Clay Warmoth and William Pitt Kellogg dominated Radical Reconstruction but remained unheralded theretofore. Still, there was continuity in all this: It centered on the question of how and under what conditions Louisiana would return to the Union. Beginning in the spring of 1867, Republicans in Congress and in Louisiana answered that question in a way that people of the day defined as "Radical." Radical meant Negro suffrage and a commitment to a biracial society based on equality and justice. This book is about the fiery trial of war and reconstruction that produced that Radical solution and the black and white Republicans who called themselves Radicals.

New Orleans is a patch of dry ground ringed by vast expanses of open water and marshland. It sits in a crescent bend of the Mississippi River some ninety airline miles from the river's mouth. In late April 1862, Union warships slipped past the Confederate river forts and blasted the Rebel fleet guarding the city. Advancing overland, General Ben Butler's bluecoats occupied the Crescent City on May Day. For the duration of the war the stars and stripes waved over the Confederacy's largest city.

Reconstruction began almost immediately. President Lincoln encouraged the Union element in New Orleans to form a collaborationist regime and restore southeast Louisiana—and symbolically the entire state—to the Union. To Lincoln's chagrin, the loyal element proved to be a slow-moving lot. After much delay, the president announced the "Ten Percent Plan" in late 1863. This was a policy that allowed as few as 10 percent of the voters to form a loyal government. Under this scheme Lincoln and General Banks created the Free State government of Michael Hahn, a German immigrant, in the spring of 1864. The Ten Percent Plan also governed occupation policy in Arkansas, Tennessee, and Florida; but the regimes set up in those states never had the local backing and chances for success enjoyed by the Hahn government. Louisiana emerged as the principal test of the president's policy.

The history of the Louisiana regime has been written mainly by political historians interested in Reconstruction and only marginally concerned with how the North won the Civil War. In most accounts military and political events on the lower Mississippi occur almost in separate realms. Writers note General Banks's long absences from New Orleans as he fought Rebels in Texas, at Port Hudson, and on the Red River; but they treat them as mere interruptions in the story of Reconstruction. That the two realms, military and political, might be intimately related has seldom been considered. Such compartmentalized history treats Union victory as a foregone conclusion and Lincoln's Ten Percent Plan as a "search for an effective postwar policy." In this view, the purpose of the Hahn government was as a tentative model for postwar reconstruction.[2] There is, however, an alternative way of looking at the problem, namely, that Lincoln's Reconstruction policy was a part of overall Union strategy against the Confederacy. By luring states like Louisiana, Arkansas, Tennessee, and Florida back into the Union with a liberal Reconstruction plan, the president would weaken the South, strengthen the North, and hasten the end of the Rebellion.[3] The evidence is not conclusive either way, but to my mind the greater wisdom lies with the idea of the Ten Percent Plan as a war policy, not as a prescription for the postwar South.

Hindsight lends an aura of inevitability to the Civil War. A mountain of evidence shows that the North started to wear the South down, almost from the first shot at Fort Sumter. After Vicksburg and Gettysburg, it is a wonder that the Confederacy did not simply roll over and die. Contemporaries, however, saw events differently. The Northern press focused public attention less on the distant West, where the war was being won, than on nearby Virginia, where Union commanders suffered years of defeat and frustration at the hands of Robert E. Lee. In the late summer of 1864 the North's armies seemed stalled on every front. Lincoln and his closest advisors gloomily concluded that George B. McClellan would be the next president of the United States. Lincoln saw himself acting under a terrible time limit: He must save the Union before McClellan took office or the nation was lost. Only

2. Peyton McCrary, *Abraham Lincoln and Reconstruction: The Louisiana Experiment* (Princeton, 1978), xi, 3–18.

3. Herman Belz, *Reconstructing the Union: Theory and Policy During the Civil War* (Ithaca, N.Y., 1969), 277–78; Hermann Hattaway and Archer Jones, *How the North Won: A Military History of the Civil War* (Urbana, Ill., 1983), 686.

the church bells tolling the fall of Atlanta in early September lifted the pall of gloom that had settled over the president and the country. To contemporaries, in other words, the outcome of the war remained in doubt until near the end. Hence it seems most unlikely that Lincoln, in the years of greatest strife, fighting for his political life and the life of the nation, was overly concerned with the postwar South. Before he could truly reconstruct the Rebel states, he had first to defeat them.

The Radical Reconstruction that the North imposed on the South two years after the war was a unique moment, not only in the United States, but in the Western Hemisphere. Slavery was abolished throughout North America and South America in the nineteenth century. Only in the United States did emancipation lead to Negro suffrage, black office holding, and bitter fights in the political arena between ex-slaves and ex-masters. Southerners, white and black, who experienced these events would have been dumbfounded by the currently fashionable notion that Reconstruction was a staid and conservative affair.[4]

Radical Reconstruction raised vital issues that cut across the entire political economy of Louisiana and the South. The crux of the matter, however, was a question of cultural identity. The Reconstruction Acts, the Louisiana Constitution of 1868, and the laws of the Radical legislature defined Louisiana as a biracial society belonging to white and black alike. Louisiana whites at every social level recoiled in horror. Radicalism meant NEGRO RULE, AFRICANIZATION, and a WAR OF RACES. For generations whites had dreaded a day of reckoning when blacks would break their chains and rise above them. Now that day had come. Louisiana after 1867 became that "appalling world turned upside down," that "crazy nonsense world of black over white," that "anti-community which was the direct negation of the community as white men knew it."[5] With a unity they had denied the cause of Southern independence, whites rejected the Radical vision. "We hold this to be a Government of White People, made and to be perpetuated for the

---

4. C. Vann Woodward, "The Price of Freedom," in David G. Sansing (ed.), *What Was Freedom's Price?* (Jackson, Miss., 1978), 93–96, 109–110; Eric Foner, "Reconstruction Revisited," *Reviews in American History*, X (December, 1982), 91–92.

5. Winthrop D. Jordan, *White over Black: American Attitudes Toward the Negro, 1550–1812* (Chapel Hill, 1968), 114.

exclusive political benefit of the White Race," asserted the state Democratic party.[6]

No middle ground existed between two such polar positions, and the political rule book went out the window. From Andrew Jackson to Ronald Reagan the idea of "legitimate opposition" has generally guided American politics. The major parties and their leaders have accepted party competition as a natural and healthy part of government.[7] Beginning in 1860, however, the South emerged as the great exception. The one-party South had its roots in secession and in white rejection of the two-party South of Radical Reconstruction. Louisiana Radicals learned at considerable cost that their opponents regarded them not as lawful rulers, but as criminal usurpers. The Democrats sought not simply to vote the Republicans from office, but to destroy them and expunge them from the polity. The Knights of the White Camellia and the White League, the Louisiana versions of the Ku Klux Klan, acted sub rosa as the Democrats' military arm. With the ascent of the Republicans, Louisiana plunged into a crisis of legitimacy, a crisis that largely explains the violent Banana Republic character of state politics, including those desperate struggles that pitted Radical against Radical. In a situation in which bullets replaced ballots, Republicans' tactics against one another increasingly resembled Democratic tactics against Republicans. The struggle to resolve the crisis of legitimacy forms a central theme of Radical Reconstruction.

In recent years books and articles on Louisiana Reconstruction have assumed the proportions of a minor growth industry. Yet, surprisingly, the state's Radical leaders have remained curiously out of focus. Historians generally agree that the scalawags in Louisiana and other states were mainly the Unionists of 1861–1865. But who were the Unionists? And why did they side with the North against the great majority of their countrymen? The notion persists that carpetbaggers wielded more power in Louisiana than elsewhere in the South. How powerful were they in fact? How did they gain and maintain their au-

6. Kenneth M. Stampp, *The Imperiled Union: Essays on the Background of the Civil War* (New York, 1980), 264–69; Kenneth M. Stampp, *The Era of Reconstruction, 1865–1877* (New York, 1965), 78.

7. Richard Hofstadter, *The Idea of a Party System: The Rise of Legitimate Opposition in the United States, 1780–1840* (Berkeley, 1969).

thority and to what ends was their influence used? We know from the studies of David C. Rankin that the old free Negro class of New Orleans largely dominated black leadership in the state. What impact did these creoles of color have on Reconstruction? And what was their relationship with the freed masses? Harboring no delusions of definitiveness, I have addressed all of these questions and suggested answers.

In the final chapter the setting shifts from New Orleans to the Red River Valley, scene of the Colfax and Coushatta massacres. The view from the Crescent City, the state capital during Reconstruction, distorts events. The Radicals finally failed in Louisiana and other states, less because they lost State Houses and governorships than because the White League, the Red Shirts, and their kin overran places like Colfax and Coushatta. Had their bases in the hinterlands remained secure, defeats at the state level would have proved only routine, temporary setbacks. For this reason, I have narrated the rise and fall of a local Republican boss: the tragic story of Marshall Harvey Twitchell and of Red River Parish.

Although I have written about most aspects of Louisiana Reconstruction and tried to depict events about which much has been written in fresh perspective, the reader should be forewarned that this is not a complete history of the subject, nor even a complete political history. A full narrative of events from the capture of New Orleans to the downfall of the Radicals would require a volume twice the length of this one. In view of the books by Peyton McCrary, Joe Gray Taylor, and others, such a work is probably not needed. In any event, I have not written it. These pages may best be described as a series of related interpretive essays on themes that have not yet received the full attention they deserve. I will leave it to the reader to judge the result.[8]

8. Some of the primary sources quoted in this book are ungrammatical. Believing the insertion of brackets and [sic] to be disruptive, I have generally left the words as they were written. On rare occasions I have added punctuation and corrected minor spelling errors. Where quoted material is in italics, in every case the emphasis is in the original document and has not been added by me.

I

The Origins of
Unionism

For sixty miles before it empties into the salty water of Lake Borgne,
between Lake Pontchartrain and the Mississippi Sound, the Pearl
River forms the southernmost boundary of Louisiana and Mississippi.
At the time of the Civil War a Danish immigrant and coastal trader
named Christian Koch lived on the eastern shore with his family. In
the fall of 1864, from Rigolets, Louisiana, Koch wrote his wife about
the course of the war. He hesitated to spend any more money on their
home, he confided, because if the South should win it would be "impossible for us to remain, even if they would allowe us; At heart, there
is not a Union man in the whole country round, with the exception of
old Mr White and perhaps a few Dutchmen. . . . It would be no place
for us to live, esp so for ouer children." The situation in the North,
though, looked somewhat better, and the Dane believed that Lincoln
would be reelected: "If so perhaps we will yet have a home for ouer
old age, if not we may as well, make up ouer mind to lose every thing
we have, and move to the West, and begin the world again; it will be
hard . . . poor mother, but we will not therefore despair, we have
good children that will not leave us in ouer old age, and God knows
best how to fix things."[1]

Koch belonged to that class of Southerners who sided with the
North in the Civil War and called themselves Unionists. His words
reveal, about as well as words can, that his decision to be a Union man
was a hard one to live with. His letters do not explain his choice; they
simply reveal that he chose the Union.

The Civil War confronted Southerners with a terrible dilemma. It
forced them to choose, in the words of David Potter, between "two

1. Christian D. Koch to Annette Koch, September 28, 1864, in Christian D. Koch
and Family Papers, Troy H. Middleton Library, Louisiana State University, Baton
Rouge.

loyalties coexisting at the same time—loyalty to the South and loyalty to the Union," or, as Emory M. Thomas would have it, between their identity as Southerners and their identity as Americans.[2] Historians have been concerned mainly with the majority who resolved the dilemma in favor of the South and made war on the North. The concern here is with the minority who, like Christian Koch, resolved the conflict in favor of the Union.

Southern Unionism, an important chapter in the story of Southern dissent, represents a vital component of Reconstruction history. President Abraham Lincoln's entire effort at wartime Reconstruction hinged on cooperation between Unionists and Northern military commanders. Under Major General Nathaniel P. Banks, Louisiana Unionists established a loyal government in 1864 and wrote a new constitution that abolished slavery. Beyond that, Union men made up the great majority of white Southerners who joined the Louisiana Republican party after the war—the scalawags of Reconstruction legend. In one postwar investigation of Louisiana affairs, for example, over fifty scalawags from all over the state were questioned. No more than a dozen of these men had voluntarily supported the Confederate cause, and even this minority represented unenthusiastic Rebels. By comparison, at least thirty-five and probably forty had been uncompromising Unionists or, in a few instances, individuals who aided the Confederacy under duress.[3] One of the latter, a merchant from St. Helena Parish, when asked if he had been a Union man, replied, "I was until they fixed up a rope to hang me." The number of Unionists remains elusive; however, a rough idea is obtained by comparing the number of Louisiana whites who served in Confederate armies (about 56,000)

2. David Potter, *The Impending Crisis, 1848–1861* (New York, 1976), 450; Emory M. Thomas, *The Confederate Nation: 1861–1865* (New York, 1979), 3–5.
3. Carl N. Degler, *The Other South: Southern Dissenters in the Nineteenth Century* (New York, 1974); *House Miscellaneous Documents*, 41st Cong., 2d Sess., No. 154, Pts. 1 and 2. A growing consensus finds that Unionism was the basic determinant of scalawaggery throughout the South (see Frank Joseph Wetta, "The Louisiana Scalawags" [Ph.D. dissertation, Louisiana State University, 1978]; Sarah Woolfolk Wiggins, *The Scalawag in Alabama Politics, 1865–1881* [University, Ala., 1977]; Carl H. Moneyhon, *Republicanism in Reconstruction Texas* [Austin, 1980]; and Gordon B. McKinney, *Southern Mountain Republicans, 1865–1900: Politics and the Appalachian Community* [Chapel Hill, 1978]).

with the number who joined Union armies (about 5,000).[4] In other words, about one white male in eleven was a Union man.

Louisiana was probably the state in the deep South most divided over secession. In the presidential election of 1860 John C. Breckinridge (Southern Democratic party) won Louisiana's electoral vote but received only a plurality of the popular vote, 55 percent of which went to John Bell (Constitutional Union party) and Stephen A. Douglas (Northern Democratic party). In every other state on the Gulf Coast Breckinridge won substantial majorities.[5] The election, of course, was not exactly a referendum on secession. Many Democrats supported Breckinridge because of party discipline, and many who voted for Bell or Douglas were cooperationists or conditional Unionists. And in any event, the election of Lincoln—who received not a single vote in Louisiana and nine other Southern states—started an immediate shift toward secession. Nonetheless, the election in Louisiana was significant. However much Breckinridge avowed his devotion to the Union, he could not, as Allan Nevins has written, divest his party of its "disunionist aroma" nor alter the plain intentions of Southern fire-eaters to use it to bring about secession. Bell's candidacy, by contrast, reflected the desires of moderates in the South and the border states to avert a sectional crisis. Excepting Lincoln, Douglas' position was least ambiguous of all: He stood unequivocally for the Union. To suppose that the mass of voters ignored the underlying realities of the parties goes against the grain of common sense. The large vote for Bell and Douglas revealed a people who were notably reluctant to embrace disunion.[6]

Map 1 describes the election of 1860 in Louisiana. Maps 2, 3, and 4 show the secession election of January 1861 and the pattern of voting

4. *House Miscellaneous Documents*, 41st Cong., 2d Sess., No. 154, Pt. 1, p. 92; John D. Winters, *The Civil War in Louisiana* (Baton Rouge, 1963), 428; Frederick H. Dyer, *A Compendium of the War of the Rebellion* (Des Moines, Iowa, 1908), 11.

5. Official returns in the New Orleans *Daily Picayune*, December 6, 1860. Breckinridge's majorities are as follows: Texas (75.5 percent), Mississippi (58 percent), Alabama (54 percent), and Florida (62 percent) (W. Dean Burnham, *Presidential Ballots, 1836–1892* [Baltimore, 1955]).

6. Allan Nevins, *The Emergence of Lincoln* (New York, 1950), II, 282. See Potter, *Impending Crisis*; Ollinger Crenshaw, *The Slave States in the Presidential Election of 1860* (Baltimore, 1945); and Peyton McCrary, Clark Miller, and Dale Baum, "Class and Party in the Secession Crisis: Voting Behavior in the Deep South, 1856–1861," *Journal of Interdisciplinary History*, VIII (Winter, 1978), 429–57.

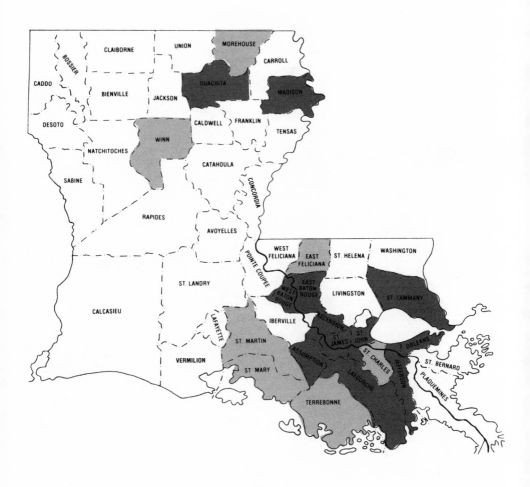

Map 1

Presidential Election in Louisiana, 1860

Total vote:
- Breckinridge 22,681
- Bell   20,204
- Douglas   7,625

☐ Breckinridge received majorities

◪ Combined vote of Bell and Douglas exceeded Breckinridge vote

■ Bell or Douglas received pluralities or majorities

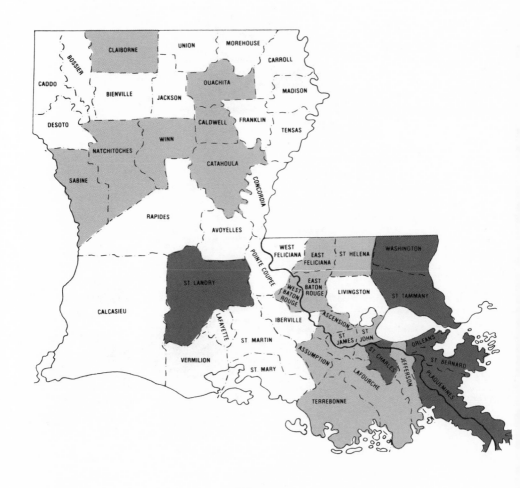

Map 2

Louisiana Secession Election, January 1861

☐ Elected entire delegation in favor of immediate secession

▨ Elected entire delegation opposed to immediate secession

◼ Elected divided delegations

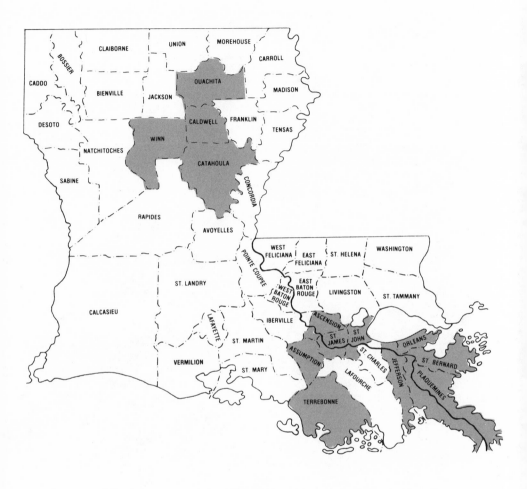

Map 3

Louisiana Secession Convention, January 1861

Seventeen delegates voted against the Ordinance of Secession. The shaded parishes are those they represented.

Map 4

Louisiana Secession Convention, January 1861

Nine delegates refused to sign the Ordinance of Secession.
The shaded parishes are those they represented.

within the secession convention. The four maps reveal a consistent pattern of opposition to disunion in three parts of the state: (1) an upstate region centered in the parishes of Winn, Ouachita, and Caldwell (and at times including Claiborne, Sabine, Natchitoches, Madison, and—though not shown by the maps—part of Rapides); (2) the sugar country of southeastern Louisiana along the Mississippi River, especially the parishes of Ascension, St. James, Assumption, and St. John the Baptist; and (3) New Orleans and its environs (Orleans and Jefferson parishes). Most wartime Unionists hailed from these areas.

It has been said that the great rivers and bottomlands of Louisiana form a giant alluvial Y in the center of the state. The Y is an irregular one, but the description is basically accurate. The western and narrow arm of the Y is formed by the floodplain of the Red River. The eastern, wide arm of the Y is created by the convergence of the Ouachita, Boeuf, Black and Mississippi rivers. Between the arms of the Y, somewhat to the left of center, lies Winn Parish, which, in antebellum times, was a region of rolling pine hills, mostly small farms, and comparatively few slaves. This was fertile ground for dissenters, and it nurtured Unionists in the Civil War, Populists in the 1890s, and socialists and Longites in the twentieth century. (Huey Long was born and raised there.) Here Bell and Douglas captured 58 percent of the vote, and in the secession election the Unionists trounced the opposition, 1,012 to 154. Nearly three years later, in the midst of war, a group of Winn farmers drafted a remarkable protest against Confederate rule and sent it to Major General Ulysses S. Grant at Vicksburg. Bearing seventy-two signatures, its major provisions asserted:

> That we have undoubted evidence that the Confederate States are designed to be very aristocratic and exceedingly oppressive in its form of government.
>
> That we hold no further allegiance to the Confederate States except when overpowered and compelled by the sword.
>
> That we believe the United States is the most democratic and best form of government now in existence.
>
> That we are certain the State of Louisiana did not secede from the United States Government by a vote of the people.
>
> That we have only been kept from our loyalty to the United States by the force of arms and oppression.

That we are willing to cordially welcome to our country the United States forces and flag of the Union.

In some degree, this protest showed resentment against the Confederate "Tax in Kind," which imposed an onerous 8 percent (later 10 percent) ad valorem tax on corn and other food staples, but more basically it dramatized the alienation of small farmers in a marginal region from slavery and the plantation system.[7]

Winn Parish, though, was an exceptional place. Most Unionists in upstate Louisiana were not alienated farmers, but small-town lawyers, planters, and editors from the alluvial bottomlands of Winn's neighboring parishes, Ouachita, Caldwell, Catahoula, Rapides, Jackson, and Claiborne. This north-central region produced a corps of loyalists who would form the nucleus of the Republican party in the area after the war. As one of them put it, becoming a Republican "was a kind of transition from being a Union man. I regarded the republican party all along as being the Union party." Their number included James Madison Wells, James G. Taliaferro (pronounced Tolliver), Wade H. Hough, Thomas S. and Isaac W. Crawford, Allen Greene, A. W. Faulkner, John Ray, John T. Ludeling, and W. Jasper Blackburn. Most of these men were lawyers, and all but two of them owned slaves (although only Wells ranked as a great planter). In the main, they had been old Whigs, but it was a Whiggery that owed as much to Alexander Hamilton as it did to Henry Clay. Thomas S. Crawford expressed it in an extreme form when he admitted that although he had acted with the Whig party before the war, he had never truly considered himself a Whig. "I claim to be a federalist of the old federal school."[8]

Opposition to disunion in southeastern Louisiana was tied to the

---

7. Roger W. Shugg, *Origins of Class Struggle in Louisiana: A Social History of White Farmers and Laborers During Slavery and After, 1840–1875* (Baton Rouge, 1939), 4; New Orleans *Daily Picayune*, December 6, 1860; Charles B. Dew, "The Long Lost Returns: The Candidates and Their Totals in Louisiana's Secession Election," *Louisiana History*, X (Fall, 1969), 369; *The War of the Rebellion: A Compilation of the Official Records of the Union and Confederate Armies* (Washington, D.C., 1880–1901), Ser. I, Vol. XXX, Pt. 3, pp. 732–33 (hereinafter cited as *OR*; unless otherwise indicated, all citations are to Series I); John Milton Price, "Slavery in Winn Parish," *Louisiana History*, VIII (Spring, 1967), 144–46; Thomas, *Confederate Nation*, 198; Winters, *Civil War in Louisiana*, 210.

8. *House Miscellaneous Documents*, 41st Cong., 2d Sess., No. 154, Pt. 1, pp. 203, 705; Appendix I, Table 1.

economics of the sugar industry. Unlike cotton planters, sugar planters had no delusions about sugar being king. The principal markets for Louisiana sugar were the states of the upper Mississippi Valley and the ports on the Atlantic seaboard. Between 1834 and 1861 over 78 percent of Louisiana's sugar went to those two areas. Moreover, the ability of sugar producers to compete in those markets depended, in part, on federal tariff protection. Except for slavery, sugar planters united on nothing else as on the need to maintain the protective tariff on sugar. With disunion, Louisiana sugar producers would compete on the world market with the more efficient growers of the Caribbean sugar islands. Until Lincoln's election, the great majority of sugar planters opposed secession.[9]

In the weeks following the presidential election, however, secessionism gained rapidly in the sugar parishes. A majority of the sugar country delegates at the secession convention were avowedly against immediate secession; when put to the test, however, they joined the militants and voted for disunion. Six sugar delegates voted against the ordinance of secession, but none of the six joined the diehards who also refused to sign it and voted against joining the Confederacy.[10] Lincoln's victory forced sugar planters to weigh the benefits of remaining in the Union against, as they perceived it, the possible or even probable loss of their slaves at some future date. The vote in the secession convention told the result.

The New Orleans area, the third center of Unionist strength, voted overwhelmingly for Bell and Douglas in 1860. In fact, Breckinridge ran a poor third in both Orleans and Jefferson parishes. But, as in the sugar country, Lincoln's triumph stoked the fires of the militants. In the secession election the immediate secessionists won twenty of twenty-five seats in New Orleans proper. To some extent, however, the closeness of the contests belied the disunionist sweep. The five vic-

9. J. Carlyle Sitterson, *Sugar Country: The Cane Sugar Industry in the South, 1753–1950* (Lexington, 1953), 178, 189, 205.

10. Dew, "Long Lost Returns," 358–69; Mary Lilla McLure, "The Elections of 1860 in Louisiana," *Louisiana Historical Quarterly*, IX (October, 1926), 697; Ralph A. Wooster, *The Secession Conventions of the South* (Princeton, 1962), 112n; Wynona Gillmore Mills, "James Govan Taliaferro (1798–1876): Louisiana Unionist and Scalawag" (M.A. thesis, Louisiana State University, 1968), 38.

torious senatorial candidates, all militants, received a total of 21,532 votes; the five losing senatorial candidates, all opponents of immediate secession, obtained 19,571 votes. The winner with the most votes received 4,327; the loser with the least votes gained 3,848. Moreover, in the environs of the city, the Right Bank of Orleans and Jefferson Parish, the opponents of immediate secession won all seven seats by overwhelming margins. In all, the New Orleans area sent twelve opponents of immediate disunion to the secession convention. Six of the twelve voted against secession, and five opposed ratifying the constitution of the Confederacy. In the end, only four refused to sign the ordinance of secession.[11]

As in the sugar parishes, economic considerations alone caused many persons in the Crescent City to doubt the wisdom of disunion. The history of New Orleans was the story of its strategic location near the mouth of the greatest river system on the North American continent. In 1860, 3,500 steamboats docked at its wharves, and the total value of its trade reached $324 million. Even if secession did not lead to war, the city's commerce might suffer irreparable damage. Perhaps the most dire threat, short of invasion, was the potential loss of northern financial backing. In the 1850s, as its trade with the upper Mississippi Valley declined proportionately to its total trade, New Orleans had concentrated on marketing the cotton and sugar of Texas, Arkansas, Mississippi, and the Louisiana interior. In 1860 it was the largest cotton market in the world; yet the credit and capital, the financial fuel that moved the crops from plantation to market, was supplied only partly by local banks. Louisiana's banking reserves—the largest in the South—were less than a quarter of New York's, which, indeed, had 38 percent more banking capital than the seven leading cotton states combined. In brief, the financial center of Louisiana and the South was in New York and, to a lesser extent, London. If the flow of Yankee credit should be cut off, New Orleans' reign as the cotton capital of the world would be imminently imperiled.[12]

11. New Orleans *Daily Picayune*, December 6, 1860; Dew, "Long Lost Returns," 362, 364–65; Wooster, *Secession Conventions*, 112n; McLure, "Elections of 1860 in Louisiana," 697; Mills, "Taliaferro," 38; *Ordinances Passed by the Convention of Louisiana* (New Orleans, 1861), 4–5.

12. Gerald M. Capers, *Occupied City: New Orleans Under the Federals, 1862–1865* (Lex-

The potential loss of trade represented only one aspect of the city's dilemma. In crucial respects, New Orleans was an anomaly in the secessionist South. The great strength of the disunionists in Louisiana (and throughout the lower South) was in cotton areas in which black slaves comprised 60 percent or more of the population. In New Orleans slaves made up only 8 percent of the people, and the total black population (counting free Negroes) was still less than 15 percent, a smaller proportion even than that citadel of agrarian radicalism, Winn Parish.[13]

The city's most pronounced peculiarity, however, lay in the fact that it was a metropolis in a plantation and village culture. A total of 181,354 people, 25.6 percent of Louisiana's general population and *43 percent of its white population*, lived in New Orleans and the adjacent cities of Carrollton, Jefferson, and Algiers (across the river). Baton Rouge, with 5,428 people, ranked as the second largest city in the state. Charleston, the next largest city in the Confederacy, was still small by comparison, with 40,000 inhabitants. The Southern people as a whole were notable for their homogeneity; the people of New Orleans were notable for their diversity. In the city proper, Irish, German, French, Swiss, and other immigrants made up 38 percent of the population (and another sizable segment counted one or both parents born abroad). The city was also home to thousands of people from the North; there were, in fact, more natives of New York and Pennsylvania than natives of any Southern state except Louisiana itself. The Yankees dominated the business community as well as the newspapers, public schools, and Protestant churches.[14] One of the most distinctive characteristics of the plantation South was the absence of a true middle class (the mass of citizens who owned no slaves were sub-

---

ington, 1965), 1–3; Harold D. Woodman, *King Cotton and His Retainers: Financing and Marketing the Cotton Crop of the South, 1800–1925* (Lexington, 1968), 30, 166–70.

13. Seymour Martin Lipset, "The Emergence of the One-party South—The Election of 1860," in his *Political Man: The Social Bases of Politics* (New York, 1959), 344–54; Potter, *Impending Crisis*, 502–505; *Eighth Census, 1860, Population*, 194–95.

14. *Eighth Census, 1860, Population*, 194–96; Capers, *Occupied City*, 6; William W. Chenault and Robert C. Reinders, "The Northern-born Community of New Orleans in the 1850s," *Journal of American History*, LI (September, 1964), 232–47; Robert C. Reinders, "New England Influences on the Formation of Public Schools in New Orleans," *Journal of Southern History*, XXX (May, 1964), 181–95.

sistence farmers). New Orleans, on the other hand, was a middle-class society of bankers, merchants, shopkeepers, mechanics, tradesmen, professionals, and free laborers. If plantations, cotton, and slaves were the preeminent symbols of Southern civilization, then New Orleans was an appendage of the middle-class North.

It is generally accepted, of course, that the Northern-born and foreign-born communities acted as a brake on the secession movement in the Crescent City. Moreover, Clement Eaton, Peyton McCrary, and Joe Gray Taylor have called attention to the Northern or foreign birth of such wartime figures as Thomas J. Durant, Benjamin F. Flanders, Michael Hahn, James G. Belden, and Anthony P. Dostie.[15] None of these accounts, however, fully assesses the significance of Northern and foreign birth as a factor in Unionism. Appendix 1 (Tables 1 & 2) contains biographical information on 172 Louisiana Unionists. The most significant statistic that emerges from these data is that 112 (65 percent) were born in the North or abroad. Add to this majority those Unionists born in the border slave states that sided with the North in 1861 (Missouri, Kentucky, Maryland, and Delaware), and the figures grow even more one-sided, 126 of 172 (73 percent). Most Unionists in Civil War Louisiana, in other words, were *outsiders*: men born and raised to young manhood in the North, or abroad, or in those parts of the upper South where slavery and the plantation system were weakest. With some variation, the pattern held true in every part of the state: in New Orleans, in the sugar country, and, with the exception of Winn Parish, in the north-central region. (The farmers of Winn represent the well-known exception that proves the rule: Excepting New Orleans, they lived in the area where the Peculiar Institution was most feeble.) Again with some variation, the pattern also characterized Union loyalists of every political coloration, from those whom historians have called Radicals, such as Thomas J. Durant, Charles W. Hor-

15. Charles B. Dew, "Who Won the Secession Election in Louisiana," *Journal of Southern History*, XXXVI (February, 1970), 18–32; Charles P. Roland, "Louisiana and Secession," *Louisiana History*, XIX (Fall, 1978), 389–99; Wooster, *Secession Conventions*, 101; Clement Eaton, *The Freedom-of-Thought Struggle in the Old South* (Rev. ed.; New York, 1964), 390–91; Peyton McCrary, *Abraham Lincoln and Reconstruction: The Louisiana Experiment* (Princeton, 1978), 96–97, 99, 125; Joe Gray Taylor, *Louisiana Reconstructed, 1863–1877* (Baton Rouge, 1974), 30.

nor, and Benjamin F. Flanders, to conservatives like Simeon Belden, Dr. Thomas Cottman, E. E. Malhiot, and Jacob Barker.[16]

This explanation accounts for most Unionists—but not all. William H. Hunt, Thomas P. May, James Madison Wells, John T. Ludeling, W. Jasper Blackburn, and James G. Taliaferro, for example, were all born in the seceder states and represent significant exceptions to the outsider pattern. Their number includes a principal founder of the loyal New Orleans *Times* (May), the governor under presidential Reconstruction (Wells), the chief justice of Louisiana throughout Radical Reconstruction (Ludeling), an associate justice of the Radical high court (Taliaferro), a congressman and state senator (Blackburn), and a state attorney general and secretary of the navy under President James A. Garfield (Hunt). Excepting May, all of these individuals were bulwarks of the Republican regime after the war.

On closer inspection, however, a familiar motif appears in the lives of these "exceptions." Although born in South Carolina, the eminent New Orleans attorney William H. Hunt lived most of his youth, from age ten to age eighteen, in Connecticut, first as a student at preparatory school and then as a student at Yale College. In the opinion of his son, the contrast between New Haven and Charleston, between slavery and freedom, between states' rights and Unionism, and between cavalierism and Puritanism made a great impact on him. From that time on he "was never again the Southerner but the American." In 1852 Hunt visited the Hudson River Valley of New York and met the woman who became his second wife; a decade later, in the midst of war, he built a summer home on the Hudson named in her honor.[17]

Contact with the North and intersectional marriage also emerges in the story of John T. Ludeling, the Louisiana-born son of a French emigrant father and a mother from Saint-Dominique. Ludeling studied at St. Louis University in Missouri and read law in his hometown of

16. As a check, I looked up the place of birth of sixty prominent Louisiana Rebels. The results came as no surprise, but the contrast with Unionists is nonetheless striking: Forty-six (76.6 percent) were born within the Confederate states, and thirty-three (55 percent) in the deep South states that went out of the Union in the first wave of · secession.

17. Thomas Hunt, *The Life of William H. Hunt* (Brattleboro, Vt., 1922), 56, 116–22, 134.

Monroe, Louisiana, with Isaiah Garrett (the same man who years later refused to sign the ordinance of secession). The 1860 census reveals that he married a New York woman, that his three-year-old son was born in New York, and that two other New Yorkers lived in his household.[18]

In 1861 Thomas P. May was a wealthy nineteen-year-old sugar planter in St. John the Baptist Parish. He had lived much of his boyhood abroad, most recently in St. Petersburg, Russia, from whence he had only lately returned because of the death of his eccentric father, who had been a follower of Charles Fourier and a close friend of Thomas J. Durant. May served briefly as a Rebel cavalryman in northern Mississippi but escaped down the Mississippi River in a skiff after the Federals captured New Orleans. George S. Denison, the agent of Secretary of the Treasury Salmon P. Chase, believed that he was the first citizen in occupied Louisiana to abandon slavery and adopt free labor on his plantation. Whitelaw Reid stayed with May in 1865 and found the young Unionist "measurably free from the ideas which slavery steadily instilled."[19]

Born in 1808 and named after the fourth president, James Madison Wells was the youngest son of a large and evidently very patriotic family (another son was named after Thomas Jefferson). He was orphaned at the age of eight and raised by an aunt, and he received a good education at a Jesuit college in Kentucky (even though the family was Episcopalian), then at a military academy in Connecticut, and finally at a law school in Cincinnati, Ohio. In Cincinnati Wells tutored in the law with an old-line Federalist named Charles Hammond, who, as editor of the Cincinnati *Gazette*, penned frequent attacks on slavery. Hammond failed to convert his pupil to antislavery, as evidenced by Wells's later acquisition of nearly a hundred bondsmen; however, the nation-

18. *Dictionary of American Biography*, XI, 488–89; U.S. Census, Manuscript returns, 1860, Population.

19. Whitelaw Reid, *After the War: A Tour of the Southern States, 1865–1866*, ed. C. Vann Woodward (New York, 1965), 227–28; George S. Denison to Salmon P. Chase, November 25, 1864, in "Diary and Correspondence of Salmon P. Chase," *Annual Report of the American Historical Association for the Year 1902* (Washington, D.C., 1903), II, 451–52 (hereinafter cited as *AHA Annual Rept.*); Joseph G. Tregle, Jr., "Thomas J. Durant, Utopian Socialism, and the Failure of Presidential Reconstruction in Louisiana," *Journal of Southern History*, XLV (November, 1979), 490.

alistic editor and jurist probably reinforced the patriotic catechism of the young man's early years. Wells returned to Louisiana and Rapides Parish around 1830, taking up a career as a planter and prominent local Whig. Evidently he never practiced law. In 1860, now one of the wealthiest men in the parish, he backed Stephen A. Douglas, believing that "the Little Giant" was the only candidate who could avert civil war. He remained a devout Unionist even after secession and the outbreak of war. Through the spring of 1863 the Confederates left him pretty much alone, and he stayed on his plantation outside Alexandria. On learning of the death of Stonewall Jackson, however, Wells incautiously expressed the hope that the hero would be buried "in a gum coffin, and that the bottom plank might be very thin, so that he might eat his way down to where it was intended that he should go." For that remark there was no forgiveness, and he fled into the uncharted thickets of Bear Wallow, a refuge for hunted Unionists and Confederate deserters. He engaged in a brief career as a guerrilla fighter or jayhawker, leading the motley inhabitants of the hideout in attacks on weakly guarded Rebel supply trains. By November even Bear Wallow was unsafe, and he fled with a handful of followers to New Orleans, where bigger things awaited him.[20]

W. Jasper Blackburn grew up in Randolph County, Arkansas, a small-farming region near the Missouri border with so few slaves (359 out of a population of 6,261) that, by comparison, Winn Parish was a pro-slavery fortress. A printer and editor by profession, he moved to Claiborne Parish in far northern Louisiana about 1848 and established the Minden *Herald*. In 1856 the *Herald* earned a place among the handful of newspapers in the South that boldly condemned the caning of Charles Sumner by Preston Brooks. Perhaps it was only coincidence, but not too long afterward Blackburn closed the *Herald*, moved to another part of the parish, and established the Homer *Iliad*. During the war the Rebels suppressed the *Iliad*, and Blackburn, like Wells, fled to the forest. Between himself and the disunionists "there is this differ-

20. Walter McGeehee Lowrey, "The Political Career of James Madison Wells," *Louisiana Historical Quarterly*, XXXI (October, 1948), 997–1008; Appendix I, Table 1; *Dictionary of American Biography*, IV, 202–203; *House Miscellaneous Documents*, 41st Cong., 2d Sess., No. 154, Pt. 1, pp. 580–81.

ence," he explained: "They worshipped slavery, and I never believed
in it, although I am a southern man. . . . They are not national in con-
tradistinction to sectional; they love the South more than the North,
and the State of Louisiana more than the United States. I have always
loved my country and worshipped the star-spangled banner."[21]

James G. Taliaferro, the last of this group, lived the first eight years
of his life in eastern Virginia at a time when the Founding Fathers still
ruled the state and the nation. His family moved to Mississippi and
then to Catahoula Parish, Louisiana. His father was, by turns, a lum-
berman, mill owner, and small planter. Young Taliaferro graduated
from Transylvania University in Lexington, Kentucky, in the nation-
alistic period after the War of 1812. In those days Henry Clay was a
trustee, and Transylvania the most distinguished institution of higher
learning west of the Appalachians. Remaining in Lexington after college, Taliaferro married a local woman, was admitted to the Kentucky
bar, and made the acquaintance of Henry Clay. He returned to Louisiana in the early 1820s and over the next forty years made a distinguished career as a jurist, editor, and planter (he owned twenty-seven
slaves in 1860). His most admired political heroes were the great Whig
leaders of New England (he named one son after Daniel Webster and
another after John Quincy Adams). The motto of his newspaper, the
Harrisonburg *Independent*, proclaimed from Cicero: "I defended the
republic in my youth; I shall not stop as an old man." In the secession
convention Taliaferro adamantly opposed disunion, predicting anarchy, war, and ruinous taxation if Louisiana left the Union. Of his sons,
one joined the Union army, another led anti-Rebel jayhawkers, and
a third served in the Louisiana constitutional convention of 1864.
The old man himself was briefly imprisoned by the Confederate
authorities.[22]

These six Unionists were characterized by an intense American na-

21. *Eighth Census, 1860, Population,* 18; *House Reports,* 39th Cong., 2d Sess., No.
16, pp. 421–23; *House Miscellaneous Documents,* 41st Cong., 2d Sess., No. 154, Pt. 1,
pp. 75–80; *Appleton's Cyclopaedia of American Biography,* I, 272–73; David Donald,
Charles Sumner and the Coming of the Civil War (New York, 1960), 305.
22. Mills, "Taliaferro," 1–45; Roger W. Shugg, "A Suppressed Co-operationist Protest Against Secession," *Louisiana Historical Quarterly,* XIX (January, 1936), 199–203;
John D. Wright, Jr., *Transylvania: Tutor to the West* (Lexington, 1975).

tionalism forged early in life. Hunt, Ludeling, Wells, and Taliaferro were Whigs; but their Whiggery expressed their nationalism as much as caused it. As a group, they represent a variant of the outsider pattern. None was "typically" Southern; although born in the seceder states, they lived for extended periods during the formative years of their youth or early adulthood in the North, or overseas, or in some part of the South where slavery was not entrenched. Two of them married Northern women.[23]

To be sure, most Southerners who traveled in the North or studied at Northern colleges did not grow soft on the South because of the experience. Had that been the case the Southern ruling class would have suffered massive defections, perhaps even losing the talents of John C. Calhoun, Jefferson Davis, and Robert E. Lee. Nonetheless, contact with the North emerged as a consistent theme in Southern dissent in the antebellum and Civil War periods. In a discussion of Southern antislavery, Carl N. Degler has been struck by the number of native-born critics of the Peculiar Institution who had had "first-hand contact with the North"; he concluded "that it required exposure outside the South to bring Southerners to an antislavery stance." Also pertinent is the fact that the slaveholding class expended much time and energy before the war ensuring that the common whites of the South were not exposed to hostile ideas from above the Potomac, their efforts resulting in what one historian has called an intellectual blockade. In fact, the fear that Lincoln's election would result in the dismantling of that blockade ranks as a principal cause of secession.[24]

23. The decision to write about these six men was largely dictated by the availability of information about their lives, not by a careful sifting of the files for individuals to fit a preconceived thesis.

24. Degler, *Other South*, 91; Eaton, *Freedom-of-Thought Struggle*, 335–52; Eric Foner, *Free Soil, Free Labor, Free Men: The Ideology of the Republican Party Before the Civil War* (New York, 1970).

2

Free State Louisiana

A crucial difference existed between reconstructing the Union *during* the Civil War and reconstructing it *after* the war. Simply put, the South had first to be defeated before the North could truly reconstruct it. President Lincoln and the Republican majority in Congress assumed that the Union would prevail, but even the most stouthearted of Republicans must, at times, have doubted that the hard-fighting Rebels would ever submit. As late as the summer of 1864, before the fall of Atlanta in early September, a war-weary public appeared certain that November to turn out of office the Union's strongest defender, Abraham Lincoln, throwing the outcome of the war in doubt. The president's Ten Percent governments, as Herman Belz has observed, "were obviously predicated on wartime conditions" because necessity forced Lincoln to consider Reconstruction mainly "as an adjunct of over-all Union strategy."[1] In essence, the Ten Percent Plan, like the Emancipation Proclamation, was a war measure that was intended, above all, to hasten an end to the Rebellion.

Major General Benjamin F. Butler occupied New Orleans on May 1, 1862. Under Confederate rule, Union men in the city had led a furtive existence: Thomas P. May, William H. Hunt, and Thomas J. Durant had been more or less impressed into the Confederate service; Anthony P. Dostie and Benjamin F. Flanders had fled to the North; the clubfooted Michael Hahn had bravely omitted a Rebel loyalty pledge from his oath of office as a notary public. Now the tables were turned, and the ruling authorities supported the Unionist minority. That summer loyal men formed the Union Association and in December elected two representatives to Congress in a special election called by Butler's military governor, General George F. Shepley. In the spring of 1863

1. Herman Belz, *Reconstructing the Union: Theory and Policy During the Civil War* (Ithaca, N.Y., 1969), 277–78.

they created the Free State General Committee, which became the focus of Lincoln's expectations for a loyal government in Louisiana.[2]

Free State Louisiana was largely the creation of the Northern-born and foreign-born communities in southeastern Louisiana. Fully 70 percent of prominent Unionists in the New Orleans area emanated from the North or abroad. The list reads like a Free State who's who: from Pennsylvania, Thomas J. Durant and Charles W. Hornor; from Washington, D.C., William R. Crane and James E. Tewell; from New York State, William R. Fish, Anthony P. Dostie,. John McNair, and J. Randall Terry; from New England, Benjamin F. Flanders, Edward H. Durell, Edward Heath, J. Q. A. Fellows, and Simeon Belden; from Germany, Michael Hahn, Max F. Bonzano, and Christian Roselius; from Ireland, James Graham and Bartholomew L. Lynch; and from Poland, Stanislas Wrotnowski. Six out of seven officials of the Free State General Committee (including the president) were Northerners or immigrants, as were two thirds of the signers of the Free State constitution. Of seven state officials elected to head the Free State government in 1864, only one, James Madison Wells, was a native of the Southern states.[3]

Early in 1863 a controversial figure emerged as the leader of the Free State movement, the brilliant, charismatic, forty-six-year-old attorney Thomas J. Durant. "He was tall, thin, sallow, cadaverous," observed Whitelaw Reid. "In Boston he would be an Abolitionist of the Abolitionists. He speaks at negro meetings, demands negro suffrage, unites with negroes in educational movements, [and] champions negroes in the courts." On the other hand, to his Radical wartime rival Anthony P. Dostie, he personified self-serving ambition. Durant arrived in New Orleans from Philadelphia in 1831 as a boy of fourteen; he

2. Amos E. Simpson and Vaughan Baker, "Michael Hahn: Steady Patriot," *Louisiana History*, XIII (Summer, 1972), 232; Peyton McCrary, *Abraham Lincoln and Reconstruction: The Louisiana Experiment* (Princeton, 1978), 95–101; Willie Melvin Caskey, *Secession and Restoration of Louisiana* (Baton Rouge, 1938), 55–69. The representatives were Michael Hahn and Benjamin F. Flanders.

3. Appendix 1, Table 1 and Table 2; officials of Free State General Committee in document dated December 17, 1863, in Salmon P. Chase Papers, Library of Congress. I have identified the place of birth of forty-nine of the seventy-eight signers of the constitution with these results: border slave states, 1; the North, 13; abroad, 20 (which adds up to 34, or 69 percent); the Confederate states, 15; (or 31 percent).

pursued publishing, the law, and Democratic party politics; his distinguished legal career spanned decades. A disciple of the French utopian socialist Charles Fourier, Durant saw the Democratic party as a tool for rebuilding society along Fourierian lines, and in the 1850s he aided the unsuccessful Fourier community at Reunion, Texas. Joseph G. Tregle has assured us that Durant hated slavery as few white Southerners ever hated it; nonetheless in 1851 he purchased for his domestic service a young black woman and her three children, holding them in bondage until March 1863. Although Durant was a Union man who campaigned for Stephen A. Douglas, he served as a private in the Confederate militia, performing cleanup duty in the streets of New Orleans near his home.[4]

In the ideology forged by Durant and other Free Staters, the war represented a clash between slavery and freedom and would continue until one or the other principle triumphed. The Rebellion, they maintained, had annulled the state's antebellum constitution, and it followed that the first step in restoring Louisiana to the Union was for loyal citizens to draft an antislavery constitution; the state's organic law must reflect the basic concept of American government that "all men are created free and equal." In May 1863 the Free State General Committee asked Governor Shepley to register loyal voters and order an election of delegates to a constitutional convention. Shepley reacted by appointing Durant state attorney general and commissioner of registration in June.[5]

The road to a convention, however, proved to be studded with obstacles. (Shepley had merely authorized registration, not set a date for an election.) For one thing, Durant revealed a legalistic bent of mind that encouraged delay. He and most Unionists, for example, assumed that for a Free State government to claim legitimacy, at least

---

4. Reid, *After the War: A Tour of the Southern States, 1865–1866*, ed. C. Vann Woodward (New York City, 1965), 232; Emily Hazen Reed, *Life of A. P. Dostie; or, The Conflict in New Orleans* (New York, 1868), 110–11, 116–17; Joseph G. Tregle, Jr., "Thomas J. Durant, Utopian Socialism, and the Failure of Presidential Reconstruction in Louisiana," *Journal of Southern History*, XLV (November, 1979), 491–99; *Dictionary of American Biography*, V, 543–44.

5. Appleton's *American Annual Cyclopaedia and Register of Important Events of the Year 1863* (New York, 1864), 589–90; McCrary, *Lincoln and Reconstruction*, 130–31.

half of the state's population would have to come under Federal rule. The Union victories at Vicksburg and Port Hudson in the summer of 1863 gained them control over the Mississippi River but did not, as expected, lead to Federal occupation of the Louisiana interior. Instead, a military stalemate developed in the Department of the Gulf that endured until the end of the war. After several months of registration, in fact, Confederate raiders overran the region around New Orleans until, by one account, "not a foot of Louisiana beyond the city and outside of the range of Union cannon was left in possession of the federal forces." An even more serious obstacle lay in the fact that the army and not the Free State party ruled occupied Louisiana. Political organization and registration of voters in the areas outside New Orleans depended on the full cooperation of the military. Governor Shepley, a timid man, had little authority outside the city; rather, the provost marshals in the parishes took orders from General Banks, who throughout 1863 concerned himself with military affairs and had little time for political matters. In fact, the provost marshals, who were intent upon restoring agricultural production, were often either indifferent or outright hostile to voter registration. In some areas they had reorganized the police juries under conservative sugar planters who were even less friendly to registration officials than the provost marshals themselves. Despite the problems, by the end of 1863 the Free State General Committee resolved to push ahead. In late November it asked Shepley to fix a date in early 1864 for an election of delegates to a constitutional convention.[6]

By this time, however, an impatient Lincoln (exasperated by Durant's legalism and unaware of the Free Staters' real problems) had also resolved to act. The presidential election of 1864 was less than a year away, and he desperately wanted a loyal government in Louisiana as a show of progress in ending the Rebellion. But more than that, the president probably could not help measuring the glacial pace of restoration in New Orleans against the alacrity with which Southerners had

---

6. LaWanda Cox, *Lincoln and Black Freedom: A Study in Presidential Leadership* (Columbia, S.C., 1981), 64–65; Appleton's *Annual Cyclopaedia (1863)*, 589; McCrary, *Lincoln and Reconstruction*, 160–66, 172–73, 182–83.

dismantled the Union in the winter of 1860–61. In sixty-one days the secessionists had taken seven states out of the Union and created the Confederate States of America. Now, after eighteen months under the protection of Federal guns, so-called Union men in Louisiana had failed to establish a loyal government. The president would give them a hand.

On December 8, 1863, Lincoln announced the Ten Percent Plan, which bypassed the problem of gaining more territory by allowing as few as 10 percent of the voters to form a loyal government. The president made another crucial decision on December 24 when he charged General Banks with the sole responsibility of giving Louisiana a free-state government, informing the commander of the gulf that he would have complete mastery over political affairs in the state. The next month Banks announced a controversial program that ignored the plans of the Free State party and changed the political configuration of wartime Louisiana. In view of the historical controversy surrounding the general's course, his instructions from Lincoln merit closer examination. The president's letter of December 24 stated "You are master" no less than four times, and a week later he repeated himself: "I intend you to be master in every controversy made with you." Those repeated words "grated harshly upon my ears," Durant complained after Banks read him the orders; he saw at once that Lincoln had all but commanded the general to take over the restoration of Louisiana from Shepley and the Free State party.[7]

In part, Lincoln's decision to take hold of Reconstruction policy himself revealed a lack of understanding of the Free State party's problems; more fundamentally, it revealed a profound lack of confidence in Southern Unionists. In the 1850s the sentiment that the majority of white Southerners (who owned no slaves) harbored latent antislavery sentiments had become a staple of Republican party ideology. Radical Republicans had spoken confidently of organizing the common whites

7. James D. Richardson (ed.), *A Compilation of the Messages and Papers of the Presidents, 1789–1897* (Washington, D.C., 1896–1897), VI, 213–15; Abraham Lincoln to Nathaniel P. Banks, December 24 and 29, 1863, in Roy P. Basler (ed.), *The Collected Works of Abraham Lincoln* (New Brunswick, N.J., 1953–1955), VII, 89–90, 95; hereinafter cited as *CWL*; Thomas J. Durant to Salmon P. Chase, January 16, 1864, in Chase Papers, LC.

of the South into state Republican parties under a Republican president. It followed that secession reflected the machinations of the slave-owning aristocracy rather than the wishes of the white masses. In his address before the special session of Congress on July 4, 1861, Lincoln blamed secession on "seceder politicians" and expressed doubt that a majority of voters in any Southern state, except South Carolina, desired disunion. Rather, reason led the president "to believe that the Union men are the majority in many, if not in every other one, of the so-called seceded States."[8]

Although this view of secession enjoyed wide popularity in the North, it found its true believers among Southern Unionists themselves. In New Orleans the story of how a minority of unprincipled traitors dragged a loyal people into disunion acquired the status of holy writ; every major political figure gave it credence at some time or other. Indeed, it probably represented the only idea that all loyal men agreed on.

In actual fact there was little substance to this idea, either in Louisiana or elsewhere. The Louisiana secession election of 1861 had been a close, essentially fair contest between immediate secessionists and so-called cooperationists who wanted secession in unison with other Southern states. Unconditional Union men had been a small minority and had had little alternative other than to support the cooperationists in the hope of averting immediate disunion. Even had the cooperationists won, secession would have been delayed only a few weeks or months.[9]

The commitment to an apocryphal version of secession was, in the main, a case of men believing what they thought ought to be true or what comported with their interests. Yet truth has a subtle way of doubling back on those who distort its lineaments too carelessly. Louisiana Unionists seldom, if ever, noted the double-edged quality implicit in the story of traitors pushing loyal men into disunion. If, in

8. Eric Foner, *Free Soil, Free Labor, Free Men: The Ideology of the Republican Party Before the Civil War* (New York City, 1970), 119–22; Richardson (ed.), *Messages and Papers of the Presidents*, VI, 29.

9. Charles B. Dew, "Who Won the Secession Election in Louisiana," *Journal of Southern History*, XXXVI (February, 1970), 18–32.

fact, Union sentiment had been so strong in 1861, how had the dis-unionists manipulated the political process with such apparent ease? How explain the minority of traitors running roughshod over the loyal majority? In short, did not this explanation of secession raise embarrassing questions about the patriotism of Southern Unionists? The logic was inescapable and few, if any, found it more disturbing than Abraham Lincoln.

In his message of July 4, 1861, the same one in which he spoke of the presumed loyalty of the Southern masses, the president reviewed some disturbing events in the border states. In Richmond, Virginia, a convention dominated by "*professed* Union men" had debated disunion during the crisis over Fort Sumter. After Sumter fell, Lincoln observed that the Unionist majority evaporated, and the convention promptly enacted Virginia's ordinance of secession. The president also found the policy of "armed neutrality," which was favored by some border state leaders, to be very troubling. Such a course, he said, "would do for the disunionists that which of all things they most desire—feed them well and give them disunion without a struggle." While many individuals who supported this plan were "doubtless loyal citizens," the results would be nonetheless damaging to the Union.[10] On July 4, then, Lincoln told Congress that the majority of Southern whites were probably loyal Union men; yet he more than hinted that such people were not really to be trusted.

The president's first impressions of Louisiana Unionists and Thomas J. Durant only intensified his suspicions. In June 1862 he sent Reverdy Johnson to New Orleans to investigate accusations made by foreign consuls against Butler's regime. A conservative Maryland Unionist, Johnson took it on himself to instruct the president on the general political situation. The abolitionist policies of General John W. Phelps, a Butler subordinate, he reported, undermined Union sentiment in the state. The people of Louisiana, Lincoln retorted, bore the responsibility for the soldiers on their soil. If they would be rid of Phelps, they had but to resume their place in the Union on the old terms. "You . . . say I apply to *friends* what is due only to *enemies*. I

10. Richardson (ed.), *Messages and Papers of the Presidents*, VI 23–24.

distrust the *wisdom* if not the *sincerity* of friends, who would hold my hands while my enemies stab me. This appeal of professed friends has paralyzed me more in this struggle than any other one thing." [11]

Several days later, through William H. Seward, a similar assessment of Louisiana affairs came to the president's attention, this time in Durant's hand. If the New Orleans attorney had wanted his views known at the top, he more than succeeded; Lincoln wrote an extensive commentary. Durant was probably right, he allowed, in blaming secession on disloyal conspirators; but, if so, the president asked, why did the majority "stand passive and allow themselves to be trodden down by a minority?" Why not have "a convention of their own, to express and enforce the true sentiment of the state?" Moreover, if such action was precluded *then*, Lincoln asked, why did not the loyal element act *now* that the Federal government protected them? "The paralysis—the dead palsy—of the government in this whole struggle is, that this class of [Union] men will do nothing for the government, nothing for themselves, except demanding that the government shall not strike its open enemies, lest they be struck by accident!" Durant, Lincoln continued, complained that Butler's bluecoats enticed the slaves away from their masters, injuring the loyal along with the disloyal; he even urged liberalized trade with the Confederacy, a policy that "would serve the enemy more effectively than the enemy is able to serve himself." Lincoln resisted saying that the Louisianian was pro-Confederate. "Still, if there were a class of men who, having no choice of sides in the contest, were anxious only to have quiet and comfort for themselves while it rages, and to fall in with the victorious side at the end . . . their advice . . . would be precisely such as his is." The Rebellion in Louisiana, he concluded, would never be put down "if the professed Union men there will neither help to do it, nor permit the government to do it without their help." [12]

Over the next eighteen months events seemed only to confirm the president's initial impression of Durant and the Union element in New

11. Abraham Lincoln to Reverdy Johnson, July 26, 1862, in *CWL*, V, 342–43.

12. Tregle, "Durant," 498; Cuthbert Bullitt to William H. Seward, July 15, 1862, in William H. Seward Papers, University of Rochester Library, Rochester, New York (Thomas J. Durant to Bullitt, July 15, 1862 is enclosed together with an endorsement by Thomas Cottman); Abraham Lincoln to Bullitt, July 28, 1862, in *CWL*, V, 344–46.

Orleans. That November, for example, found Lincoln upbraiding military governor Shepley that "nothing had been done about congressional elections." The president wanted congressmen who represented the people of the region and not "our military and quasi-military, authorities there." Yet "knots must be cut," and if the loyal element "stand idle not seeming to know what to do, do you fix these things for them by proclamation. And do not waste a day about it." A year later the chief executive remained bitterly disappointed at the lack of progress. He urged General Banks to obtain results from Shepley and the Free State party, warning direly that the longer they delayed, the greater the danger that a "few professedly loyal men" would act first, organize the disloyal, and establish a proslavery government. In early 1864 General Banks deposed Durant as the head of Free State Louisiana, and when Durant protested, Lincoln ignored him. The protests against his program, Banks maintained, playing on the president's fears, emanated from "men professing loyalty" who, for their own selfish reasons, did not want immediate restoration.[13] To an unfortunate degree Durant reaped in 1864 the suspicion that he had helped plant in the first months of the occupation.

Major General Nathaniel Prentice Banks replaced Butler as commander of the gulf in December 1862. Like Butler, Banks was a political general from Massachusetts; unlike Butler, he was a Republican. A self-made man, "the Bobbin Boy" of Waltham, he was cut from the mold of American politicians that, for better or worse, had run American governments since the Jacksonian period. His not unsympathetic biographer, Fred Harvey Harrington, describes his political career:

> Banks . . . too often looked at issues with the myopic gaze of the professional politician. He mixed in reform movements, only to drop out when it seemed expedient. He sought the Irish vote, then turned anti-foreign, and later became pro-Fenian. Although he deplored strife within the Union, he used antislavery agitation to catch votes. He was a moderate on reconstruction, then a radical, then a moderate, then a radical. He was a Democrat, a Coalitionist, an American or Know Nothing, a Re-

13. Abraham Lincoln to George F. Shepley, November 22, 1862, in *CWL*, V, 504–505; Lincoln to Nathaniel P. Banks, November 5, 1863, in *ibid.*, VII, 1–2; Banks to Lincoln, January 22 and March 6, 1864, in Abraham Lincoln Papers, Library of Congress.

publican, a Liberal Republican, a Labor Reformer, an Independent, a Republican once more.

Bewildering as these shifts may seem, they all fit into a political pattern of ambition and survival. Banks needed to hold office in order to pay his bills, and he desperately desired to be a famous man. In consequence, he was usually willing to reshape "principles" to suit the occasion, to deal in compromises and reversals, catch phrases, weasel words, and politicians' tricks.

Banks had the good fortune to look and talk the way antebellum Americans expected a statesman to look and talk. And though he lacked the talent as well as the training for military command, his imposing good looks and resonant voice enabled him to make the transition to the warrior class with remarkable aplomb. Indeed, Banks probably made an even more impressive-looking captain at arms than he did a statesman. If tailored uniforms and sitting right in the saddle won battles, he would never have wanted for military glory.[14]

Under the Ten Percent Plan Banks announced a new program for Louisiana on January 11, 1864: A loyal governor and other state officials would be elected on February 22; an election of delegates to a constitutional convention would follow in April. Until the new constitution was written and approved, the constitution of 1852, excepting its slavery provisions, remained in force.[15] This program and the general's implementation of it emerged as the subject of immense controversy. The governor elected that winter was Michael Hahn, not Thomas J. Durant, and the commander of the gulf used the full weight of the army to ensure Hahn's election. The Hahn Free State government was, in reality, the Banks-Hahn government, which also dominated the constitutional convention. In short, Banks ousted Durant from the leadership of Free State Louisiana and installed his own man in power.

The Massachusetts general miscalculated badly. Durant had moved to the left in 1863 and emerged as an unusually able Radical leader. His abrupt dismissal split the Free State party into warring factions and, of

14. Fred Harvey Harrington, *Fighting Politician: Major General N. P. Banks* (Philadelphia, 1948), vii–viii, 4, 62.

15. Nathaniel P. Banks to Abraham Lincoln, January 11, 1864, in Lincoln Papers, LC.

greater consequence, stirred up trouble on the Potomac. Durant, along with Benjamin F. Flanders and other allies, protested Banks's heavy-handed action at the highest levels of government and found Senator Charles Sumner and other Radical Republicans sympathetic to their pleas. These skillful protests helped to crystallize congressional opposition to presidential Reconstruction and led directly to the defeat of Lincoln's Louisiana policy in early 1865.[16]

A widely accepted view holds that these events stemmed from an ideological conflict over Negro suffrage. In this interpretation, Durant and Flanders emerge as revolutionary Radicals who united the Free State party behind a sweeping program of black suffrage. Banks and Hahn, on the other hand, reveal themselves as moderates or liberals who favored a reconstruction for whites only. Alarmed by the drift to the left, Banks seized on the Ten Percent Plan as a pretext for purging the Radical leadership of the Free State party. For reasons not entirely clear, Lincoln accepted Banks's actions and swung the weight of the national government behind his moderate strategy. The Unionist movement never recovered from these blows, and Lincoln's Louisiana policy never recovered its credibility with Congress. In the final analysis, wartime Reconstruction failed because wrongheaded moderates—Banks, Hahn, and Lincoln—discarded the root and branch Radicalism of Durant in favor of politics as usual. In the skillful hands of Peyton McCrary all of this sounds very plausible, but it is essentially rooted in the intellectual experience of the 1960s instead of in that of the Civil War era.[17] Negro suffrage (more accurately, *partial* Negro suffrage) was, however, a subject of controversy in wartime Louisiana.

The issue arose in November 1863 when free men of color petitioned Governor Shepley to enfranchise black Louisianians "born free before the rebellion." The Crescent City's *gens de couleur* were well known for their light skin, education, and air of respectability. They regarded themselves and were regarded by most whites as a people apart from the slaves. Historians have sometimes confused enfranchis-

16. McCrary, *Lincoln and Reconstruction*, 200–209, 232–34, 270; Tregle, "Durant," 510–11.
17. McCrary, *Lincoln and Reconstruction*, xi–xii, 7–8, 16–18, 185–86, *passim*; see also Tregle, "Durant," 507, 510–12.

ing this small community with general Negro suffrage. It is essential to realize that Negro suffrage in Civil War Louisiana meant some form of *partial* suffrage. Until the end of the war white policy makers neither endorsed nor seriously debated giving all blacks the vote.

Cautiously at first, Durant emerged as the main supporter of free black hopes. Calling himself a *"radical Abolitionist,"* he observed at a Union rally in early December that because the United States attorney general had declared free Negroes citizens, "the area of citizenship was likely to be extended." He pointedly stated, however, that nothing in the attorney general's decision applied to slaves. The following day he wrote to Secretary of the Treasury Chase on the subject; his business dealings with the people of color were of an intimate and long-standing nature, and he shared their confidence. They believed "that the persons of African descent born free before the rebellion . . . should be admitted to the registration. I think the claim well founded in justice, and have advocated it in my public speeches here." Two weeks later Durant made his last-known public statement on the suffrage question as the leader of Free State Louisiana. He predicted that after slavery the civil rights of the ex-slaves would be safeguarded "by extending the elective franchise to the free colored citizens, most of whom were men of education and property." [18]

December 1863 was an eventful time in New Orleans. Ten days before Christmas the Free Staters met in a Friends of Freedom convention. They intended to select envoys for an antislavery meeting of Southern Unionists in Kentucky; however, the appearance of eighteen free blacks asking entry to the convention plunged the delegates into controversy. When the names of the Negroes were read, Anthony Fernandez, president of the Union Republican Club, remarked that many

18. New Orleans *Times*, December 4 and 20, 1863; Thomas J. Durant to Salmon P. Chase, December 4, 1863, in Salmon P. Chase Papers, Historical Society of Pennsylvania, Philadelphia. Durant talked ambiguously about extending the area of freedom three times in his December 3 speech. Tregle, "Durant," 507, has seen in this evidence of general support of Negro suffrage. As noted above, Durant specifically denied such an interpretation, and his letter to Chase the next day also mentioned only free blacks. Finally, anything as revolutionary as general Negro suffrage would have made a strong impact on members of the audience; yet John F. Morse and John Hutchins, who heard the address, interpreted it only as an antislavery attack (Morse to Chase, December 12, 1863 and Hutchins to Chase, December 6, 1863, in Chase Papers, LC).

of these men "were personally known to him; they were gentlemen—men of education. This was a Convention of the Friends of Freedom, and he saw no reason for excluding these men." With Durant forcefully presiding, a hefty majority rejected the report of the credentials committee and seated the black delegates. Controversy erupted again when someone proposed that Stephen W. Rogers, one of the black delegates, deliver the opening prayer. By a narrow margin this too passed. A group of diehards attempted to eject the Negroes at the second session, and one delegation walked out when the effort failed.[19]

Seating the free blacks was a bold move, but not so bold as to support the claim that four fifths of the delegates endorsed Negro suffrage and put the Union movement "on record" behind that policy. After admitting the men of color, the Unionists proceeded to their original purpose. The resolutions that they adopted pertained wholly to slavery and the Rebellion; in fact, the official record of the meeting makes no mention of Negro suffrage, not even a hint. Nor did the New Orleans *Times*. Its headline announced simply: "FREE COLORED MEN ADMITTED TO SEATS." The Friends of Freedom could hardly have gone on record in behalf of a policy they never even discussed.[20] The Unionists, in brief, admitted the black delegates and went no further. And as events shortly demonstrated, a wide gap existed between seating blacks in a meeting and Negro suffrage.

After receiving no reply from Shepley or Banks, the free people of color directed their suffrage appeal to President Lincoln and Congress in early January. One thousand free blacks signed the revised petition, and sympathetic loyal whites added their names as well. Several hundred politically active Unionists lived in the New Orleans area; the names of 138 appear on the roll of the Friends of Freedom; but only Durant, Fernandez, and 20 others signed the suffrage memorial. Conspicuously absent are the signatures of Flanders, Ezra Heistand, Thomas J. Earhart, John S. Whitaker, and other Radical warhorses. Indeed, of the dozen-odd individuals identified by Peyton McCrary as

19. *Proceedings of the Convention of the Friends of Freedom* (New Orleans, 1863), 5–16.
20. *Ibid.*; New Orleans *Times*, December 16 and 22, 1863; McCrary, *Lincoln and Reconstruction*, 194–99.

the chief Radicals in New Orleans and Durant's stongest allies, fewer than half signed the petition.[21]

Instead of a Union movement solidly committed to Negro suffrage on the eve of restoration, the record shows the Free State party edging hesitantly toward a limited partial suffrage for the *gens de couleur*—and still some distance even from that goal.[22] The whole question, in fact, remained secondary to emancipation; the term *Radical*, more than anything else, still denoted militant opposition to slavery.

If the ideological view pushes Durant too far to the left, it pushes Banks too far to the right. Officially, the general made no reply to the free black petition in the early winter of 1863–1864, but behind the scenes, he and Judge Edward H. Durell of the United States Circuit Court considered a plan. In Banks's words, it called for Durell ruling that any person "with a major part of white blood, should possess all the rights of a white man. Upon this decision I should have ordered all persons of that class . . . to be enrolled as voters. . . . It would have given the rights of representation to 30,000 colored people." Why Banks backed off from the plan is unclear. He complained that "a few men, who wanted to break the bundle of sticks without loosening the band, defeated it." (This was no doubt a reference to Durant.) He also complained that he simply had too much to do that winter to accomplish everything. Perhaps, as he confided to Lincoln in late December, he feared raising questions about the Negro, "beyond emancipation," that while acceptable in Louisiana might prove unacceptable to Northern voters in an election year.[23] Or perhaps, counting the white signatures on the January petition, he concluded that enrolling free blacks would prove no more popular among Union men in Louisiana than among Northern voters. In any event, the scheme never saw daylight.

The subject, however, remained on the general's agenda. Several

21. Boston *Liberator*, April 1, 1864; McCrary, *Lincoln and Reconstruction*, 166, 197, 218, 229, 239, 244.

22. LaWanda Cox has arrived at similar conclusions (*Lincoln and Black Freedom*, 75–79, 92).

23. Appleton's *American Annual Cyclopaedia and Register of Important Events of the Year 1864* (New York, 1865), 479–80; Harrington, *Fighting Politician*, 114; Nathaniel P. Banks to Abraham Lincoln, December 30, 1863, in Lincoln Papers, LC.

days after the Free State elections of February 22, he assured Lincoln that the upcoming constitutional convention in New Orleans would abolish slavery and "provide such extension of suffrage as will meet the demands of the age." By the time the convention met in April, Banks had marched up the Red River, intent on taking Shreveport. Aware that Judge Durell would likely be chosen president of the convention, Banks wrote to him from Grand Ecore on April 6. He stressed Washington's interest in broadening the suffrage and urged the importance of extending the vote to blacks on the basis of intelligence or taxation.[24] Similar instructions went to Thomas Bangs Thorpe, a trusted subordinate and also a member of the assembly. Thorpe replied in mid-April. He reviewed the special status of the free colored people and suggested that they might "form a link between the white and the slave emancipated populations." A property qualification modeled after the New York State Constitution seemed the best means of enfranchising them. He correctly predicted, however, that any suffrage proposal would meet with stout resistance from the other delegates.[25]

In the meantime, the petition from the *gens de couleur* had arrived in Washington. At the insistence of Radical Republicans in Congress, its bearers broadened its range to include the vote for all Louisiana Negroes, especially Union soldiers. It reached Lincoln's desk on March 12. The very next day the president wrote that famous letter to Michael Hahn encouraging the Louisiana convention to enfranchise exceptionally intelligent Negroes and those who fought in the Union army. Lincoln's critics have often deplored the letter's hesitant tone ("I barely suggest for your private consideration," he had written), but in fact by including black soldiers the president liberalized the suffrage issue in Louisiana beyond anything that Durant or Banks had considered. Far from spurning Lincoln's advice, when the constitution makers took up this most touchy subject, Hahn lobbied effectively for a liberal exten-

24. Nathaniel P. Banks to Abraham Lincoln, February 25, 1864, in Lincoln Papers, LC; LaWanda Cox discovered this important Durell letter (*Lincoln and Black Freedom*, 98).

25. Thomas Bangs Thorpe to Nathaniel P. Banks, April 12, 1864, in Nathaniel P. Banks Papers, Library of Congress.

sion of the vote, showing Lincoln's letter to many of the delegates.[26] It remains a matter of record that the convention—pushed by Banks, Hahn, and Lincoln—empowered the legislature to give blacks the vote on the basis of property, intelligence, and military service.

This provision has been described as a "vague and hollow promise," but that was not the intent of its backers. Two bills were introduced in the Free State legislature in the fall of 1864; the first revived Banks's plan of the previous winter and proposed treating mulattoes as whites; the second would have explicitly carried out the voting authorization of the new constitution. But the legislature met in October, and Banks had left Louisiana in September. His aides kept the suffrage issue alive through the winter, but without the general's presence their efforts ended in failure.[27]

Differences of course had existed between Durant and Banks. In temperament the two men were fundamentally dissimilar. Nor was that all; whatever he said or did in private in the winter of 1863–1864, the commander of the gulf had not forthrightly supported the free black petition; he also countenanced some ugly race baiting by Hahn supporters in the February governor's election. Still, such differences were no greater than existed within Durant's own circle. The overall record simply fails to sustain the notion that Banks—or Lincoln or Hahn—stoutly opposed giving free blacks the vote, and no direct evidence supports the claim that anything to do with Negro suffrage caused Durant's removal. Whether from principle or expediency, Banks too saw the Crescent City's *gens de couleur* as a special class meriting some form of enfranchisement. By mid-1864, at Lincoln's behest, this consensus also embraced black soldiers. All of which raises a critical question: If the Durant-Flanders faction was not in fundamental disagreement with the Banks-Hahn party over Negro suffrage, what did they disagree on, except as to who controlled Reconstruction in Louisiana? Their rhetoric, we are told, was basically the same. Both

26. Abraham Lincoln to Michael Hahn, March 13, 1864, in *CWL*, VII, 243; New York *Times*, June 23, 1865; Cox, *Lincoln and Black Freedom*, 100–101.

27. C. Peter Ripley, *Slaves and Freedmen in Civil War Louisiana* (Baton Rouge, 1976), 173; see Chap. 4.

"described the war against slavery as a revolutionary struggle—and each saw itself as revolutionary"; the difference lay in their conflicting ideas about the nature of the revolution. The difference escaped George S. Denison. The principles of the two parties seemed identical, he reported to Secretary Chase. "The only distinction I feel able to make is, that one is a Banks and the other an anti-Banks party." The treasury agent admired Durant but was "sorry he is such a good hater."[28]

If not ideology, what then explains Banks's shakeup of the Free State party on the eve of restoration? As noted earlier, most historians interested in the Bay State general's Louisiana career have been concerned mainly with Reconstruction. Their interpretations have stressed political factors without really considering that political decisions in an occupied territory deep behind enemy lines were also military decisions. Lincoln entrusted the commander of the gulf with dual responsibilities: He was to help save the Union by defeating the enemy, and he was to help save the Union by giving Louisiana a Free State government. No doubt existed as to which of these goals held the priority; defeating the enemy came first, because if the Rebels could drive the Union army from the state, a loyal government in New Orleans became irrelevant. The priority of military necessity also recommended itself to the general's personal ambition. What William Herndon said of Lincoln was equally true of Banks: "He was always calculating and planning ahead. His ambition was a little engine that knew no rest." And for a man already three times governor of Massachusetts and Speaker of the United States House of Representatives, only one world remained to conquer, the one now ruled by the rail-splitter from Illinois.[29] Banks had many flaws, but lack of intelligence failed to make

28. McCrary, *Lincoln and Reconstruction*, 16, 224; George S. Denison to Salmon P. Chase, February 5 and March 5, 1864, and January 13, 1865, in *Annual Report of the American Historical Association for the Year 1902* (Washington, D.C., 1903), II, 430, 433, 455.

29. Historians have been all but unanimous in believing that Banks had serious presidential ambitions. See David Donald, *Charles Sumner and the Coming of the Civil War* (New York City, 1960), 363–64; Harrington, *Fighting Politician*, 125–27, 138; Tregle, "Durant," 502; McCrary, *Lincoln and Reconstruction*, 209–210; Gerald M. Capers, *Occupied City: New Orleans Under the Federals, 1862–1865* (Lexington, 1965), 175; and Shelby Foote, *The Civil War: A Narrative* (New York, 1958–74), III, 25–26.

the list. No general had ever become president riding a desk in the rear echelon; for a soldier, the road to the White House was paved with victories on the battlefield.

Accustomed to thinking of the Department of the Gulf as a military backwater, we forget that Banks and the president could not afford the luxury of such thoughts; stretching from the Rio Grande to Florida, the gulf represented the largest Union theater of the war, with responsibilities commensurate to its size. Banks went there as the highest-ranking Union general in the West; his orders directed him to cooperate with General Grant in opening the Mississippi River and then to capture Mobile, Alabama. They also stressed the vital importance of returning north Louisiana and Texas to Union control. As Shelby Foote has observed, this was an awesome agenda for a commander who had yet to win a battle. Banks started work on it the day he arrived in New Orleans; he recaptured Baton Rouge in December, led his army up the Bayou Teche and the Red River in the spring, captured Port Hudson in July after a siege, and that fall campaigned in Texas.[30]

No wonder the Free Staters had trouble getting his attention in 1863; from March until the end of the year he remained almost continually in the field. When he returned to New Orleans in December, moreover, he learned that the president held him responsible for the political inertia in New Orleans. It was no wonder, too, that he complained that Lincoln gave him more to do than any other Union general. His expressions of vexation and surprise were probably genuine; he had been fighting Rebels, after all, leaving the nonentity Shepley to deal with Reconstruction. But because the president did charge him with the task, he would perform it with dispatch. In short order he took matters in hand and arranged for state elections and a constitutional convention. True, he shunted Durant and Flanders aside, leading Lincoln to believe that they had no immediate plans for restoration; but he was *master* of the gulf; the president wanted results and Banks gave them to him.

30. *The War of the Rebellion: A Compilation of the Official Records of the Union and the Confederate Armies* (Washington, D.C., 1880–1901), *Atlas*, plates 166 and 168 (hereinafter cited as *OR*; unless otherwise indicated, all citations are to Series I); *ibid.*, XV, 590–91, 602–603, 613–14, 618–19, 626; Foote, *Civil War*, II, 54, 389, 616–17, 870–72.

All the while he prepared for the spring campaign. In early March General William T. Sherman visited New Orleans to discuss the coming offensive. The plan called for Banks to move up the Red River, rendezvous with General Frederick Steele at Shreveport, and march west into Texas, liberating all of Louisiana and warning the French away from the Lone Star State. Banks delayed a few days until after Michael Hahn's inauguration on March 5, and then he set out for the Red River (his army already en route). In early April he entered Grand Ecore with 30,000 troops. In the meantime, General Grant had drafted new orders for him. At the fall of Shreveport, the commander of the gulf would return to New Orleans, organize a minimum force to hold Louisiana and the Rio Grande, and then strike overland against Mobile with 25,000 men. Thus, while Grant moved on Richmond, and Sherman hit Atlanta, Banks would create a third front against the Rebels. By the time these orders reached him, the Massachusetts commander had suffered a humiliating defeat at Sabine Crossroads, and the Red River campaign and his military career were effectively over. During the retreat, he endured the taunting voices of Union soldiers singing to the tune of "When Johnny Comes Marching Home":

> In eighteen hundred and sixty-one
> We all skedaddled to Washington.
> In eighteen hundred and sixty-four
> We all skedaddled to Grand Ecore.
> Napoleon P. Banks![31]

The modern writer easily forgets that, for a time, Banks was the master of his fate; had he taken Shreveport and Mobile, in all probability he would have earned the military glory he so desperately craved.

An intimate connection existed between military operations and Reconstruction in the gulf. Durant, Flanders, and their allies accused Banks of creating a military-dominated regime in Louisiana. They were exactly right. Negro suffrage arises infrequently in the general's correspondence in the winter of 1863–1864; on the other hand, his

---

31. *OR*, XXXIV, Pt. 2, pp. 15–16, 45–47, 55–56, 430–31, 494, 514–16; Ulysses S. Grant, *Personal Memoirs of U. S. Grant* (New York, 1885), II, 130–32 n, 559–60; Ludwell H. Johnson, *Red River Campaign: Politics and Cotton in the Civil War* (Baltimore, 1958), 206, 242–43.

letters reveal an almost obsessive fear of civilian interference with the army. When Banks returned from Texas in December 1863 and learned of Lincoln's dismay at the lack of political progress, he lamented in reply, "I am only in partial command. . . . There are not less than *four* distinct governments here, claiming and exercising original and independent powers based upon instructions received directly from Washington, and recognizing no other authority than their own." The general then inventoried his grievances against civilian officialdom.[32]

At the top of the list stood the federal and city courts in New Orleans, particularly Judge Durell's United States Circuit Court. Durell and the officers of his court, Banks charged, had interfered with the army's use of the *Alabama*, a draft vessel that had proved invaluable during military operations in Texas; they had tried to make the military submit to the court's authority, and soldiers had literally to seize the vessel. The army had also wrangled with Durell's court over the steamer *Leviathan*, which, according to Banks, was additional evidence of judicial prejudice against the military. The city courts of New Orleans were almost equally subversive of the army's authority. During his absence in Texas, complained the commander of the gulf, a city court actually decreed that its rulings took precedence over military orders. More recently, city courts claimed the right to try soldiers who violated city ordinances. Where the judiciary was so openly prejudiced against the army, Banks concluded, "the just military influence is impaired. Even in a department like this where military or martial law, is the foundation of all proceedings civil or judicial, it is greatly injurious to the public service."[33]

The New Orleans police also earned a prominent position on Banks's grievance list. The army needed the assistance of the police in ferreting out deserters from the city's many places of concealment, he said. Without this aid a thousand runaway soldiers could find refuge there. Indeed, the general argued that the influence of the police, for the army or against it, equaled a force of two or three thousand troops. Of necessity, the police ought to be "friendly to the interest of the army if

32. Nathaniel P. Banks to Abraham Lincoln, December 16, 1863, in Lincoln Papers, LC.
33. *Ibid.*

it be not under military direction. But it is not so here. As at present organized it is useless."[34]

The commander of the gulf preferred to avoid using the full powers granted him under martial law: "I came here to fight rebels, and not to enter into conflict with the officers of your government. . . . I desire to avoid it. It exhausts my mental and physical energy. My duties in this city are more appalling than the most perilous service in the field. . . . I earnestly ask that the powers of the different officers may be more closely defined, or that they be concentrated in single hands with direct responsibilities, and especially that what is called the 'State Government' may be lifted out of the deep ruts . . . into which it has fallen."[35]

Lincoln made it plain that he wanted a loyal government in Louisiana, and soon. In the wrong hands the new government would pose a serious threat to the general's power. All but ignored by the commander of the gulf, the Free State movement had developed on its own and owed Banks nothing. Durant, Flanders, and their associates breezily went about their business, registering voters, holding conventions, and signing controversial petitions without a by-your-leave from the general. Worse than independent, Flanders had the reputation of being outright hostile. B. Rush Plumly, a Banks lieutenant, informed Secretary Chase of Flanders' "open and outspoken opposition" before the controversy arose: "He dislikes Banks generally! I think he is unjust to Genl Banks, but [even] if he were right in his judgment, it is worse than folly to make war on the General."[36] To avert the threat of an uncontrolled Unionist government operating at his rear, contradicting his authority, delaying his plans, and hassling his officers, Banks pushed Durant aside and made Michael Hahn governor. A German lawyer in his mid-thirties, Hahn owed his position

34. *Ibid.*
35. *Ibid.*
36. R. Bush Plumly to Salmon P. Chase, December 1, 1863, in Chase Papers, LC. Banks had earlier removed Flanders from the New Orleans *Era* (George S. Denison to Chase, November 6, 1863, in *AHA Annual Rept.*, II, 416). The general and the treasury agent had also quarreled over confiscated property and labor policy (Ripley, *Slaves and Freedmen*, 54–56). A state of open hostility existed between Flanders and most of Banks's most trusted aides (John Hutchins to Chase, December 12, 1863, and Thomas Bangs Thorpe to Chase, December 19, 1863, in Chase Papers, LC).

entirely to Banks; with him running affairs in New Orleans, the general would not have to keep looking over his shoulder as he advanced on Shreveport. Personally, Banks no doubt preferred the more conservative German to the dynamic, Radical-talking Durant and certainly to the hostile Flanders; but as he had made clear in his grievance list of that December, to earn his enmity, civilians had only to get in the army's way.

The Bay State commander misled the president about his role in promoting Hahn over Durant, but as to his ultimate purpose he revealed himself clearly. He sent Lincoln a copy of his Louisiana proclamation in January; the enclosed order, he explained, "provides for the gradual restoration of power to the people, in such manner as to leave the control of affairs still in the hands of the commanding general." The proclamation itself made the same point. "The fundamental law of the State is martial law. It is competent and just for the Government to surrender to the people . . . so much of military power as may be consistent with the success of military operation." The general addressed the president again on the subject the day after Hahn's inauguration. It was accepted here, he stated matter-of-factly, "that Mr. Hahn represents a popular power entirely subordinate to the armed occupation of the state." The German could, therefore, safely be entrusted with the powers of a military governor "without impairing in the slightest degree, the military authority . . . of the general government." He continued:

> The problem, to be solved, in the restoration of insurgent States is to bring the people into harmonious co-operation with the government without risking the loss of its authority in any possible degree. This is accomplished by the measures adopted here. The election perilled nothing. Had it resulted in the election of an opponent, he would be without power. The election of a friend of the government, on the other hand, who acts in harmony with the military authorities, gives them the great benefit of the direct support of the People, without impairing their authority. Other measures . . . such as the adaptation of Constitutions to the new condition of things can proceed steadily without producing any shock between the people and the government, and without risking the power of the latter.[37]

37. Nathaniel P. Banks to Abraham Lincoln, January 11 and March 6, 1864, in Lincoln Papers, LC.

Banks could hardly have been more blunt; he had created a puppet regime.

No mystery surrounds Lincoln's acceptance of all this. His knowledge of the deposed Free State leaders was limited and tinged with suspicion; Durant had failed to do his job, and Flanders, though once trusted, was known as a supporter of Salmon P. Chase's presidential hopes. On the other hand, Lincoln and Hahn had evidently gotten along well during the months that the Louisianian had spent in Washington in the winter and spring of 1863.[38] More to the point, though, the president essentially accepted Banks's military priorities and had no intention of overruling the ranking commander in the West for the benefit of dissident Unionists.

The priority of military operations in the gulf was apparent in the subsequent treatment of Banks. The Bay State general gave the president his loyal government in Louisiana, but when he failed to take Shreveport, he was stripped of field command and reduced to the level of a high-ranking Shepley, presiding over civil affairs in New Orleans. There he endured a new superior, Major General E. R. S. Canby, who evidently relished his discomfort. By September Banks could endure it no longer and returned to Washington on a three-week pass, which was subsequently extended until the end of the war. In the capital he worked loyally for congressional approval of the Louisiana government, all the while pathetically attempting to regain his lost command. "I know you are dissatisfied," Lincoln responded in December, but "I have told you why I can not order Gen. Canby from the Department of the Gulf." Yet, "I do believe that you, of all men, can best perform the part of advancing the new State government of Louisiana; and therefore I have wished you to go and try. . . . This is certainly meant in no unkindness; But I wish to avoid further struggle about it."[39]

The clearest evidence of Lincoln's priorities comes from his tolerance of Banks's successors in the gulf, Canby and General Stephen A.

38. Ripley, *Slaves and Freedmen*, 167; Simpson and Baker, "Hahn," 233–34; Cox, *Lincoln and Black Freedom*, 49–50.

39. *OR*, XXXIV, Pt. 3, pp. 409–411, 491–92, 644; Harrington, *Fighting Politician*, 163–65; Abraham Lincoln to Nathaniel P. Banks, December 2, 1864, in *CWL*, VIII, 131.

Hurlbut. Professional soldiers, Hurlbut and Canby were openly contemptuous of the Hahn government and repeatedly interfered in its affairs in the most arbitrary manner. In November, citing specific examples, an exasperated Lincoln lectured Hurlbut that the hostile treatment of the Louisiana government by himself and Canby comprised a shameful record. Why two Union commanders should side with John Slidell and the advocates of slavery who hoped to see the new regime fail was beyond all understanding. At the same time, he assured Hurlbut that he did not want the army "thwarted by the civil authority; and I add that on points of difference the commanding general must be judge and master." He warned, however, against using "military necessity" as an excuse "to crush out the civil government." Some weeks later, the president upbraided Canby. "It is conceded," he said, "that the military operations are the *first* in importance; and as to what is indispensable to these operations," the general in command must have the final say. The state government, however, was also important, and Lincoln appealed to Canby for a more tolerant attitude toward it.[40] Plainly, a president who tolerated outright subversion of his Reconstruction policies would hardly balk at the behavior of Banks.

Free State Louisiana was not created as a model for the postwar world. It grew out of the exigencies of war, and its central conflict, civil versus military authority, remained peculiar to the war years. Durant, Flanders, and others attacked the Hahn government because the army dominated it. Though understandable, the charge was naïve. New Orleans was not located in the Hudson River Valley or on Cape Cod Bay; it was a pocket of Union control enclosed by hundreds of miles of enemy territory. In modern terms, moreover, Durant, Flanders, Hahn, and other Unionists were "collaborationists." In such a situation, no military commander (in that war or any other) intended giving independent power to such people. Banks handled the situation badly, but Durant, if anything, acted worse. The role of the military excepted, his differences with Banks, Hahn, and the president were more matters of style than of substance. Unable to alter Banks's course, Durant played the spoiler, boycotting the Free State elections, the con-

40. Abraham Lincoln to Stephen A. Hurlbut, November 14, 1864, and Lincoln to E. R. S. Canby, December 12, 1864, in *CWL*, VIII, 106–107, 163–64.

stitutional convention, and assailing the new regime before Congress.
The issue was power, and the Radical leader basically decided that if he
could not be king of the Free State mountain then he would demolish
the mountain. A very human decision by a very able man, and regret-
tably he succeeded.

3

To Save
the Union

In October 1862 General Godfrey Weitzel invaded the Lafourche River country southwest of New Orleans with 5,000 Federal troops. There ensued scenes that would be repeated wherever Union armies marched. "What shall I do about the negroes?" the exasperated Weitzel asked headquarters. "You can form no idea of the vicinity of my camp, nor . . . the appearance of my brigade as it marched down the bayou. My train was larger than an army for 25,000 men. Every soldier had a negro . . . carrying his knapsack. Plantation carts, filled with negro women and children . . . and of course compelled to pillage for their subsistence, as I have no rations to issue to them. I have a great many more negroes in my camp now than I have whites. These negroes are a perfect nuisance."[1]

The following spring General Banks marched up the Bayou Teche and the Red River. A planter in St. Mary's Parish wrote dejectedly, "The drum & bugle, are the general, almost the only sounds, & the passing of troops almost the only sight to be seen—all the inhabitants depressed in spirits & discouraged with regard to the future—The slaves demoralized, refractory, leaving their owners & going to the enemy, who receive them with open arms—Violence committed on aged & unprotected persons—Many of my negroes have left me & some of them I have dismissed owing to refusing to work as usual."[2]

A planter named John H. Ransdell informed his absent neighbor, Confederate governor Thomas O. Moore, about the Federal invasion of Rapides Parish: It "turned the negroes crazy. They became utterly demoralized at once. All business was suspended and those that did not go on with the army remained at home to do *much worse*." The Yankees told the blacks they were free and could do as they pleased,

---

1. James Parton, *General Butler in New Orleans* (New York, 1864), 580.
2. J. Carlyle Sitterson, *Sugar Country: The Cane Sugar Industry in the South, 1753–1950* (Lexington, 1953), 210.

Ransdell stated. "I assure you that for the space of a week they had a perfect jubilee." He could not even guess at the number of cattle, sheep, and hogs the hands killed. "There was no white man on C's place below me," Ransdell continued, "and of course the devil was let loose there and on my place too. . . . Your boy Wallace and two others . . . forcibly put a Confederate soldier in the stocks at your place on Saturday night." Although Ransdell thought the soldier suffered much abuse, it did not prevent him from escaping early Sunday morning. Frightened by their own actions and fearing retaliation, or so Ransdell assumed, Wallace and about thirty-five other hands went off in the rear of the Federal army. "Four of mine went also. All my mules and horses . . . wagons, carts, bridles, saddles, etc. were taken." Shortly afterwards, "a train of negroes camped in your yard and some of yours showed them where everything was, and then they soon made away with it."[3]

Free State Louisiana emerged against this backdrop of social and economic disintegration. In the early days of General Butler, loyal men united in their devotion to the Union and their hatred of secession traitors. The sweep of events, however, forced them to grapple with the upheaval of Southern society. For two years after the fall of New Orleans, emancipation remained the central issue in the state; during that time the term Radical signified a staunch antislavery stand. Individuals like Thomas J. Durant and Joseph Ad. Rozier, who would be poles apart after abolition, were coupled together as men of Radical principles.[4]

In early 1864 General Banks took over Reconstruction and produced a schism in the Free State party between the old leadership and the new leaders whom the general himself elevated to power. There emerged that spring, however, a much more fundamental ideological cleavage, which only partially conformed to the political split and for which Banks was not responsible. Its basis was simple: Agreeing to

3. John H. Ransdell to Thomas O. Moore, May 24, 1863, in Thomas O. Moore Papers, Troy H. Middleton Library, Louisiana State University, Baton Rouge.
4. George S. Denison to Salmon P. Chase, January 29, [1864], in Salmon P. Chase Papers, Library of Congress.

end slavery was one thing, but agreeing on the place of the freedmen in postemancipation society was quite another. By the time the constitutional convention of 1864 met in New Orleans in April, all but the most extreme reactionaries conceded the doom of slavery. The new issue, however, bore down on the delegates with unstoppable momentum. Emancipation, in short, opened the door to a host of divisive issues that had little to do with Banks and which, indeed, would have developed had no one in Louisiana ever heard the name of the Massachusetts general.

The administration party took a less militant pose than its critics, but neither side had a monopoly on Radicalism, or conservatism. The oft-repeated claim that Banks was a moderate ignores an important fact of geography. It was true that the general thought and acted like a moderate Republican, moderate, *that is*, in the light of Massachusetts and Lincoln's Washington. The same description generally fits a number of his top aides, Thomas Bangs Thorpe, B. Rush Plumly, Alfred C. Hills, and Thomas W. Conway, all of whom had come South with the Union army. By the standards of conservative New Orleans, which was a slave metropolis, however, Banks and his lieutenants stood far to the left of center. Their restoration program would include emancipation, limited Negro suffrage, black education, and blacks in the militia. If this was "moderation," pray, what was Radicalism? Durant, on the other hand, adopted a political style modeled more after Radical Republicanism and abolition, but in fact the ex-slaveholder and his coterie, which included a number of ex-masters, remained considerably to the right of a Charles Sumner, a Thaddeus Stevens, and in most cases Lincoln. Wartime Reconstruction might have taken a different turn if the two factions, agreeing on so much, had not remained so intolerant of one another.

The Radical element, however they characterized themselves, set the dominant tone in both parties. Slavery, they agreed, had caused the war, and the war was revolution. From these premises, Durant, Flanders, Ezra Heistand, Anthony P. Dostie, Edward H. Durell, Alfred C. Hills, Thomas Bangs Thorpe, J. Randall Terry, and others approached the problem of the Negro's place in postemancipation society. "The Rebellion," Durant maintained in late 1863, "was based on the idea of

53

universal slavery and Union men were, necessarily, compelled to take the antagonistic idea, and proclaim universal freedom and an equality of the human race." It was axiomatic that "revolutions never leave nations as they find them," and this revolution would result in the enlargement of the area of freedom. According to Flanders, men did more in a time of revolution than in centuries of ordinary life. Everyone had the sense that this revolution had already lasted ten years instead of three. Those who claimed we go too fast, he argued, did not want to come in the first place. Those who said they did not like Negro equality or did not understand it—yet proclaimed themselves Union men—took the oath only to protect their property. As president of the constitutional convention, Edward H. Durell admonished his fellow delegates against being blinded by prejudice: "Nothing goes backward in times of revolution. You must go with the current or it will overwhelm you." In an age of progress the old must give way and things be made new. "We are to work no distinction of races, no distinction of color." [5]

These ideas were not exclusive to white Unionists. They formed part of the broader current of thought in wartime New Orleans and Civil War America. Educated free blacks and Northern military and government officials also talked matter-of-factly about the revolution. General Banks wrote effusive letters on the subject. On the whole, there is little reason to doubt the sincerity of so many who coupled human equality to the engine of revolution. There is, however, reason to ask exactly what all the rhetoric meant. When Banks, for example, informed John Hay that "we have changed all the elements of society" and the "revolution is complete," his meaning remained vague. On the other hand, there was no mistaking the free Negro newspaper, *The Union*, when it urged blacks to be done "with the craven behavior of bondage!" [6] When Durant spoke of equality, he clearly meant that blacks merited an education and that the better-educated and successful free blacks deserved the franchise. Did he also mean that *all* Ne-

5. New Orleans *Times*, December 4 & 18, 1863; *Debates in the Convention for the Revision and Amendment of the Constitution of the State of Louisiana* (New Orleans, 1864), 543.
6. Nathaniel P. Banks to John Hay, March 28, 1864, in Abraham Lincoln Papers, Library of Congress; James M. McPherson (ed.), *The Negro's Civil War: How American Negroes Felt and Acted During the War for the Union* (New York, 1965), 62.

groes should vote and their children sit in the same classroom with his children? Yet again, did he mean that he would accept a black lawyer as his professional equal in a court of law? Well, perhaps, but as regards most Radical Unionists, it is clear that however much they believed in equality, they also believed in Negro inferiority. Asked by Northerners what Southern Unionists intended to do with the freedmen, Ezra Heistand replied, "We will put them in a situation to sustain themselves by their own industry—then if they do not sustain themselves the fault will be theirs. If they will not make the proper effort, why let them go down and disappear from the earth as other worthless races have done before them." Flanders gave an identical answer to the same question: If the Negro would not work, "then let him starve." The Radicals, in discussing the subject, spoke often about fair play, struggle, the race for life, and giving every man his chance on the platform.[7] Too often their concept of equality was like a footrace where blacks and whites lined up together at the start, but only whites finished the race.

For inspiration in reshaping Southern society, Radical Unionists looked above the Potomac; to their minds, the North was the progressive section of the country. In particular, they never tired of contrasting, to the South's disadvantage, the economic progress of Yankee civilization. The broad-based prosperity of the free states, declared Ezra Heistand, upon his return from a Northern trip, convinced him "that we never really had any prosperity in the Southern States, except that which was confined to a privileged class." In *Freedom vs. Slavery* Anthony P. Dostie compared the economic growth and prosperity of the free states since 1789 with that of the slave states. Despite an equal start, by every index the South lagged behind. The South, Dostie concluded, was the land of "ignorance, poverty and imbecility," while the North was the land of "freedom . . . intelligence, wealth, prosperity and happiness."[8]

Radicals of the Durant-Dostie mind-set, however, were never a ma-

7. New Orleans *Times*, November 3, 18, and 26, 1863; *Debates in the Convention (1864)*, 543.
8. New Orleans *Times*, November 3, 1863; as read into the *Debates in the Convention (1864)*, 168.

jority. Most Unionists were conservatives who accepted revolutionary changes in the social and political world only under extreme pressure. Moreover, like political figures in other ages, Unionists were rarely completely consistent. Radicals in 1864, Durant and Michael Hahn had taken conservative or centrist positions earlier in the war. At the opposite end of the Unionist political spectrum from the Radicals stood the Unionist reactionaries, a class of men who pursued contradictory ends: preservation of the Union on the one hand, and preservation of slavery and the antebellum social order on the other.

All three—Radicals, conservatives, and reactionaries—met in the constitutional convention that assembled in New Orleans from April to July of 1864. Numerically, conservatives and reactionaries dominated the membership; however, the Banks-Hahn administration supported the Radical minority. Aware that Lincoln and Congress would not approve a reactionary constitution, at crucial moments Banks brought the full weight of his authority down on the side of the Radicals, overturning reactionary measures or forcing concessions on Negro suffrage or black education.

By general consensus, the Unionists in the convention believed that slavery had caused the war and that the institution was now dead or dying and must be legally abolished. But when discussion centered on the nature of slavery, its rightness or wrongness, and its effects on Negroes and Southern society, Unionist thought became a tangle of contradictions. Part of the reason was that so many Unionists, including members of the convention, had themselves owned slaves. Not surprisingly the most spirited critique of slavery and the Slave Power delivered in the sessions came not from a native Unionist but from Alfred C. Hills, who had come South to report on the war for the New York *Herald*.[9] Many delegates believed that slavery was wrong, and some, like J. Randall Terry, spoke eloquently of the "downtrodden African." Others professed no guilt over the institution. William Tompkins Stocker averred that he had lived in a slave state all his life and never encountered "the horrors that have been pictured to this Convention." As for the "downtrodden African," Stocker remarked,

9. *Debates in the Convention (1864)*, 170–80, *passim*; Peyton McCrary, *Abraham Lincoln and Reconstruction: The Louisiana Experiment* (Princeton, 1978), 166 n.

"I have never seen him." Such sentiments were not limited to conservatives. The Radical Ezra Heistand had told a New York audience in 1863 that he had owned slaves for as long as he had been able to own them without any pangs of conscience. He believed that Providence had willed Southern slavery in order to bring the "rude, brutish, barbarous" Africans under the tutelage of a superior civilization.[10]

Still, few Unionists were fully at peace with the moral and political implications of slavery. Most believed it controverted the Declaration of Independence and the gospel of Christ's redemption, and that it opposed the progress of American and Christian civilization. Even Edmund Abell, who belabored the convention for days with the proslavery argument, felt compelled to declare that he "never saw a day or a moment in my life when I was in favor of slavery as an abstract principle."[11]

Fortunately, the convention did not have to agree on the morality of slavery in order to abolish it. Indeed, for the majority, as for R. King Cutler, John Henderson, and William Tompkins Stocker, the question was largely irrelevant. Cutler did not favor emancipation merely as a boon to humanity, nor was he there "to discuss whether a state of slavery or a state of freedom is more beneficial to the Negro . . . but I do say that the slaves in every State of this rebellious country should be set at liberty, for the purpose of crushing out this odious rebellion." In point of fact, he declared, there are no slaves in Louisiana, and no power on earth can "resurrect slavery among us." Once he would have ended slavery gradually, he said, but "the world demands the abolition of it now, in order to save the Union. So I say down with it!" Stocker also supported abolition not out of any sentimental or conscientious feelings against slavery, "but because I believe our country demands it of us." On May 11, 1864, Louisiana Unionists voted seventy-two to thirteen to save the Union by abolishing slavery (which they agreed was already dead).[12]

Abolition cleared the ground for the real battle over what to do with

10. *Debates in the Convention (1864)*, 168, 181; New Orleans *Times*, October 6, 1863.
11. *Debates in the Convention (1864)*, 166.
12. *Ibid.*, 160–61, 169–70, 181; *Official Journal of the Proceedings of the Convention for the Revision and Amendment of the Constitution of the State of Louisiana* (New Orleans, 1864), 74.

Negroes now that they were free. Did the safety of the Union also require that blacks should vote and send their children to school? When they confronted these questions, Louisiana Unionists were immeasurably influenced by assumptions regarding the Negro past. To Unionists, as to other Southern whites, the Negro's African origins linked him to savagery and barbarism, setting him off from the progressive Christian culture of the West. Many times in the convention, delegates referred not to the Negro, or the black man, but to the African. For all its negative connotations, the concept of the Negro's barbaric past was amenable to both Radical and conservative political stances. As I have observed, Ezra Heistand believed that Providence had willed Southern slavery in order that a barbaric people might eventually reap the rewards of constitutional government. This grand design, he asserted in 1863, had in large part been realized all over the South. Much more intelligent than whites conceded, Southern Negroes, he suggested, were probably better prepared for the responsibilities of representative government than the ignorant peasantry of some European states. Heistand had met many intelligent, well-dressed free Negroes in the North and saw no reason why Southern blacks could not be raised to a similar level.[13]

Yet, in the main the weight of the black man's African origins worked against his freedom. While the convention debated, the loyal New Orleans *Times* protested the too-rapid elevation of the Negro. The African race, the newspaper averred, inhabited much of the earth in a condition little removed from barbarism untouched by the enlightenments that had swept other lands. Though much had been done for the Negro in the United States, the distinctive characteristics of the race would hold them back for generations. After slavery the black man's advancement would depend on the benign supervision of the "superior race." In the convention Joseph Hamilton Wilson asked what place the freed slaves would assume in society. For himself, Wilson did not think that "the African is the EQUAL of the white man, either socially or politically." Citing the work of a recent traveler to the dark continent, he remarked that he did not wish to amalgamate

13. *Debates in the Convention (1864)*, 158, 168, 181, 190, *passim*; New Orleans *Times*, October 6 and November 3, 1863.

with a race that displays "human flesh for sale in their public markets, whose domiciles are surrounded by piles of human bones and skulls . . . who sell each other to foreign traders, and make sheaths for their knives from human skin." Barbarism, he concluded, was inherent in the Negro race. "Look at the free negro in his native jungles, sir, what do you find?" asked Edmund Abell. "A mere bug-eater; a fruit-eater." [14]

As the sessions progressed, the three basic Unionist positions emerged. On the extreme right a hard core of fifteen to twenty delegates opposed granting blacks any rights at all. To Edmund Abell, the main theorist and spokesman of the reactionaries, the blacks were a vile, degenerate race for whom slavery was not oppression but a benign and necessary evil. Removed from the patriarchal discipline of bondage, they would fall prey to vice, dissipation, disease, and death. Paradoxically, they would at the same time overwhelm the white population "with a natural increase unparalleled in the history of any race." Less verbose than Abell, William Tompkins Stocker concerned himself solely with the welfare of whites: "My hand is against the African, and I am for pushing him off the soil of this country." [15]

The piecemeal program the reactionaries put before the convention was wholly negative. They opposed emancipation without compensation of loyal slaveowners; Negro suffrage in any form; blacks entering the state; Negro education, but most emphatically the use of white tax money for such purposes; and, the entry of blacks into legal practice, medicine, or any other trade or profession. [16]

Conservative Unionism, the second position, included the majority of Louisiana Unionists and a majority in the convention. The more flexible conservatives, like R. King Cutler, were capable of growth. Others differed from the reactionaries only in small degree. As the proceedings got under way in New Orleans, the conservatives found themselves occupying the middle ground in a tug-of-war between the reactionaries on the one side and the Radical lieutenants of the admin-

14. New Orleans *Times*, June 23 and 26, 1864; *Debates in the Convention (1864)*, 156, 182–83.
15. *Debates in the Convention (1864)*, 142, 165–66, 181.
16. *Ibid.*, 210–11, 224, 394, 501–502, 602–606; *Official Journal* (1864), 68–71.

istration on the other. Left to their own inclinations, they heeded the shrill cries of miscegenation, Negro equality, and other bogeys conjured up by Edmund Abell. On May 10, for example, Abell stampeded the conservatives en masse into supporting a ban on black suffrage. Fortunately the Radicals did not have to rely on numbers or humanity; they had Banks. Abell's amendment was overturned the following day.[17]

The basic difference between the conservatives and the reactionaries was the willingness of the former to accord the freedmen *some* rights and take *some* steps, however slight, for the betterment of their lot. The New Orleans *Times* consistently espoused the conservative position during the convention. On the important question of Negro education, the Unionist newspaper maintained that world history led to the conclusion that blacks would continue to be mainly "hewers of wood and drawers of water." This was the station assigned them by the God of nature, and while a few would rise above it, the great majority would not. The freedmen should be educated, the *Times* believed, but they should be educated for the lowly positions they would hold. Self-supporting industrial schools, it concluded, fitted the Negro's peculiar needs and would achieve all that his warmest friends could hope.[18]

In the convention, John Henderson, R. King Cutler, Benjamin H. Orr, and Joseph Hamilton Wilson acted as the main spokesmen of conservative Unionism. In varying degree, all conceded that blacks ought to be educated, provided that Louisiana whites were not burdened with the entire cost. "We are scarcely in a condition to educate those of our own color," Cutler explained, "letting alone those who have . . . been emancipated from their state of bondage." Emancipation, he observed, had eliminated one of the two main sources of tax revenue, the tax on slave property (the other being real estate). Cutler

17. On most important issues, eighty to eighty-four members voted. Counting fifteen to twenty reactionaries and a like number of Radicals, the conservatives averaged forty to fifty delegates. For key votes see *Debates in the Convention (1864)*, 211–12, 222, 450, 499, 502, 556, 607. Peyton McCrary provides a valuable roll call analysis in *Lincoln and Reconstruction*, 373–80. The vote on May 10 was sixty-eight to fifteen; the overturn vote on May 11 was sixty to twenty-four (*Debates in the Convention [1864]*, 211–12, 222).

18. New Orleans *Times*, June 22 & 23, 1864.

looked to the Federal government for aid in educating the freedmen and opposed making it mandatory on the legislature to educate "any but the superior race of man—the white race." Despite the obvious racial implications, there was substance to his argument. Louisianians conceded that, outside New Orleans, the antebellum public school system was a huge failure.[19] With abolition a reality, a state that had been unable to educate rural whites confronted the additional burden of educating an even larger number of rural blacks.

Barring federal aid, the school system most acceptable to conservative Unionists was that embodied in the proposal of J. Randall Terry: White tax money would support white schools, while Negro taxes would support black schools. The convention, in fact, adopted the Terry proposal and it stood for three weeks until, on July 22, the members approved a substitute (also by Terry) that simply required the state to educate all children, six to eighteen years of age. A similar proposal had previously lost sixty-six to fifteen.[20] The unseen hand of Banks was evident in the reversal.

While conservative Unionists conceded that Negroes ought to benefit from some form of education, they strongly opposed even partial black suffrage. John Henderson spoke for all of them: "I believe that a negro should possess his wife, his house and his horse, but that a negro shall have the same elective franchise as a white man, is impossible." On the first test, the conservatives voted as a bloc against any form of black suffrage. The vote, however, was overturned, and six weeks later Henderson, Cutler, and thirty-odd conservatives voted with the Radicals and empowered the legislature to enfranchise "such other persons" as qualified "by military service, by taxation . . . or by intellectual fitness." On intimate terms with administration leaders, George S. Denison recognized that only the untiring behind-the-scenes efforts of Banks and Hahn had reversed the decision on the suffrage article. Under the circumstances, he wrote, it was all that "reasonably could have been expected."[21]

19. *Debates in the Convention (1864)*, 161; Raleigh A. Suarez, "Chronicle of Failure: Public Education in Antebellum Louisiana," *Louisiana History*, XII (Spring, 1971), 109–22.
20. *Official Journal (1864)*, 143; *Debates in the Convention (1864)*, 499, 502, 601.
21. *Debates in the Convention (1864)*, 212, 450, 633; George S. Denison to Salmon P.

The Radicals in the convention comprised a bloc that was about the same size as that of the reactionaries; but in contrast to the Negro-phobes, they controlled the chair and at least seven of seventeen committee chairmanships, including the emancipation, education, and legislative (Negro suffrage) chairs.[22] The liberal clauses of the constitution showed their work. Left to themselves, they almost certainly would have provided some form of direct Negro suffrage.

They professed themselves to be shocked at the intransigence of the reactionaries. Hearing proslavery talk in a free-state convention, J. Randall Terry felt a desire to consult the heavens for an adequate reply. Alfred C. Hills expressed shame that any man as well educated as Edmund Abell should, in the second half of the nineteenth century, try and "make us believe that slavery is in accordance with the precepts of religion." Slavery, Hills said, belonged "to the rude ages of mankind, before the light of Christianity and civilization had fallen upon the human family." The proslavery argument appeared particularly offensive in view of the Negro's military service. While the convention listened to cries of "enslave him," Terry intoned, "the Negro bleeds and dies for us at Fort Pillow. See him fighting there to uphold the folds of the glorious banner of the Union."[23]

To be sure, such rhetoric won few votes in that convention, and the Radicals usually combined their appeals to humanity with even lengthier ones to the self-interest of Louisiana whites. To Radicals, the curse of the South was not merely slavery but all that slavery entailed: the economic and political dominance of the slaveholding oligarchy and the degradation of the white masses. Hence, the freeing of the African, stated one, "will prove to be . . . the true liberation and emancipation of the poor white laboring classes of the South." Akin to this idea was

---

Chase, November 25, 1864, in "Diary and Correspondence of Salmon P. Chase," *Annual Report of the American Historical Association for the Year 1902* (Washington, D.C., 1903), II, 451–55 (hereinafter cited as *AHA Annual Rept.*).

22. These were: Max F. Bonzano (Emancipation), George A. Fosdick (Legislative), William R. Fish (Executive), Joseph Gorlinski (Internal Improvements), Alfred C. Hills (Education), Alfred Shaw (Ordinance), Thomas Bangs Thorpe (Enrollment). In addition, John Purcell (Printing), Rufus K. Howell (Judiciary), R. King Cutler (Mode of Revising), and William Davis Mann (General Provisions) usually voted with the Radicals (*Official Journal [1864]*, 28–29; McCrary, *Lincoln and Reconstruction*, 373–80).

23. *Debates in the Convention (1864)*, 167–68, 171–72.

another: That Negroes could be made safe and useful to whites only if they were uplifted. Educating the freedmen was a duty, asserted Hills, and "a matter of self-preservation." Treat them fairly "and they will never imbue their hands in your blood." Whites need not fear blacks, said another Radical; they will find their "proper place," provided they be educated and made useful. Thomas M. Wells, the lieutenant governor's son, put the idea in its baldest form: "I am for the education of the negro, for the simple reason that I believe he will be better to himself and more useful to the country and the white race."[24]

Humanity, duty, self-interest—the Radicals spoke easily of these things because of a crucial difference between themselves and the other members: They did not fear the Negro. Underlying the hatred and recalcitrance of conservatives and reactionaries was fear, the fear of race war, of Negro equality, of this bogey or that; fear, above all, that amalgamation would subvert their sense of themselves as Christian men, living in a civilized Christian culture. To Hills, on the other hand, Negro equality seemed a mere phantom. He did not fear it "because I believe that the white race is the dominant race in this country, and always will be." The liberation of blacks in the free states, he observed, had not led to Negro equality and amalgamation. He asked Abell if that gentleman thought our young men and women would suddenly be seized by a desire to marry Negroes. Amid laughter from the other delegates, he remarked, "I have no taste for that sort of equality myself, and accordingly have no fear of it." The incessant talk about Negro equality, claimed another Radical, amounted to cowardice. "Are you, sir, afraid lest the so greatly despised African, your proclaimed '*inferior*,' shall become your equal or superior?" Does anyone actually fear this? "If I am wrong, let that voice answer. Not one responds, Sir!"[25]

In the end, though, the Radicals always fell back on necessity. President Lincoln, General Banks, and other important people, Thomas Bangs Thorpe told the delegates, played important parts in making this convention possible. "If we fail to come up to their expectations, and the expectation of the North, what will be the result?" The protec-

24. *Ibid.*, 158, 190, 214, 495.
25. *Ibid.*, 178–79, 190; see also 158, 215–16.

tion of the United States, he answered, would not again be extended to any rebellious state.[26] Thorpe's words were more than an appeal for men to act for the good of the country; they were an unsubtle reminder of just where power in Louisiana really resided. Louisiana Unionists abolished slavery to aid the Union. In the end, they voted for black education and partial Negro suffrage in the service of the same master.

The historian, Joseph G. Tregle has observed, is at times compelled to overcome his scruples and "play the game of 'might have been.'" Had Banks not deposed the former leaders of the Free State party, might not Louisiana's wartime convention, perhaps held a month or two earlier, have been a more Radical body; might it not have directly enfranchised part of the black population rather than merely authorizing the legislature to do so? Certainly the writings of Tregle and McCrary suggest that this would have been the case. Perhaps so, but there are reasons for skepticism. Although Durant (by choice) and Flanders missed the convention, the left wing of Louisiana Unionism was not excluded; on the contrary, Radicals showed up in numbers roughly equivalent to their overall strength. The convention, in other words, represented a fair sample of Unionism in the state, and of its members one thing is clear: Their votes may have yielded to Banks, but their hearts belonged to Edmund Abell. Abell free-lanced his way into the assembly, where his presence was most unwelcome by the administration. Perhaps Durant and Flanders could have dealt with him much more effectively than Alfred C. Hills and Thomas Bangs Thorpe. The fact remains that what finally prevailed against the pugnacious old reactionary was military power and deception; the Radical leadership carefully waited until he absented himself from the floor before pushing a final "sneak" vote on the suffrage question.[27]

Another area of speculation concerns the military eclipse of Banks. As LaWanda Cox has observed, the general's humiliating defeat on the Red River unfortunately coincided with the convention and undoubt-

26. *Ibid.*, 140.
27. Joseph G. Tregle, Jr., "Thomas J. Durant, Utopian Socialism, and the Failure of Presidential Reconstruction in Louisiana," *Journal of Southern History*, XLV (November, 1979), 512; McCrary, *Lincoln and Reconstruction*, 263–64.

edly reduced his influence.[28] But what *if* Banks had taken Shreveport and then, amid national fanfare, marched to victory in Alabama. The mood in New Orleans would have been entirely different, the position of the left in the convention immeasurably strengthened, and a truly Radical Free State constitution enters the realm, not of possibility, but of probability. Perhaps, though, we attach too much significance to wartime Louisiana. To imagine counterfactual actions of Durant or Banks altering the overall history of Reconstruction in the state or the nation, we must imagine another event that did not occur: the misfiring of Booth's pistol that fateful night at Ford's Theater.

The loyal electorate ratified the constitution in September by a vote of 6,836 to 1,566.[29] The next month, the Free State legislature met in New Orleans. Although it deliberated until the last days of the war, it accomplished nothing of importance, establishing no schools and enfranchising no one. In its makeup, the legislature resembled the constitutional convention; the difference was the absence of Banks. Frustrated and humiliated at the loss of field command, that worthy had returned to Washington, leaving the gulf in the hands of General Canby and General Hurlbut, neither of whom had any use for the Unionist government of Louisiana. Michael Hahn protested bitterly against constant military interference, to no avail.

Although the constitution makers took little notice, their debates had been followed closely, and with mounting anger, by part of the black community. Desiring political equality with whites, free Negro leaders in New Orleans interpreted the assembly's reluctant concessions to their race not as triumphs but as rebuffs. And in retrospect, while the convention of 1864 did not significantly alter the course of presidential Reconstruction, it marked a critical shift in the history of black thought and action during Reconstruction.

---

28. LaWanda Cox, *Lincoln and Black Freedom: A Study in Presidential Leadership* (Columbia, S.C., 1981), 102.

29. Appleton's *American Annual Cyclopaedia and Register of Important Events of the Year 1864*, (New York, 1865), 479.

4

The Black
Elite

At the close of the Civil War, Whitelaw Reid, a young Radical Republican journalist, visited New Orleans in the retinue of Chief Justice Salmon P. Chase. A skillful reporter, Reid inspected Negro schools and churches, observed the brash behavior of defeated Rebels, and talked with local Union men about the political situation. One morning Thomas J. Durant arranged an interview between Chief Justice Chase and representatives of the "old Louisiana free-negro stock," the *gens de couleur*, in the residence where Reid was staying. Leaving his lunch, the journalist found Chase and a delegation of free blacks talking in the library. On first impression, Reid could hardly believe "that these quiet, well-bred gentlemen, scarcely one darker than Mr. Durant himself—many of them several shades whiter—were negroes." He even imagined that there was some mistake, "that some other party had got into the library by accident—some delegation of Rebel lawyers, perhaps, to remonstrate against the test oath." The free blacks asked the chief justice to explain to President Andrew Johnson "that they paid heavy taxes" to maintain public schools that their children could not enter, and that they contributed to the support of city and state government "and were without voice in either." These facts, they believed, did not accord with the president's "well-known ideas of genuine democracy." What reply could men give who claimed to accept the Declaration of Independence, Reid asked.[1]

Before the war, the journalist noted, the free Negroes "held themselves aloof from the slaves, and particularly from the plantation negroes." This attitude, he believed, no longer prevailed; as one free black candidly told him, "We see that our future is indissolubly bound up with that of the negro race in this country; and we have resolved to

1. Whitelaw Reid, *After the War: A Tour of the Southern States, 1865–1866*, ed. C. Vann Woodward (New York, 1965), 259–60.

make common cause, and rise or fall with them. We have no rights which we can reckon safe while the same are denied to the field-hands on the sugar plantations." When he compiled his narrative for publication the following year, Reid failed to note that his informant's remarks and the tone and spirit of the interview between Chief Justice Chase and the "well-bred gentlemen" in the library were not entirely harmonious.[2]

The individuals described by Reid represented the elite of what had been the largest free black community in the deep South. In 1860, 18,647 free Negroes had lived in Louisiana, 10,689 of them in New Orleans. First as black Unionists, then as black Republicans, they played a critical role in Louisiana during the Civil War and Reconstruction. From their number came Oscar J. Dunn, P. B. S. Pinchback, James H. Ingraham, Ceasar C. Antoine, Louis and J. B. Roudanez, Francis E. Dumas, and other black leaders. Although the slave population of New Orleans numbered 13,385 at the time of the Civil War, the city's black political leaders in the Reconstruction period, almost to a man, were former free men of color.[3]

From French colonial days down to the Civil War, the *gens de couleur* occupied a comparatively secure place in Louisiana society. True, they endured rigid social discrimination, but it was also true, as the state Supreme Court ruled in 1856, that "in the eyes of the Louisiana law, there is . . . all the difference between a free man of color and a slave, that there is between a white man and a slave." Moreover, "it has been settled doctrine here," the high court had held a decade earlier, that light-skinned "persons of color are presumed to be free." Free Negroes owned real and personal property (including slaves), contracted legal marriages, testified against whites in courts of law, learned trades and professions, and participated in music and the arts. Their achievements rested on a solid economic base. Federal census figures from

2. *Ibid.*, 243–44.
3. *Eighth Census, 1860, Population,* 194–96. Starting with a list of 240 Negro politicians, David C. Rankin identified the prewar status of 174 of the Crescent City's Reconstruction black leaders; he found that 169 had been free men of color ("The Origins of Black Leadership in New Orleans During Reconstruction," *Journal of Southern History,* XL [August, 1974], 419–21). The great majority of the 260,000 free Negroes in the slave states lived in the upper South and in the border states (Ira Berlin, *Slaves Without Masters: The Free Negro in the Antebellum South* [New York, 1974], 136).

1850 list the occupations of 1,792 free Negro males in New Orleans. The enumeration includes 355 carpenters, 278 masons, 156 cigar makers, 92 shoemakers, 82 tailors, 64 merchants, 41 barbers, 18 butchers, 12 teachers, 11 overseers, 4 doctors, and 1 architect. Only 179 are classified as unskilled laborers.[4]

Throughout much of their history the people of color relied upon a unique institution to safeguard their rights in society: the free Negro militia. In 1729 a handful of black bondsmen, motivated by the promise of freedom, helped put down a savage uprising of the Natchez Indians. Thereafter free Negro militia fought in every battle against the foreign and domestic enemies of colonial Louisiana. From 1779 to 1781 they engaged the British as Spanish allies of the American revolutionists. After 1803 the Americans disbanded the black militia, but events soon led them to reconsider the decision. In 1811 free men of color volunteered to fight against rebellious slaves marching on New Orleans. Although white militia and American regulars put down the revolt, the territorial governor used a company of free Negroes to relieve the white units. The loyalty of the *gens de couleur* in that crisis led the government to revive the Battalion of Free Men of Color, and in late 1814, with the British threatening New Orleans, it created a second battalion. Both units fought with distinction under Andrew Jackson in the Battle of New Orleans, winning the respect and approval of the hostile Americans. Their bravery in that last and greatest battle of the War of 1812, which was commemorated annually in antebellum New Orleans, helped secure the rights and privileges of free blacks down to the Civil War.[5]

4. Berlin, *Slaves Without Masters*, 110–114, 128–30; Helen Tunncliff Catterall (ed.), *Judicial Cases Concerning American Slavery and the Negro* (5 vols.; Washington, D.C., 1926–1937), III, 392–93, 447–48, 570–71; (in Louisiana 81 percent of Free Negroes were mulattoes); Negro Population 1790–1915 (Washington, D.C., 1918), 511. See John W. Blassingame, *Black New Orleans 1860–1880* (Chicago, 1973); David C. Rankin, "The Impact of the Civil War on the Free Colored Community of New Orleans," *Perspectives in American History*, XI (1977–1978), 379–416; and H. E. Sterkx, *The Free Negro in Ante-Bellum Louisiana* (Cranbury, N.J., 1972).

5. In most years during the 1850s Negro veterans of the Battle of New Orleans marched or rode in the annual victory parade. Roland C. McConnell, *Negro Troops of Antebellum Louisiana: A History of the Battalion of Free Men of Color* (Baton Rouge, 1968), 5–8, 15–20, 43–45, 48–54, 69–70, 89–90, 108–115; Berlin, *Slaves Without Masters*, 112–13, 117–30.

Over the years the relationship between free Negroes and slaves was an uneasy one. Free Negroes too often achieved their gains at the expense of slaves, as they did in the slave revolt of 1811. In the colonial period the free black militia had constituted white society's strongest ally against servile revolt. Nor did the origins of the free Negro population make for harmony with the slave masses. In the wars and rebellions that ravaged Saint-Domingue in the 1790s and 1800s, light-skinned Negro freemen often fought as allies of the French, or after 1803 simply as enemies of the blacks. Free Negroes fled the island in ever-increasing numbers and thousands eventually made their way to Louisiana. Largely as a consequence of that immigration, the free Negro population of Louisiana grew from 1,300 in 1785 to nearly 8,000 in 1810. The second battalion of Negro militia formed during the Battle of New Orleans was comprised almost entirely of émigrés who had fought for the French in Saint-Domingue. There also developed a class of black slave owners. In 1830 some 750 free Negroes in New Orleans owned 2,351 slaves. Rural Louisiana evolved a larger class of slaveholding free blacks than any other Southern state. Whether it was true, as many slaves believed, that free Negroes made cruel masters or simply that psychologically it was more painful to serve a black master than a white one, the quip "You be's as bad as a free nigger" was a common rebuke among bondsmen of antebellum New Orleans.[6]

Initially free Negroes in Louisiana reacted to the outbreak of war between North and South in 1861 as if the British had once again landed on the Gulf Coast. In Pointe Coupee, Natchitoches, and Plaquemines parishes, slave-owning free blacks organized militia companies for protection against slave revolts and defense of the homeland. Well-to-do men of color in New Orleans contributed to the defense fund of the Committee on Public Safety, and the city's free Negro men offered their military services to the Confederacy. In re-

6. Berlin, *Slaves Without Masters*, 108–16, 128; McConnell, *Negro Troops of Antebellum Louisiana*, 46–48, 69–70; Charles Barthelemy Rousseève, *The Negro in Louisiana: Aspects of His History and His Literature* (New Orleans, 1937), 45; Donald Edward Everett, "Free Persons of Color in New Orleans, 1803–1865" (Ph.D. dissertation, Tulane University, 1952), 250.

sponse, Confederate governor Thomas O. Moore authorized the formation of a regiment of free Negro militia, called Native Guards, for the defense of New Orleans. In subsequent months the Native Guards expanded until in early 1862 they numbered over 3,000. At that time, a considerably larger proportion of the state's free Negroes were under arms for the Confederacy than white Louisianians.[7]

After New Orleans fell to the Federals in May 1862, free Negroes maintained that they had sided with the Confederacy under duress. Little evidence exists to support that contention. The initiative for the Native Guards clearly came from the *gens de couleur*, and while the Confederates accepted their assistance, they remained suspicious of their Negro allies, limiting their military service to ceremonial duties. In the end, these suspicions proved thoroughly justified. When the Rebels abandoned New Orleans, the free Negro regiments remained behind. General Butler had not been in the city a month before the former Native Guardsmen asked him about fighting for the Union.[8]

Butler demurred, but late that summer, desperate for troops, he began recruiting Native Guards for the Union Army. The following spring General Banks established the Corps d'Afrique and initiated the mass recruitment of Louisiana blacks. By the end of the war 24,052 Louisiana Negroes had served in the Union Army. That is an impressive figure, and it becomes considerably more so when one recalls that most blacks in the state lived within Confederate lines throughout the war. Within Union territory, moreover, Federal policy forced

7. Everett, "Free Persons of Color in New Orleans," 268–69; Blassingame, *Black New Orleans*, 33–34; Donald E. Everett, "Ben Butler and the Louisiana Native Guards, 1861–1862," *Journal of Southern History*, XXIV (May, 1958), 202–204; Mary F. Berry, "Negro Troops in Blue and Gray: The Louisiana Native Guards, 1861–1863," *Louisiana History*, VIII (Spring, 1967), 166–67; Gary B. Mills, "Patriotism Frustrated: The Native Guards of Confederate Natchitoches," *Louisiana History*, XVIII (Fall, 1977), 440–41. By the winter of 1862, Louisiana had raised 20,000 regular troops and 15,000 militia (probably including the Native Guards) out of a white population of 357,629. By comparison, free blacks raised 3,000 militia from a population of 18,647, meaning that whereas 10 percent of the white population was under arms, 16 percent of free Negroes were so arrayed (*Eighth Census, 1860, Population*, 194; John D. Winters, *Civil War in Louisiana* [Baton Rouge, 1963], 71).

8. James Parton, *General Butler in New Orleans* (New York, 1864), 516–17; Everett, "Free Persons of Color in New Orleans," 273–76; Berry, "Negro Troops in Blue and Gray," 166–73; Mills, "Patriotism Frustrated," 440–41; Berlin, *Slaves Without Masters*, 386–87.

thousands of Negro males of military age to labor as field hands for "loyal" masters or government lessees. In fact, in proportion to the men available, the number of Louisiana blacks who carried arms for the Union was comparable with the estimated 56,000 Louisiana whites who served in the Confederate armies.[9]

Historians may quarrel about whether or not the Civil War was a revolution, but no Louisianian, white or black, ever doubted its reality from the first time he saw black men in dark blue uniforms marching in rank along the road or through the streets of New Orleans. To whites the sight aroused, as nothing else could, fears of race war and Negro domination that were as ancient as the South. But the scene was nonetheless revolutionary to blacks, raising up in reverse proportion to the fear and hatred of whites the hopes and dreams that were as old as slavery. "To Arms!" urged the Crescent City's black newspaper, *The Union*: "It is an honor understood by our fathers who fought on the plains of Chalmette [in 1815]. He who defends his fatherland is the real citizen, and this time we are fighting for the rights of our race. . . . We demand justice. And when an organized, numerous, and respectable body which has rendered many services to the nation demands justice—nothing more, but nothing less—the nation cannot refuse." Some weeks later the newspaper declared, "From the day that bayonets were placed in the hands of the blacks . . . the Negro became a citizen of the United States. . . . This war has broken the chains of the slave, and it is written in the heavens that from this war shall grow the seeds of the political enfranchisement of the oppressed race."[10]

For the *gens de couleur*, as for other Southerners, the Civil War was the most important event in history. The enlistment of several thousand fathers and sons in the Union Army firmly tied the free Negro family as an institution to the Northern side of the war. That, in turn, profoundly affected other institutions: the fraternal orders and mutual assistance societies, and the Protestant churches. Probably no event of the war better illustrates this development than the funeral in July 1863

9. Joseph T. Wilson, *The Black Phalanx: A History of the Negro Soldiers of the United States in the Wars of 1775–1812, 1861–'65* (Hartford, 1890), 142; Winters, *Civil War in Louisiana*, 428.

10. James M. McPherson (ed.), *The Negro's Civil War: How American Negroes Felt and Acted During the War for the Union* (New York, 1965), 169–70, 281–82.

of Captain André Cailloux, the fallen black hero of the Port Hudson campaign. After a Catholic service in the Church of St. Rose of Lima, the march to the cemetery began, accompanied by the dirges of the 42d Massachusetts regimental band. Beside the flag-draped hearse walked six Negro army officers and six members of the Friends of the Order, Cailloux' fraternity, which had handled the funeral arrangements. Behind the hearse, the procession included a group of sick and wounded Negro soldiers, two companies of Native Guards, the carriages of the Cailloux family, and the fully liveried representatives of thirty-seven black societies:

Friends of the Order
Society of Economy and Mutual Assistance
United Brethren
Arts' and Mechanics' Association
Free Friends
Good Shepherd Conclave, No. 2
Artisans' Brotherhood
Good Shepherd Conclave, No. 1
Union Sons' Relief
Perseverance Society
Ladies of Bon Secours
La Fleur de Marie
St. Rose of Lima
Children of Mary Society
St. Angela Society
Immaculate Conception Society
The Sacred Union Society
The Children of Jesus
St. Veronica Society
St. Alphonsus Society
St. Joachim Society
Star of the Cross
St. Eulalia Society
St. Magdalen Society
God Protect Us Society
United Sisterhood

Angel Gabriel Society
St. Louis Roi Society
St. Bénoit Society
Benevolence Society
Well Beloved Sisters' Society
St. Peter Society
St. Michael Archangel Society
St. Louis de Gonzague Society
St. Ann Society
The Children of Moses
St. Theresa Society.

Along the route the members of those societies lined Esplanade Street for over a mile.[11] Such demonstrations became common in New Orleans during the war on a lesser scale. In January 1865 a newspaper advertisement notified "all colored citizens and societies" to assemble at Lafayette Square "in full Regalia" to celebrate the emancipation of Missouri and Tennessee. The previous week a meeting had been called at the School of Liberty to read a letter from President Lincoln that acknowledged the gift of a special Bible from the colored people of New Orleans: "All citizens, pastors and officers of churches . . . all presidents, officers, and members of different societies are respectfully invited to turn out in full Regalia. Our most distinguished colored speakers will be selected for the occasion."[12]

As the names of their societies suggest, most free Negroes in New Orleans were Catholics. White Southerners controlled the positions of authority in the Catholic Church and, while some free black Catholics abandoned their faith during and after the Civil War, the majority did not.[13] An important reason, then, why Negro societies played vital political roles in the community was that, unlike black Protestants, black Catholics could not convert their churches into independent forums for social and political organization.

Negro Protestants, slave and free, on the other hand, did precisely

11. William Wells Brown, *The Negro in the American Rebellion* (Boston, 1867), 186–91.
12. New Orleans *Tribune*, January 17 & 24, 1865.
13. Robert C. Reinders, "The Churches and the Negro in New Orleans," *Phylon*, XXII (Spring, 1961), 242–43, 247; Blassingame, *Black New Orleans*, 148–49.

that when the Federal occupation freed them from white supervision. Several thousand blacks promptly deserted the Southern Methodist Episcopal Church and formed Negro congregations affiliated with the Methodist Episcopal Church North. The African Methodist Episcopal (AME) Church, the AME Zion Church, and the African Baptist Church also grew rapidly during the war. Protestant church buildings constituted the largest property holdings of the Negro community[14] and, quite logically, became the centers where most social, charitable, and political community business was transacted. A religious writer complained in early 1865 that some churches had closed their doors against efforts at providing relief for Union soldiers: "As an excuse, we are told that churches are not the place to hold meetings in, except for religious purposes; granted. But what other places are we to assemble in?" The writer urged church officials to make their buildings available to the community.[15]

Under such conditions black ministers emerged as important political figures. In July 1864, for example, Negro leaders met at St. James AME Church to consider the expansion of the National Union Brotherhood Association, a black Unionist society. After the opening remarks, clergymen so dominated the discussion that an uninformed stranger coming in off the street would probably have mistaken the proceedings for a preachers' meeting. At length, the assembly approved a motion "to call a Ministerial Meeting and invite the ministers of all colored churches and denominations to meet in (St. Paul's) Wesleyan Chapel" and consider the question further. Beginning in early 1865, two prominent AME ministers, William A. Dove and Robert McCary, edited a newspaper column called the "Religious Department," in which they repeatedly stressed the vital importance of a "Religious and Political Union of Our People."[16]

The formation of the Louisiana National Equal Rights League revealed the full extent to which the war politicized the social and reli-

14. Blassingame, *Black New Orleans*, 148–49; church directory in New Orleans *Tribune*, February 1, 2, and 5, 1865, *passim*; Everett, "Free Persons of Color in New Orleans," 226–27.
15. New Orleans *Tribune*, February 17, 1865.
16. *Ibid.*, July 21, 1864; January 31, February 17 and 26, March 22, April 9, May 18 and 21, and June 11, 1865.

gious institutions of free Negro society. In October 1864 Negroes from eighteen states (among them James H. Ingraham of Louisiana) met in a National Convention of Colored Citizens of the United States at Syracuse, New York, and established a National Equal Rights League. After Ingraham's return to New Orleans, black leaders formed a Louisiana NERL and made preparations for a state convention. They announced that any Negro society with 100 members was entitled to one representative in the convention; societies with over 120 members received two representatives. In January 1865 some 100 delegates met for a week in New Orleans. At one session, the first order of business was a proposal to investigate the churches that had not contributed to the expenses of the convention. "The influence of ministers is very great," William A. Dove asserted in support of the motion; "every minister of the Gospel has to favor every thing tending to the elevation of his race. . . . If the elders or deacons of the churches do not concur in this move let them be removed." The delegates approved the investigation and later elected Dove and Robert McCary to the NERL Executive Committee.[17]

Traditionally, French Catholics, so-called creole Negroes, comprised the black elite in New Orleans and, indeed, exerted a major influence in the community during the war. Paul Trévigne, for example, editor of *The Union* (1862–1864) and an editor of the New Orleans *Tribune* (1864–1869), had formerly taught at a Catholic school for free Negroes. His father had fought in the Battle of New Orleans in 1815. Dr. Louis and J. B. (Jean Baptiste) Roudanez, the proprietors of the *Tribune*, were the sons of a French merchant and a free Negro woman. A graduate of the Medical Faculties of the University of Paris and Dartmouth College, Louis practiced medicine in New Orleans throughout the Civil War and Reconstruction. His brother J. B. was a skilled mechanic. In mid-1864 the brothers obtained control of the faltering *Union* and reorganized it into the *Tribune*. From that time until the newspaper's demise in 1869, they took part in every major racial controversy in the state.[18]

17. *Ibid.*, November 24 (French edition) and December 27, 1864, and January 14, 1865.
18. Everett, "Free Persons of Color in New Orleans," 330; Roussève, *Negro in Louisi-*

As the crisis of the Union deepened, though, leadership roles opened up to new men—individuals like Oscar J. Dunn, James H. Ingraham, and P. B. S. Pinchback, for example. By his own account, Dunn was born in 1826 and could never remember being anything but a free man. According to stories in the New Orleans press after his death, he was the son of a free Negro woman who owned a rooming house for white actors and a mulatto stage carpenter. By those accounts, the future lieutenant governor learned elocution and rhetoric as a boy from the actors and singers in the boardinghouse. It is certain that he was apprenticed to a plastering firm as a youth and that such was his profession in antebellum New Orleans. A small property owner of modest means, he ran an employment agency after the war, supplying servants and field hands to planters. "I am a creole," he declared, and explained that anyone born in New Orleans, regardless of color, was a creole.[19]

Born a slave, James H. Ingraham was freed at the age of six. He owed his political prominence to a good war record. In May 1863 two regiments of Native Guards attacked a Rebel strongpoint at Port Hudson. Tactically, it was an ill-conceived assault that led to pointless slaughter. Its significance lay in the revelation that Negro soldiers would suffer themselves to be slaughtered like whites. ("They fought splendidly!" General Banks informed his wife. "No troops could have been more determined or more daring.") The battle made a dead hero of Captain Cailloux and a live one of Captain Ingraham. He was introduced to the National Convention of Colored Citizens in Syracuse the

ana, 43–44, 118–20. Dr. Roundanez had been one of the backers of the *Union* (Finnian Patrick Leavens, "*L'Union* and the *New Orleans Tribune* and Louisiana Reconstruction" [M.A. thesis, Louisiana State University, 1966], 12–16; Boston *Liberator*, April 15, 1864; William P. Connor, "Reconstruction Rebels: The *New Orleans Tribune* in Post-War Louisiana," *Louisiana History*, XXI [Spring, 1980], 160–65). One of the *Tribune* editors was Jean-Charles Houzeau, a white Belgian astronomer and political Radical (unfortunately the *Tribune* staff did not write under by-lines). See his autobiographical "Le Journal Noir, Aux Etats-Unis, de 1863 a 1870," *Revue de Beligique*, II (May, 1872), 5–28 and (June, 1872), 97–122.

19. *House Reports*, 39th Cong., 2d Sess., No. 16, pp. 68–69; *House Miscellaneous Documents*, 41st Cong., 2d Sess., No. 154, Pt. 1, pp. 178–81; New Orleans, Mayor's Office, Register of Free Colored Persons Entitled to Remain in the State, 1840–1864, New Orleans Public Library; Marcus B. Christian, "The Theory of the Poisoning of Oscar J. Dunn," *Phylon*, VI (Fall, 1945), 254–55 *nn.* 4–10; A. E. Perkins, "Oscar James Dunn," *Phylon*, IV (Spring, 1943), 105; New Orleans *Tribune*, November 30, 1865.

following year as that bold young officer from Louisiana who had led his unit over the ramparts at Port Hudson. President of the NERL convention in 1865, Ingraham emerged as a skillful leader.[20]

P. B. S. (Pinckney Benton Stewart) Pinchback represented a small but important class of free black leaders who migrated to Louisiana during the war. The eighth child of a white Mississippi planter and his manumitted mulatto mistress, Pinchback attended high school in Cincinnati, Ohio. His father died soon after his return to Mississippi, and Pinchback's mother fled to Cincinnati with her illegitimate children to escape their father's heirs. From that time until the Civil War, Pinchback worked on canal boats and riverboats, eventually becoming a steward. He also learned to gamble. In *Forty Years a Gambler on the Mississippi*, George H. Devol recalled, "He was my boy. I raised him, and trained him. I took him out of a steamboat barber shop. I instructed him in the mysteries of card-playing, and he was an apt pupil." In particular, the gambler remembered the lucky streak that began the night "we sent Pinch to open a game of chuck-a-luck with the niggers on deck, while we opened up monte in the cabin." Less credibly, Devol has young Pinchback claiming, "Ise going to get into that good old Legislature; and I'll make Rome howl if I get there." One concludes that Pinchback was more than a casual acquaintance of such cardsharps as Devol.

In 1862 Pinchback jumped ship in Yazoo City, Mississippi, and made his way to occupied New Orleans. There he stabbed a free Negro, who reputedly was his brother-in-law, and served a month in jail. Light enough to pass for white, he joined the Federal army after his release. When General Butler recruited Negro troops, Pinchback left his white unit and raised a company of Native Guards. In 1863 General Banks forced the resignations of black officers, including Captain Pinchback. Though Pinchback later recruited a company of Negro cavalrymen, Banks refused to recommission him. Following that disappointment, he left the army.[21]

20. Rankin, "Origins of Black Leadership in New Orleans," 421–22; Harrington, *Fighting Politician*, 112; New Orleans *Tribune*, October 25, 1864.

21. William J. Simmons, *Men of Mark: Eminent, Progressive and Rising* (Cleveland, 1887), 759–63; Agnes Smith Grosz, "The Political Career of Pinckney Benton Stewart Pinchback," *Louisiana Historical Quarterly*, XXVII (April, 1944), 527–31; George H. Devol, *Forty Years a Gambler on the Mississippi* (New York, 1887), 216–17.

Whatever their origins, the initial political goal of free Negroes during the war was to obtain the suffrage for the *gens de couleur*. But what started as the free Negro suffrage issue gradually became the Negro suffrage issue, and as it did the Crescent City's men of color confronted two of the most difficult questions of Reconstruction: To what extent would whites determine the interests of blacks? And to what degree would former "free" Negroes decide the interests of "freed" Negroes?

In preparation for the wartime restoration of Louisiana to the Union, the registration of loyal white voters commenced in the early summer of 1863. The following November free men of color met at Economy Hall in New Orleans and adopted resolutions calling on military governor George F. Shepley to register free Negroes as voters. The petitioners described themselves as men of property who contributed to the commerce and industry of the state. Their forefathers had defended New Orleans in 1815, and under Butler and Banks they had taken up arms for the Union: "We are men, treat us as such."[22] Shepley—and Banks—failed to respond, and the Free State government of Michael Hahn was elected in early 1864 without black participation.

Blocked in Louisiana, the *gens de couleur* appealed to President Lincoln and Congress, asking that black Louisianians, "born free before the rebellion," be registered as voters. Charles Sumner and other Radical Republicans received the petition favorably but were disturbed that it ignored the slave masses. They persuaded J. B. Roudanez and Arnold Bertonneau (a wine merchant and ex-captain of Native Guards), who were the bearers of the petition, to add a section asking the suffrage for all Louisiana Negroes, "whether born slave or free, especially those who have vindicated their right to vote by bearing arms." Lincoln was also moved by the entreaty. The Louisiana constitution convention of 1864 was scheduled to meet in April; the day after the president received the petition, he wrote Governor Michael Hahn suggesting privately that the convention enfranchise part of the colored population, "as, for instance, the very intelligent, and especially those who have fought gallantly in our ranks."[23]

22. Appleton's *American Annual Cyclopaedia and Register of Important Events of the Year 1863* (New York, 1864), 589–90; New Orleans *Times*, November 6, 1863.
23. Boston *Liberator*, April 1 and 15, 1864; McPherson (ed.), *Negro's Civil War*,

Free Negroes probably did not expect much from the constitution makers in New Orleans. If so, they were not disappointed. Left to themselves, the delegates showed a decided preference for the coarse fare of the proslavery argument, served up in generous portions. But they were not left to themselves. Aware of the expectations in Washington that the Louisiana constitution make some concessions to blacks, General Banks and Governor Hahn forced the convention, beyond abolishing slavery, to provide for Negro schools and to authorize the legislature to enfranchise blacks on the basis of military service, exceptional intelligence, or payment of taxes.

Even the New Orleans *Tribune* conceded that the new constitution was an improvement over the constitution of 1852. That did not make it acceptable to the *Tribune* or to the *gens de couleur*. Free Negroes were already free, many of their children attended private schools, and a limited extension of the suffrage was merely authorized—not actually granted. As well as anyone else, they could see the means by which General Banks and Governor Hahn had wrung concessions from the convention majority, a perspective that did not inspire confidence in a legislature composed of similar men actually carrying out the educational and suffrage provisions of the constitution. Probably as important as anything else was the tone of the debates: the proslavery harangues; the endless talk about amalgamation, race war, Negro degeneracy and savagery; the enthusiastic response of the majority for measures that would exclude free Negroes from the state, deny them the suffrage or bar them from learning trades or professions. Even the Negro's "friends" in the assembly compiled a record of gratuitous insults.[24] Under such leadership, Lincoln and Banks proposed to restore Louisiana to the Union. Black leaders were outraged.

Four days before the convention adjourned, and twelve days after the *Union* stopped publication, the first issue of the New Orleans *Tribune* appeared. In most respects, the *Union* had been a Radical and egalitarian newspaper. Taking its stand on the Declaration of Independence and trusting in Christian reform, it had attacked the abuses of society

278–79; Abraham Lincoln to Michael Hahn, March 13, 1864, in Roy P. Basler (ed.), *The Collected Works of Abraham Lincoln* (New Brunswick, N.J., 1953–1955), VII, 243.

24. New Orleans *Tribune*, July 28, 1864; *Debates in the Convention (1864)*, 142, 156, 165–66, 182–83, 210–11, 224, *passim*.

from slavery to capital punishment. What it had not done was challenge the Reconstruction policies of Lincoln and Banks.[25] All that now changed. Had the South "desired a conservative President in 1860," the *Tribune* charged angrily, "neither North nor South of the Potomac could they have found one who would have more zealously protected their rights of property in man; no one who would have lent the whole weight of the executive of the nation to the rigid enforcement of the Fugitive Slave Act; no one who would have preserved more inviolate the rights of the people of the Southern states under the Constitution than Abraham Lincoln." The record in Louisiana made plain what loyal men could expect from the president. The hidden goal of the Free State constitution was to secure Louisiana's electoral votes for Lincoln in the presidential election of 1864. That document was "*based on Executive usurpation*" and drafted by individuals "who had no higher principle of action than hatred of their fellows of African descent." Like the authors of the Wade-Davis bill, the *Tribune* concluded that Reconstruction was a job for Congress, not the president.[26]

The second phase of the Negro suffrage controversy in Louisiana began when the Free State legislature met in the fall. Very probably at the instigation of Federal officials, Charles Smith of St. Mary Parish introduced a bill in the senate that provided that "every person having not more than one-fou[r]th negro blood, shall be considered and recognized as white, in the State of Louisiana." Smith expressed concern that men who were three-fourths white were treated as Negroes, but it was not a concern shared by his fellow lawmakers. Most agreed with the senator who asked, "Does Mr. Smith wish the legislature to declare a colored man a white man? This bill is an absurdity." The senate disposed of the measure on November 14, but the very next day Smith returned with a new bill. He now proposed extending the suffrage to blacks who qualified by "intellectual fitness," a year in the army, or the payment of thirty dollars a year in taxes. Because this merely carried out the explicit authorization of the new constitution,

25. See, for example, *The Union*, December 1, 1863. Most of the surviving copies of the *Union* are in French. Some excellent excerpts have been translated in McPherson (ed.), *Negro's Civil War*.

26. New Orleans *Tribune*, August 13 and 25, 1864.

Smith perhaps expected a more sympathetic hearing. However, a big change had occurred in Louisiana since July: General Banks had returned to Washington; in his absence, Louisiana Unionists voted their prejudices unmolested. They rejected Smith's second bill on its first reading by a convincing vote of fifteen to five.[27]

Considering the finality of the vote in the senate, the whole question ought to have died down until after the war. It did not because the question of Negro suffrage in Louisiana had become adjoined to the national issue of congressional recognition of presidential Reconstruction. When General Banks undercut Durant and engineered the election of Michael Hahn as Free State governor, he stirred up more trouble than he ever thought could arise. Durant and his allies complained to Congress persistently and articulately that Banks had created a puppet regime in Louisiana. So effective was the charge, that congressional support for the Hahn government was badly damaged. At the time the Louisiana senate rejected the Smith bills, however, Congress was not in session and the fate of Free State Louisiana was still undecided. When Congress met in December, Lincoln fought hard for the readmission of Louisiana to the Union. For weeks the administration and its supporters appeared on the verge of victory, but in late February 1865 a Radical filibuster, led by Charles Sumner, doomed the Louisiana resolution by preventing it from coming to a vote.[28]

Throughout the controversy General Banks remained in Washington and lobbied for the Hahn government. Back in Louisiana the general's loyal lieutenants, the "Banks oligarchy"[29]—Major B. Rush Plumly, Thomas W. Conway, Anthony P. Dostie, and others—attempted to influence the readmission struggle in Congress: From December

27. The senate indefinitely tabled Smith's first bill by a vote of twenty to four. *Louisiana Senate Journal*, 1864, pp. 56–59; *Louisiana Senate Debates*, 1864, pp. 45–50; New Orleans *Daily True Delta*, November 16, 1864. The Smith bills were the basis of the New Orleans *Tribune*'s somewhat misleading discussion of a "Quadroon Bill" (November 10 [French edition], 12 and 16, 1864, *passim*).

28. Herman Belz, *Reconstructing the Union: Theory and Policy During the Civil War* (Ithaca, N.Y., 1969), 190–94, 267–72; Peyton McCrary, *Abraham Lincoln and Reconstruction: The Louisiana Experiment* (Princeton, 1978), 207–210, 232–33, 293–302; James M. McPherson, *The Struggle for Equality: Abolitionists and the Negro in the Civil War and Reconstruction* (Princeton, 1964), 308–310.

29. The description is James H. Ingraham's. New Orleans *Tribune*, March 18, 1865.

through February they urged the black community in New Orleans to petition the legislature for the franchise. In view of the state senate's action on the Smith bills, that strategy requires an explanation. Perhaps they believed that the lawmakers might change their minds and receive such a petition favorably. But because the intelligence of Plumly, Conway, and Dostie is not in question, the answer must lie elsewhere. The only explanation that makes sense is that they expected Banks to return to New Orleans before the Louisiana question came to a vote in Congress—return and force concessions from the recalcitrant Unionists in the legislature as he had forced concessions in the constitutional convention. In fact, Banks did return, but too late. The Radical filibuster in the United States Senate had ended. Governor Hahn had resigned, and the reactionary James Madison Wells was governor of Louisiana.

Ironically, for the *gens de couleur* the petition question turned into the most divisive issue of the war. While most black leaders opposed petitioning the legislature, a determined minority supported the move. The two factions closely resembled each other; both included prominent French Catholics, ex-soldiers, and Protestant ministers.[30] The major confrontation between the two occurred at the NERL convention when a special committee issued a divided report: a majority report in favor of petitioning the legislature and a minority report opposed to it. The supporters of the majority position argued that a petition was the logical step before appealing to Congress and that certainly nothing could be lost by trying. The opposition maintained that even if the legislature was inclined, which it plainly was not, it could only make a limited extension of the suffrage as authorized by the constitution of 1864. And beyond that, how could they appeal to a government that had systematically treated them with contempt? "If we have blood in our veins," James H. Ingraham asserted, "we will not seek to be once more rebuked." Under Ingraham's determined leadership, the convention overturned the majority report by a vote of

30. An interesting division occurred among the Protestant clergy. Despite initial support, the AME and AME Zion pastors ended up against the petition while the African Baptist ministers backed the propetition minority throughout (New Orleans *Tribune*, January 14, February 5, 9, and 15, 1865; New Orleans *Black Republican*, April 15, 22, & 29, 1865).

fifty-one to twenty-two. Motions to reconsider the question were urged on subsequent days and voted down, but not so decisively. A proposal that the petition be held back until Congress readmitted Louisiana to the Union lost by the narrow margin of thirty-seven to thirty-two. In late January and throughout February, the issue continued to come up at public meetings and in the local chapters of the NERL. [31]

As the official organ of the NERL, the *Tribune* vigorously supported the antipetition faction. The newspaper was now convinced that a congressional extension of the suffrage to Southern Negroes was all but inevitable, because by themselves white Unionists would be overwhelmed after the war by the defeated Confederates. Should the conflict end in a month, it predicted, "the first general election . . . would place the government of the state in the hands of . . . the open foes of the Union." Hence, only by enfranchising Southern freedmen could the North prevent Rebel domination of the postwar South. "Why then to be in such a hurry?" the journal asked the petitioners. "Can we not wait a little longer, in order to obtain the franchise for all, without distinction of classes?" Is any black man "bold enough and selfish enough to go to the ballot-box and exercise the right of voting, when thousands of his brethren, as good citizens as he, would be lookers on . . . declared unfit to be men?" Despite the *Tribune*, the NERL, and charges of race treason, the petitioners persisted; and on February 17 a sympathetic senator introduced their petition, bearing some five thousand signatures, in the upper chamber. The senate consigned the memorial to a special committee, never to be heard of again. [32]

Throughout the petition controversy, relations between the NERL and the *Tribune*, on the one hand, and the "Banks oligarchy," on the other, had steadily worsened. Nor was the petition the only cause of conflict. The Union Army, no less than generations of white Southerners, had practiced widespread discrimination against Louisiana Negroes throughout the occupation. In addition, many free blacks were

31. New Orleans *Tribune*, January 14, February 5, 1865, *passim*.
32. *Ibid.*, December 9, 1864, and January 24, 1865; *Louisiana Senate Debates*, 1865, p. 158.

outraged over the treatment of freedmen under the "free labor" program established by General Banks. But, whereas those issues united
free Negroes, the petition question divided them. With some justice,
the antipetition leaders blamed Plumly, Conway, and Dostie for the
split in the black community. By March the petition was history, but
relations between black leaders and occupation officials did not improve; on the contrary, overnight the two antagonists found themselves locked in another bitter conflict. This time the cause was "free
labor."

Because blacks in occupied Louisiana refused to work as slaves,
Butler and Banks established wage systems to ensure a stable work
force and exploit the state's agriculture for the Union. The program
that emerged in 1863 was so oppressive that, by comparison, the notorious black codes adopted after the war appear merely as extensions
of Federal policy. "Free labor" assumed that Negroes would not work
without compulsion; hence, it bound them to yearly contracts enforced by the army; its restrictive rules governing travel, assembly,
firearms, and whiskey showed the same obsession with race control
that had dominated generations of Southerners. Banks's provost
marshals ran the program to meet the needs of the army, the war effort, and the planters. The hopes and aspirations of black men and
women little influenced their decisions.[33]

Although widely condemned by abolitionists and Radical Republicans in the North, the New Orleans *Tribune* emerged as the program's
most persistent critic. In late 1864 the black journal compared a set of
"free labor" regulations, adopted by a recent conference of planters,
with Louisiana's antebellum slave code:

> If we except the lash, which is not mentioned in these communica-
> tions, one is unable to perceive any material difference between the two

33. The program is outlined in *The War of the Rebellion: A Compilation of the Official
Records of the Union and Confederate Armies* (Washington, D.C., 1880–1901), Ser. I, Vol.
XV, pp. 592–95, 602, 619–21, 666–67, Vol. XXXIV, Pt. 2, pp. 227–31 (hereinafter
cited as *OR*, unless otherwise indicated, all citations are to Series I); and Parton, *Butler in
New Orleans*, 522–28. Its repressive nature is amply documented by C. Peter Ripley,
Slaves and Freedmen in Civil War Louisiana (Baton Rouge, 1976); Louis S. Gerteis, *From
Contraband to Freedmen: Federal Policy Toward Southern Blacks, 1861–1865* (Westport,
Conn., 1973); McCrary, *Lincoln and Reconstruction*; and William F. Messner, *Freedmen
and the Ideology of Free Labor: Louisiana 1862–1865* (Lafayette, La., 1978).

sets of regulations. All the important prohibitions imposed upon the slave, are also enforced against the freedmen. The free laborer, as well as the slave, has to retire into his cabin at a fixed hour in the evening; he cannot leave on Sunday, even to visit friends or simply to take a walk in the neighborhood [without] a written authorization. . . . It is true that the law calls him a freeman; but any white man, subjected to such restrictive and humiliating prohibitions, will certainly call himself a slave.

Banks's policy, the newspaper concluded, created "mock-freedmen." [34]

To most black leaders the continuation of the system in the present form was unthinkable. Nonetheless, in March General Stephen A. Hurlbut renewed the program in its entirety. The NERL immediately condemned the decision and called on Hurlbut to reconsider. The *Tribune* argued that the renewal blasted the hope that the freedman would learn to take care of himself, because if nothing was done that year, he would be in the same condition in 1866, "and the same arguments will once more be used to keep him down. . . . When, then, will progress come? Is this apprenticeship to be perpetual?" [35] Incensed by the criticism, Hurlbut lashed out at the NERL, and Conway intrigued against the *Tribune*. Failing to deter their critics, the Federals financed the old propetition faction in setting up a short-lived weekly newspaper, the *Black Republican*, as a rival to the *Tribune*. [36]

Over months of controversy in the winter and spring of 1865, the *Tribune* perceived a common pattern; whether the issue was the petition or "free labor," white officials like Plumly, Conway, and Hurlbut acted as if they knew better than Negroes themselves what was in the best interests of black Louisianians. Negroes, those officials assumed, be they ex-slaves or freemen, ought to remain passive, letting whites decide policy and relying on their white friends and protectors to deal fairly with them. When blacks challenged those assumptions, the Federals typically reacted as Conway did at a March meeting of the NERL Executive Committee: "Gentlemen, I differ with you. I believe your present course to be ruinous, and you will find it out to your sorrow." Hurlbut at the same time urged Negroes to "wait and work" and "not

34. New Orleans *Tribune*, December 8, 1864.
35. *OR*, XLVII, Pt. 1, pp. 1146–48; New Orleans *Tribune*, March 14 and 18, 1865.
36. New Orleans *Tribune*, March 18, 28, 29, and 30, 1865. The ultra pro-Federal editorials of the *Black Republican* leave no doubt as to the source of its income.

call meetings and pass resolutions." The *Tribune* called this pattern of Federal paternalism tutelage: "At the first step—not very material in itself—that we attempt to make, we find tutors around us, who take upon themselves to redress our conduct, and try to prescribe what we have to do. We have asserted our manhood, and we will do it again. We need friends . . . but we do not need tutors. The age of guardianship is past forever, and we shall act for ourselves." Of all the would-be tutors, none angered the *Tribune* more than Superintendent Conway of the Bureau of Free Labor. The NERL convention of January, the newspaper averred, had barely adjourned before Conway expressed disapproval of its decision on the petition question. "He seemed unwilling to understand that the Convention felt as colored men feel, while Mr. Conway could only feel as a white man feels." Thus, as the war drew to a conclusion and the minds of public men turned increasingly to the tasks of Reconstruction, the *Tribune* repeatedly warned the Federals that Negroes intended to run their own affairs. "There is no man in the world so perfectly identified with our interests as to understand it better than we do ourselves." [37]

Which Negroes would decide the interests of black Louisianians? Quick to see the paternalism of the "Banks oligarchy," free Negroes were much less perceptive about their own paternalism. To James H. Ingraham, as to most free blacks, the answer was self-evident: "Unless [the] people of refinement and education act for the benighted ones, the ignorant will be trodden down." The *Tribune* developed the idea more fully. "Louisiana is in a very peculiar situation," it said. "Here, the colored population has a twofold origin. There is an old population, with a history and mementos of their own, warmed by patriotism, partaking of the feelings and education of the white. The only social condition known to these men is that of freedom. . . . There is, on the other hand, a population of freedmen, but recently liberated from the shackles of bondage. All is to be done yet for them." It was essential, the newspaper believed, that the two populations work together. "The emancipated will find, in the old freemen, friends ready to guide them, to spread upon them the light of knowledge, and teach

37. New Orleans *Tribune*, January 20, March 15, 23, and 28, 1865.

86

them their duties as well as their rights. But, at the same time, the freemen will find in the recently liberated slaves a mass to uphold them; and with this mass behind them they will command the respect always bestowed to number and strength."[38] Put more bluntly, free Negroes knew better than ex-slaves what were in the interests of black Louisianians. In the tasks ahead, the former bondsmen ought to remain passive, letting the old freemen make policy and trusting in their more enlightened brethren to deal fairly with them.

A crucial aspect of free Negro paternalism was a concern for "elevation" of the freedmen—a subject that was ubiquitous in the minds of black leaders. Negro clergymen, for example, talked incessantly about "the great work to be accomplished [in] the elevation of the African Race." Similarly, the *Tribune* assured its readers that free Negro planters could offer the ex-slaves inducements that white planters could not: "We can give the freedmen, under the influence of liberty, moral benefit and social enjoyment, all that he estimates and contend[s] for. Let us go to work, organize labor-colonies, and elevate our emancipated brethren, at the same time that we take our legitimate share in the cultivation of the country." Did a General Hurlbut question the commitment of the old freemen to the black masses? There then appeared a "Junius" to assure him that "the old free colored people . . . have done and are doing all that is in their power to morally and physically improve the condition of the new freedmen."[39]

Religious uplift was a vital part of that program. The majority of our people, asserted the *Tribune*, "newly acquainted with the blessings of freedom, do not only need an intellectual education, but a religious guidance, too. On this point there must be no disputing. We have for some time contemplated to add to our paper a Religious Department, devoted to religious news and to the elucidation of religious points, in relation to moral education and improvement of the people." The "Religious Department" generally consisted of inspirational poetry or

38. *Ibid.*, December 27 and December 29, 1864. In this same editorial the newspaper claimed that "the emancipated shall really be free only when we will see him associated with the educated and intelligent [free Negroes] who can better appreciate the value of freedom." See also *ibid.*, "Our Duty," December 16, 1864.
39. *Ibid.*, July 21 and November 30, 1864, and March 31, 1865.

uplifting articles, such as "Earnestness in Prayer," "True Test of a Christian," or "How to Become a Blessing," reprinted from religious periodicals and reflecting the religious sensibilities of middle-class free blacks. Not infrequently, however, the editors or other local people, "Light" or "M.B.A.," wrote pieces that revealed the immediate concerns of free Negro Protestants in New Orleans: These articles emphasized the vital importance of religious and political unity; of parents sending their children to school; of teaching the freedmen about the sanctity of marriage; of keeping young people out of the city's haunts of wickedness; and, most important, of churches being led by qualified pastors. Without qualified ministers, none of those other goals could be met; the pulpit could not become "the great lever to inculcate a 'Union' of our people," nor could the great truths of scripture be properly taught. "Let us examine our pulpits," urged "Light," "and see if 'intelligence' is in them. . . . One ignorant man in the pulpit at this time is a mountain that retards our progress and development." On the other hand, "every Church that passes into the hands of a worthy and competent minister is a lever of great moral power, that will exert a great influence in our behalf and be the means of *elevating our people* out of the present *chaos* of affairs." Competent ministers, he made plain, revealed themselves not only by their learning but also by "their correct deportment and gentlemanly conduct."[40]

Properly trained pastors were crucially important if the newly emancipated slaves were to learn the benefits of Christian marriage. To respectable free Negroes, as to other reformers—and no doubt to the slaves themselves—among the worst features of the Peculiar Institution was that it had made marriage "a mere cohabitation among the slaves." With slavery gone, men of color looked for ways to undo the damage and make marriage an honored institution among the former bondsmen. If true progress was to be made, the marriage rites had to be performed by real ministers of the Gospel and not by the bogus kind. In this community, warned "Light," "there are [a] great many intruders who perform the marriage ceremony" in violation of religious law. No clergyman, he argued, "has any right to unite a man

40. *Ibid.*, January 21 and 31, February 4, 14, 17, 21, and 25, March 17 and 28, 1865.

and woman in holy matrimony unless he has been regularly ordained
to one of the following offices: Bishop, Elder, or Deacon. Among our
colored Protestant churches there are but few men in this city now,
that have the requisite qualifications to perform the duties." Negro
men and women married "by incompetent authority," he cautioned,
risked losing all the benefits and safeguards of lawful marriage, including the right to inherit one another's property and to have their children protected as legal heirs. He urged those "unlawfully united to
immediately rectify their mistake . . . before it is too late."[41]

The concern over qualifications of ministers is understandable. The
great majority of freedmen, and many free Negroes as well, had very
different concepts of Christianity than the "Religious Department" of
the *Tribune*. Those differences were made all the more apparent by the
number of runaway slaves who had crowded into New Orleans during the war. General Butler had put the figure at ten thousand in September 1862, and that number had doubled by February of the following year.[42] Under such conditions, crude makeshift churches appeared
all over the city. George H. Hepworth, a Federal chaplain, left an account of just how different those freedmen's churches were. In February 1863 Hepworth visited a "rude church" in a Negro camp outside
New Orleans. Inside the low-built structure "a full hundred blacks, of
all shades . . . were gathered together; and, for a few moments, perfect silence prevailed. . . . At length, however, a single voice, coming
from a dark corner of the room, began a low, mournful chant, in which
the whole assemblage joined by degrees. It was a strange song, with
seemingly very little rhythm. . . . It seemed more like a wail, a mournful, dirge-like expression of sorrow. . . . I was overcome by the real
sadness and depression of soul which it seemed to symbolize." After
half an hour of singing, "an old man knelt down to pray. His voice was
at first low and indistinct; the prayer was purely an emotional effort.
He seemed to gain impulse as he went on, and pretty soon burst out
with an 'O good, dear Lord! we pray for de cullered people. Thou
knows well 'nuff what we'se been through: do, do, oh! do gib us

41. *Ibid.*, February 17 and 25, 1865.
42. Parton, *Butler in New Orleans*, 526; Messner, *Freedmen and the Ideology of Free Labor*, 48.

free!'" When the old man spoke these words, "the whole audience swayed back and forward in their seats, and uttered in perfect harmony a sound like that caused by prolonging the letter 'm' with the lips closed. One or two began this wild, mournful chorus; and in an instant all joined in, and the sound swelled upwards and downwards like waves of the sea."[43]

The preaching represented the high point of the meeting. The first speaker whipped himself into a frenzy, "took flights of rhetoric which would have made Whately dizzy, and produced logic which brought tears—of laughter—to my eyes." When he resumed a seat, a hush fell over the room. After an interval, a tall figure stepped forward, a gifted individual who swayed "his rude audience with most perfect control; subdued them, excited them . . . did what he pleased with them." The man addressed himself to the plight of blacks in the camp working for the army without pay. Having labored thirty-six years for a master and never having received more than half a dollar, "'surely I can work for Uncle Sam a little while,—just a little while,—until he can find a fitting place for me, for nothing.'" The spellbinder informed his listeners that he no longer cared about his own bondage: "'I have reached maturity, and can endure it: but' (and here his voice fell almost to a whisper) 'I have in yonder cabin a child, a boy . . . whom I love as I do my life; and I thank God, I thank God, that I am a freeman, *for his sake.*'"[44] The men and women who listened to this eloquent man were not such as to be concerned about ministerial credentials or swayed by exhortations to "Earnestness in Prayer" or, even less, inspired by a free Negro version of the white man's burden.

In four years of war, free Negroes in New Orleans made a series of dramatic shifts: from Rebel militia to soldiers of the Union; from the suffrage for free blacks to the suffrage for all blacks; from acquiescence in slavery to criticism of Federal "free labor"; from support of wartime Reconstruction to approval of the Wade-Davis bill; from unconcern with the slave masses to elevation of the freedmen. These changes reflected in part a genuine awakening of liberal conscience, but even

43. George H. Hepworth, *The Whip, Hoe, and Sword; or, The Gulf-Department in '63* (Boston, 1864), 163–65.
44. *Ibid.*, 165–68.

more they resulted from a realistic perception of class interest, a perception that had remained remarkably in focus since 1729. So considered, the controversy over the petition in the last winter of the war reveals itself as a dispute over the best means of advancing that interest. The propetition leaders, in effect, pursued the old plan of asking the suffrage for the free Negro elite. Their opponents in the NERL and at the *Tribune*, decrying the selfishness and shortsightedness of that approach, championed the vote for all blacks, little doubting that once enfranchised, the freedmen would turn to the *gens de couleur* for political guidance. This belief was only partly illusory; in the unfolding drama of Reconstruction, free Negroes would play a greater role in Louisiana than any in any other Southern state.

Part II

Interregnum

1865–1867

5

The Governor and
the Rebels

But for the necessities of wartime Reconstruction, declared Whitelaw Reid, "this sallow-faced little official . . . would never have risen from the obscurity of his remote Red River plantation." He "is a political trickster," General Philip H. Sheridan charged. "His conduct has been as sinuous as . . . a snake." His administration, asserted the New Orleans *Tribune*, would give the North a true picture of postwar Louisiana: "The spirit—pro-slavery; the loyalty—null; the status—States rights above the National Constitution."[1] He was also a courageous Unionist who had defied the Confederacy as few men dared. James Madison Wells was a paradoxical man.

He fled Confederate Louisiana in late 1863. In New Orleans he won recognition as the leader of the Union element from the Rebel-held interior and found himself an available candidate on the eve of the Free State election of 1864. Both the Durant and the administration factions were sensitive about the Free State movement representing only a fraction of the state—little more, in truth, than the region around New Orleans. Both parties sought to enhance their legitimacy by nominating Wells, the most prominent upstate leader, for lieutenant governor. Seeing only the brave Unionist, no one in either party asked questions about the Red River planter, and Wells tactfully kept the larger corpus of his social and political views to himself.[2] When Michael Hahn resigned as governor in March 1865, Union men in New Orleans learned what sort of man their new governor was.

With unseemly haste Wells reshaped the political face of Free State

1. Whitelaw Reid, *After the War: A Tour of the Southern States, 1865–1866*, ed. C. Vann Woodward (New York, 1965), 237; Philip H. Sheridan to Edwin M. Stanton, June 3, 1867, in *Senate Executive Documents*, 40th Cong., 1st Sess., No. 14, p. 213; New Orleans *Tribune*, June 17, 1865.
2. Walter McGeehee Lowrey, "The Political Career of James Madison Wells," *Louisiana Historical Quarterly*, XXXI (October, 1948), 1008–1014.

Louisiana. He summarily evicted the "Banks oligarchy" and in its place appointed a new administration made up of reactionary Unionists and returning Rebels. J. Randall Terry, Alfred Shaw, Anthony P. Dostie, Mayor Stephen Hoyt, and others lost their jobs. The governor replaced Judge Ezra Heistand of the first district court with Edmund Abell. General Banks returned to New Orleans in April and attempted to reverse Wells's course. The governor appealed to President Johnson, and in May Johnson relieved Banks of his command. When the Confederate surrender brought the entire state under the government in New Orleans, Wells appointed police jurors, sheriffs, recorders, and other local officials by the hundreds, even thousands. By fall he had restructured the whole of state and local government in Louisiana.[3]

In September General Carl Schurz visited New Orleans on a fact-finding tour for the president. Though his reports disappointed Johnson, Schurz accurately assessed the situation in Louisiana. The governor and his aides, notably Mayor Hugh Kennedy of New Orleans, were a thoroughly reactionary group who wanted to set aside the Free State constitution of 1864. Mayor Kennedy even opposed the Thirteenth Amendment to the Constitution. The general called the president's attention to the black codes recently adopted in Louisiana towns. The Opelousas ordinance of July imposed a pass system and a curfew on Negroes; the law also prohibited blacks from renting houses or living in the town unless they were in the employment of whites. It barred blacks from holding public meetings, preaching or exhorting, carrying firearms, bartering, or selling goods without special permission. The ordinances adopted by the towns of Franklin and Monroe differed only in slight degree. These repressive measures, Schurz argued, revealed the true convictions of the people whom Wells had restored to power. They "study, not how to build up and develop a true system of free labor, but how to avoid it."[4]

3. New Orleans *Times*, April 1, May 3, July 3, 1865, *passim*; Lowrey, "Wells," 1028–33; Fred Harvey Harrington, *Fighting Politician: Major General N. P. Banks* (Philadelphia, 1948), 166–68; Peyton McCrary, *Abraham Lincoln and Reconstruction: The Louisiana Experiment* (Princeton, 1978), 308–312.
4. Carl Schurz to Andrew Johnson, September 4 & 15, 1865, in the Andrew Johnson Papers, Library of Congress. The Opelousas and Franklin ordinances are in the appendix of Henry Clay Warmoth, *War, Politics and Reconstruction: Stormy Days in Louisiana* (New York, 1930), 273–77. The Monroe ordinances, which Schurz was unaware of, are in the New Orleans *Tribune*, July 30, 1865.

Schurz expressed particular concern about the plight of Union men under Wells. With the state under the sway of the "disloyal and pro-slavery element," true Union men feel beaten; "they feel like the conquered people, and men who stood by the rebellion until the hour of its final downfall, act like conquerors." Such represented more than the view of the Radical element in New Orleans; on the contrary, the general stated that Radicals and conservatives united in their opposition to Wells. He enclosed letters from R. King Cutler and Thomas P. May, prominent conservatives, that blasted the governor as a "traitor" and a "copperhead."[5]

After three weeks in New Orleans, the German officer set out to investigate conditions in the interior, but illness forced him back to the city. Had he completed that journey his reports would probably have grown even more alarming. The New Orleans *Tribune* reported that summer and fall that white assassins murdered Union men and Negroes with impunity in many parts of the state. The black newspaper perhaps exaggerated such accounts, but agents of the Freedmen's Bureau also reported widespread violence. Lieutenant Edward Ehrlich in Amite City, the heart of the Florida parishes, informed his superiors in December that two blacks had recently been killed and hardly a day passed without whites committing some murderous assault on freedmen. On the evening of December 19 whites chased Negroes with knives and pistols, and later the same night Ehrlich arrested a white man in the act of assaulting a Negro with an ax. Ehrlich's predecessor had been attacked with brickbats, and two days before Christmas someone fired a shot at Ehrlich himself. The local militia, the agent observed, patrol every night, often in a state of intoxication. Other agents reported a similar state of affairs.[6] Governor Wells was not directly responsible for such lawlessness; nevertheless, officials he had appointed to power refused to punish the guilty parties.

Behind Wells's conciliatory policy lay a number of factors. The old Whig had sided with the North in the war, yet, paradoxically, he de-

5. Carl Schurz to Andrew Johnson, September 4, 1865, Johnson Papers, LC.
6. *Ibid.*, September 23, 1865; New Orleans *Tribune*, July 26 and 28, December 13, 1865; Lt. Edward Ehrlich to Lt. D. G. Fenno, December 19, 20, and 23, 1865, in Bureau of Refugees, Freedmen and Abandoned Lands, Record Group 105, CCIII, National Archives; John A. Carpenter, "Atrocities in the Reconstruction Period," *Journal of Negro History*, XLVII (October, 1962), 243–44.

spised Northerners and Northern influence in the state. We are grateful
for all that "you Northern gentlemen have done," he told an army
officer, "but now that you are successful, you had better go home.
Louisiana must be governed by Louisianians!" Still more bluntly, he
confided to his wife after President Johnson dismissed Banks, that
with the general eliminated, the state would no longer be troubled
with "Yankee adventurism." He described the former commander of
the gulf as a wretched "miserable man" who danced with Negroes at
army balls and was unaccustomed to "the society of decent people."
Wells then reviled Northern speculators, vowing that "no miserable
thieving Yankee shall rob us with impunity."[7] When one recalls that
Free State Louisiana was in good part the creation of the Northern-
born community, the significance of these anti-Northern prejudices
becomes apparent.

Class and regional differences also separated Wells from the New
Orleans Unionist leadership. The governor belonged to the planter
elite that had dominated the state before the war. Vastly overrepre-
sented in the state government, the slaveholders of the alluvial regions
had ruled in cooperation with wealthy bankers, merchants, and factors in New Orleans, yet they had held the city's power in check. The
war had opened the doors of political advancement to new men such
as Thomas J. Durant, Benjamin F. Flanders, Michael Hahn, Anthony P. Dostie, J. Randall Terry and others. One of these new leaders, Simeon Belden, a nonslaveholder from St. Martin Parish and a
native of Massachusetts, honored by his selection as speaker of the
house in 1864, remarked, "We all understand perfectly well that, three
or four years ago, I should have had scarcely a shadow of a chance" for
such a position. The newcomers, representing mainly the Northern-
born and foreign-born communities, had reformed the political system in their own interest. Basing electoral representation on the number of qualified voters—as opposed, under the antebellum constitution,
to total population—the constitution of 1864 had substantially increased the representation of New Orleans in the legislature and
changed the seat of government from Baton Rouge to New Orleans.[8]

7. Reid, *After the War*, 238; Lowrey, "Wells," 1032–33.
8. Roger W. Shugg, *Origins of Class Struggle in Louisiana: A Social History of White
Farmers and Laborers During Slavery and After, 1840–1875* (Baton Rouge, 1939), 139–40;

Wells and his top officials, then, sought to replace the nouveaux war-time leaders, as Mayor Kennedy put it, with "representative men of the old parties of the pre-rebellion times; men of irreproachable integrity, of suitable age, social importance, and proper educational qualifications."[9]

Finally, Wells entertained the inchoate notion that a new conservative political party, much resembling the Whig party, would emerge after the war under President Johnson's leadership. Returning to New Orleans after a visit with the new president in Washington, Wells predicted that the future belonged to men who had advocated conservative doctrines during the war, the principles of the old Whig party and of conservatives in the Republican and Democratic parties. Conservatives in Louisiana must look to President Johnson and adopt his policy as their guide. Some months later Wells informed the president of his nomination for governor by the Louisiana Democratic party. He believed the "old Whig element" had predominated in the Democratic convention. Knowing "the tenacity with which an old Whig clings to his creed," the president, Wells said, could appreciate the sacrifice that Louisiana Whigs had made in joining their old enemies.[10]

Despite initial success, by fall Wells was in trouble. He had looked to the president for direction and support, but as the months wore on, Johnson's program—"My Policy"—became almost as inscrutable to the Louisiana governor as to Radical Republicans in the North. Wells wanted to repudiate the constitution of 1864. But unless the president appointed him a provisional governor, putting Louisiana under Johnson's proclamation of May 29, the Free State constitution remained the only legal basis of government in the state. For months Wells entreated the president to make the appointment. In August and September, Johnson repeatedly appeared on the verge of complying but, unaccountably, backed away each time. On September 25 Wells confronted

---

Louisiana House Debates, 1864, p. 6; in the 1850s Orleans Parish had been allotted five of thirty-two senate seats (15.6 percent) and twenty-three of eighty-eight positions in the house (26 percent). The constitution of 1864 accorded the urban parish nine of thirty-six senate seats (25 percent) and forty-four of one hundred eighteen places in the house (37 percent).

9. Hugh Kennedy to Andrew Johnson, September 16, 1865, in Johnson Papers, LC.

10. New Orleans *Times*, June 18, 1865; James Madison Wells to Andrew Johnson, October 6, 1865, in Johnson Papers, LC.

a deadline—the last day on which he could legally call a general election in 1865; if he did not receive his appointment by that date, he would have to act independently. Despite last-minute appeals, Johnson remained inexplicably indecisive. The governor accepted defeat and called a general election for November.[11]

Outwardly, Wells's position remained strong. Nominated for governor by both reactionary Unionists and the dominant branch of the Democratic party, he easily defeated ex-Confederate governor Henry Watkins Allen in the election. That victory, however, was deceptive; between Wells and his Democratic allies there existed vital differences that would soon become apparent. A loyal man, the governor never doubted that the Union cause had prevailed "not because it was strong, but because it was right." The goal of his conciliatory policy, he explained, was not to reverse the decision of the war but to reconcile "our people to the condition of the country as we found it at the time of the surrender." He assumed that the returning Rebels would behave like practical men, accepting and resigning themselves to defeat and getting on with peacetime affairs. For months he and Mayor Kennedy blithely assured the president (and probably one another) that the ex-Confederates on whom they so casually bestowed positions of public trust were indeed loyal. The returning Rebels, the governor maintained in July, were eager to comply with the president's amnesty proclamation and obey the laws. Of the Democrats who nominated him for governor, Wells assured Johnson that they were "true, sincere and loyal men, who have renewed their allegiance in good faith." Kennedy likewise assured the president that the returning Rebels were almost universally well behaved and respectful of national authority.[12]

In actual fact, though, the ex-Confederates were only as reconciled as they had to be, and they soon decided under the forgiving rule of

11. James Madison Wells to Andrew Johnson, August 16 & 25, 1865, and Johnson to Wells, August 12 and September 18, 1865, all in Johnson Papers, LC. Johnson did not appoint a provisional governor in any of the states organized during the war under the Ten Per Cent Plan (Eric L. McKitrick, *Andrew Johnson and Reconstruction* [Chicago, 1960], 124–28).

12. Appleton's *Annual Cyclopaedia (1865)*, 510–13; Lowrey, "Wells," 1053–61; *House Reports*, 39th Cong., 2d Sess., No. 16, pp. 439–40; James Madison Wells to Andrew Johnson, July 3 and October 6, 1865, and Hugh Kennedy to Johnson, July 21, 1865, all in Johnson Papers, LC.

President Johnson and Governor Wells that they need not be reconciled at all. In the months after the surrender they punished Union men, adopted black laws, murdered Negroes, defied the army, and generally behaved or misbehaved as they deemed fit. If the army or the Freedmen's Bureau interfered, they trusted Wells to put their case before Johnson and achieve their ends. The governor, one former Confederate official informed another, had been to Louisiana what President Johnson had been to the South. The President had shielded the region from the oppressor, and the governor had protected the state. In his view, Wells might still emerge "the head and front of the conservative party of Louisiana."[13]

When the legislature met in November 1865, the Whig Unionist in the governor's office and the unregenerate Rebels in the State House collided. Shortly before Christmas Wells vetoed two pieces of legislation. The first reimbursed a judge who had refused to take the oath of allegiance to the United States during the war. The second and more important measure deferred state taxes for the war years in upstate Confederate Louisiana but not in the southeastern Union part of the state. This bill, Wells lectured sternly, was surely adopted in haste, else the lawmakers would have seen that its provisions sanctified rebellion and treason. It made a "monstrous" distinction between the Rebels who tried to destroy the government and the faithful, "pre-eminently deserving" Union men who supported it through the war.[14]

The rift with the legislature assumed ominous meaning because of another development: the growth of secret political societies whose members reportedly swore strange oaths and greeted one another with secret signs and passwords. During the entire period that Wells and Kennedy had assured the president of the good intentions of Louisiana whites, they had, paradoxically, repeatedly expressed apprehension at the spread of secret political clubs. In November the governor revealed his concern to the legislature, asserting that he considered all

13. H. M. Hyams to Thomas O. Moore, September 10, 1865, in Thomas O. Moore Papers, Troy H. Middleton Library, Louisiana State University, Baton Rouge. On the black laws adopted by the legislature, see Theodore Brantner Wilson, *The Black Codes of the South* (University, Ala., 1965), 77–80; and William Melvin Caskey, *Secession and Restoration of Louisiana* (Baton Rouge, 1938), 185–92.
14. *Louisiana House Journal*, 1865, pp. 74–75.

members of such societies to be "public enemies." Early in 1866, through an informer, Mayor Kennedy obtained a report on the Southern Cross Association, a clandestine Rebel organization. To Wells and Kennedy the secret order and its kin presaged a revival of the mob tradition of antebellum New Orleans politics. In the latter half of the 1850s New Orleans had been swept by a wave of xenophobia that had given rise to the Native American or Know-Nothing party. In the elections of those years the rival Democrats and Native Americans more nearly resembled armed mobs than political parties. In the 1858 election, for example, eleven men were killed and hundreds of vigilantes seized the state arsenal in an attempt to take over the city.[15]

In January 1866 the legislature pushed forward the next regularly scheduled New Orleans election from June to March. In the event of a Democratic sweep, which now seemed likely, Mayor Kennedy would lose his job and Wells would lose the city administration and find himself isolated in the governor's office. But also important, in conjunction with the growth of secret Rebel clubs, the specter of disloyal lawmakers demanding an early election aroused fears of impending violence. Wells vetoed the election bill and appealed to the president for support. He explained:

> For years before the rebellion the elections of New Orleans were a disgrace to civilization. . . . A branch of the know-nothing party, known and called from their practices "thugs," were accustomed before every election to go, painted and otherwise disguised, into the poorer quarters of the city and shoot down innocent and inoffensive citizens, and repeat their assassinations if these atrocious and diabolical outrages failed.
>
> I would infinitely prefer to renounce the governorship than be compelled to witness a revival of such things. . . . The old bodies . . . are organizing in the main the new secret societies; and it follows, therefore, that the old modes of controlling elections will again be resorted to.

Heeding only the pleas of Louisiana Democrats, however, Johnson ordered Wells to call a city election immediately, or General Sheridan would do it for him. The governor obeyed.[16]

15. Hugh Kennedy to Andrew Johnson, July 21, September 1, and November 23, 1865, in Johnson Papers, LC; *Louisiana House Journal*, 1865, p. 13; *House Reports*, 39th Cong., 2d Sess., No. 16, pp. 520–21; Shugg, *Origins of Class Struggle*, 146–47; John Hope Franklin, *The Militant South, 1800–1861* (Cambridge, 1956), 43–44.
16. *Louisiana House Journal*, 1866, pp. 43–44; James Madison Wells to Andrew

As feared, the March election removed the last remnants of Unionism from the Crescent City. John T. Monroe, the elected mayor, was an ex-stevedore, ex-Native American, ex-Rebel mayor of the city, and a former occupant of a Federal military prison. General Canby considered the unregenerate Monroe unfit to take office and promptly suspended him, but Johnson just as promptly issued the mayor a special pardon. Monroe, Lucian Adams, and other leaders of the new administration were veterans of the Know-Nothing mobs of the 1850s. Having elected thugs, lamented Thomas Cottman, the people of New Orleans have completely discredited themselves. Adams, Monroe, and their bullies "are as well known to the different Commanders of the Department as they are to the *poor Dutch & Irish* they have permitted to live on the condition of keeping away from the polls or casting their obligatory suffrage for the *Thugs*, who stood by as wolves ready to devour them." Among its first acts, the new city administration reorganized the police department.[17]

Conciliation had failed, and the dark fears that had haunted the Wells regime for months were now to be realized. Excluded from power for a year and frankly desperate, Free State Unionists, in cooperation with an equally desperate Wells, set in motion a plan to reconvene the constitutional convention of 1864. Left alone, members of the convention would have reassembled and demanded Negro suffrage and Rebel disfranchisement. Without outside help, they could have accomplished little in Louisiana, and the measure of their probable impact outside the state may be judged by the fact that when Edward H. Durell, president of the 1864 convention, sounded out Republican leaders in Congress about the plan in June, they did not even answer his telegram.[18] The new regime in New Orleans, however,

Johnson, February 10 and March 6, 1866, and Johnson to Wells, March 2, 1866, all in Johnson Papers, LC.

17. Edwin X. deVerges, "Honorable John T. Monroe—The Confederate Mayor of New Orleans," *Louisiana Historical Quarterly,* XXXIV (January, 1951), 25–34; Lowrey, "Wells," 1075; Shugg, *Origins of Class Struggle,* 147–48; *House Reports,* 39th Cong., 2d Sess., No. 16, pp. 494, 537–40; Thomas Cottman to Andrew Johnson, March 15, 1866, in Johnson Papers, LC; Joe Gray Taylor, *Louisiana Reconstructed, 1863–1877* (Baton Rouge, 1974), 81–82.

18. James Madison Wells to Andrew Johnson, [April] 1866, in Johnson Papers, LC; *House Reports,* 39th Cong., 2d Sess., No. 16, pp. 263, 439–40.

would, on July 30, 1866, convert a rash scheme of doubtful legality into a national incident that discredited presidential Reconstruction.

Although none had served in the 1864 assembly, black leaders in New Orleans made preparations to demonstrate their support of the convention. Observing the reconvocation movement, city and state officials warned darkly of revolution and anarchy, but their actions bespoke anticipation, not fear; here at last was a chance to punish Unionists and, above all, get even with blacks for obtaining their freedom. In Louisiana, as elsewhere in the South, blacks had become the main scapegoats for the frustration and rage that white Southerners had inflicted upon themselves since 1861: "By God, we are going to hang Dostie and Hahn," said a policeman. "Do you think so?" another asked. "Yes," came the answer, and "we are going to shoot down all these God damned niggers."[19]

The weekend preceding the convention, city authorities prepared feverishly. Between midnight Sunday and early Monday morning, policemen left their regular beats and, by prearranged plan, gathered at their station houses, heavily armed with pistols, bowie knives, and clubs. Many carried new revolvers that had been loaned to them by local gunshops. At one precinct house several patrolmen advised the Negro porter to stay away from the convention "if you know what is good for you." Over the morning nearly the whole uniformed force moved to assembly points near the convention; there they awaited the ringing of the city fire bell—the signal to move on the convention and put down the expected riot. At eleven o'clock a police sergeant and his men passed an open doorway; one of them exclaimed, "Now, God damn you, we have got the convention at last." Independent of the police, Sheriff Harry T. Hays commissioned scores of special deputies ("Hays' Brigade"); and ordinary citizens, firemen, members of secret Rebel societies, and assorted thugs and bullies armed themselves for any eventuality.[20]

Convention leaders were aware of the danger. As early as mid-July a Confederate friend advised one Unionist not to attend the assembly, warning that no one would leave alive. On Friday, July 27, a conven-

19. *House Reports*, 39th Cong., 2d Sess., No. 16, p. 124.
20. *House Executive Documents*, 39th Sess., 2d Sess., No. 68, pp. 39–41; *House Reports*, 39th Cong., 2d Sess., No. 16, pp. 109–110, 143, 201–202, 402.

tion member's small son asked, "Why they were going to kill all the Union men and negroes in the city on Monday," explaining to his father that "the children were talking about it at school." J. Randall Terry's clerk, an ex-Confederate, warned him on Saturday that everyone at the convention would be killed. There were other such warnings; in fact, the city was rife with rumors of violence over the weekend. Some, like Terry, Thomas J. Durant, and William Mithoff, took the warnings with deadly seriousness and remained at home or in their offices on Monday. On the other hand, Michael Hahn, Anthony P. Dostie, R. King Cutler, and others expected trouble but discounted the danger of violence. They arrived at the joint decision to go unarmed to the convention, and if the authorities interfered they would submit quietly to arrest.[21]

Monday morning the gunshops in New Orleans did a brisk business selling pistols and ammunition. At about eleven o'clock the director of a commercial college near the Mechanic's Institute, the site of the convention, dismissed his students and told them to go home, because "there's going to be a riot here today." The convention met at twelve o'clock and temporarily adjourned for want of a quorum. By this time a crowd of hostile whites had gathered outside the institute, including policemen and members of Hays' Brigade. At about twelve-thirty a procession of a hundred or more Negroes marched up Burgundy Street in support of the convention. Fights broke out between blacks in the procession and angry white onlookers, and shots were fired, but the procession continued until it stopped outside the Mechanic's Institute. Another fight started, and this time the whites fired a volley of pistol shots into the blacks, some of whom were armed and returned the fire. Outnumbered and outgunned, the blacks scattered, many making the fatal mistake of entering the convention hall where delegates and visitors, black and white, sat about awaiting their absent brethren.[22]

By now the fire alarm bell had rung and the massed police de-

21. *House Reports*, 39th Cong., 2d Sess., No. 16, pp. 4, 7, 18, 35, 124–27, 325, 361–62, 370, 464.

22. *Ibid.*, 5–6, 29, 35; Donald E. Reynolds, "The New Orleans Riot of 1866, Reconsidered," *Louisiana History*, V (Winter, 1964), 11–12; see also Gilles Vandal, "The Origins of the New Orleans Riot of 1866, Revisited," *Louisiana History*, XXII (Spring, 1981), 135–65.

scended on the institute. The police and the crowd commenced firing pistols indiscriminately through the windows of the building. Then, abetted by the mob, police broke open the doors of the institute, rushed to the top of the steps leading into the hall, and discharged their revolvers into the crowded room. When their pistols emptied, blacks with chairs and sticks beat them back down the steps and out of the building. Reloading, the police and the mob again invaded the building, once more emptied their pistols, and once more were beaten out with chairs and clubs. This grim scene was, in fact, twice more re-enacted. At some point the conventionists attempted to surrender and allowed their assailants into the institute, believing their capitulation had been accepted; upon gaining entry, however, the police and the mob again opened fire. At length, the mob stormed the building, shooting, stabbing, and clubbing Negroes as they fled, jumped from windows, or tried to surrender. One witness observed four furniture wagons carted away that were piled with dead and wounded men "thrown in like sacks of corn."[23]

The massacre spread over many blocks. Whites dragged blacks from streetcars, shot them down on the street, and pulled them from shops and assaulted them. The carnage finally ceased at about three o'clock when federal troops arrived on the scene. The army commander had mistakenly believed that the convention intended to assemble at six o'clock that evening—an assumption that the perpetrators of the riot had been aware of and exploited. Throughout, white Unionists, though wounded and abused, were allowed to surrender. Consequently, only three or four whites died from their wounds, among them, notably, the much-hated Dr. Dostie. The police and the mob, however, showed almost no mercy to blacks. The official report estimated that forty-six blacks died and another sixty suffered severe wounds. Of the assailants, ten received slight wounds and one was killed (probably by his own side). No historian has ever rendered a sounder verdict about the riot than the 1866 army board of investigation. In its judgment, anyone "examining the evidence must come to

23. *House Executive Documents,* 39th Cong., 2d Sess., No. 68, p. 41; *House Reports,* 39th Cong., 2d Sess., No. 16, pp. 5–11, 29–30, 343.

the conclusion" that the massacre resulted from "a prearranged and preconcerted programme."[24]

Combined with other events (including a similar massacre in Memphis), the carnage in New Orleans helped undermine Johnsonian Reconstruction. When Congress adopted the Reconstruction Acts in the spring of 1867, it assigned Louisiana to the Fifth Military District (along with Texas) under the command of General Philip H. Sheridan. Sheridan promptly removed Mayor Monroe, Judge Edmund Abell, and the state attorney general for their part in the massacre. In June he also removed Wells, whom he considered an embarrassment ("He has not a friend who is an honest man," Sheridan noted) and appointed Benjamin F. Flanders provisional governor.[25] Throughout that summer the registration of loyal voters, black and white, proceeded under Sheridan's strict interpretation of the disfranchisement provisions of the Reconstruction Acts. In September the new electorate chose delegates to attend a constitutional convention. When it met in November, the revolution started by secession reached its zenith; meeting ahead of the South Carolina convention, the Louisiana convention was the first major elective body in Southern history dominated by a black majority.

---

24. *House Reports*, 39th Cong., 2d Sess., No. 16, pp. 176, 444–45; *House Executive Documents*, 39th Cong., 2d Sess., No. 68, pp. 37–48.
25. *Senate Executive Documents*, 40th Cong., 1st Sess., No. 14, pp. 201–202, 213–15.

Part III

Radical
Reconstruction

1867–1877

6

Blueprint for Radicalism

Governor Wells testified before the United States House of Representatives committee that investigated the New Orleans massacre. Unlike the Tennessee Unionist in the White House, the Louisianian recognized that conciliation had failed. He urged that Congress reorganize the Rebel states under the loyal element. "To accomplish this," the governor maintained, "it is a necessity, as well as a measure of justice, that the right of suffrage should be extended to the colored man." Some whites still believed that only freeborn, educated, or propertied Negroes should vote, but Wells could see no middle ground; only universal suffrage would save the South from Rebel rule.[1]

The governor was a recent convert. In September 1865 a coalition of Unionists, free Negroes, and carpetbaggers organized the Louisiana Republican party on a platform of universal suffrage and "the equality of all men before the law." Initially, former Free Staters dominated the new party. Portentous of the future, however, when Thomas J. Durant declined nomination as Louisiana's unofficial "territorial" delegate to Congress, the nomination went to a young carpetbagger named Henry Clay Warmoth.[2]

The free blacks comprised the most Radical element in the party: Oscar J. Dunn, Paul Trévigne, P. B. S. Pinchback, James H. Ingraham, Dr. Louis Roudanez, and others. These ambitious and articulate men of color rejected white tutelage and demanded an equal role in the party. In October 1866 party leaders decided that half the seats on the state central executive committee would henceforth go to blacks. During the ensuing June, at the inception of Radical Reconstruction, the Republican state convention adopted a controversial platform; it

1. *House Reports*, 39th Cong., 2d Sess., No. 16, p. 439.
2. *Proceedings of the Convention of the Republican Party of Louisiana* (New Orleans, 1865).

pledged the party to an equal division of offices between white and black Republicans and refused support to any candidate who denied the principle. This was no empty promise, as the constitutional convention of 1867–1868 would show.[3]

The Republican platform addressed another controversial question, vowing that in the selection of black officeholders, no distinction would be made between free men of color and ex-slaves.[4] This issue was probably more sensitive in Louisiana than in any other Reconstruction state. During the war free blacks in New Orleans often spoke and acted as if the slaves were a tabula rasa to be filled in by enlightened men of color. Expressions of this attitude had drawn sharp criticism from Federal officials, and free Negro leaders learned a measure of circumspection. Yet the assumption remained, expressed more subtly. At the time of the NERL convention in early 1865, the New Orleans *Tribune* urged blacks to choose "our best men" for the meeting, leaders of ability, sincerity, and respectability. The last quality was the most important, the newspaper stated revealingly, because it would give authority to the proceedings "not only among our political enemies, but among ourselves also." Nine months later, on the eve of the first Republican convention in the state, the journal enjoined black people to select representatives of "intelligence and wealth" and not be dissuaded because such individuals were unaccustomed to "mingling with politics." The *Tribune* printed similar advice before the June 1867 Republican convention: "Above all do not forget to choose a large number from the ablest and most respectable colored citizens."[5] In these editorials, "our best," "intelligence and wealth," and "most respectable" were but code words for free men of color. As events would show, most blacks who attained positions of prominence in the Radical party represented that 5 percent of Louisiana Negroes who had been free in 1860.

In late November 1867 the Radical convention met in New Orleans. The members were an extraordinary group: blacks and whites; ex-slaves and ex-slave owners (of both colors); Northerners and Southerners; Protestants and Catholics; elder statesmen and young men barely old enough to vote; famous men and obscure men, some from

---

3. New Orleans *Tribune*, October 19 (see also November 9), 1866, and June 18, 1867.
4. *Ibid.*, June 18, 1867.
5. *Ibid.*, January 4 and September 10, 1865, June 5, 1867.

the Confederate South's only metropolis and others from its most isolated rural areas; men of wealth and men who never before or ever again after would earn as much as the state paid them for attending the convention. By occupation they were clerks, shop owners, grocers, planters, farmers, lawyers, judges, journalists, doctors, politicians, tradesmen, and jacks-of-all-trades. Yet, for all their diversity, they shared common bonds: loyalty to the Union, membership in the Radical Republican party, and a similar view of recent history.[6] At the close of the Civil War, when loyal people expected their due, Governor Wells and President Johnson had all but allowed the Rebellion to gain in defeat what it had lost on the battlefield. For two long years in Louisiana and the South, Rebels vilified, purged, and massacred loyal citizens. But Congress had at last intervened, crushing "My Policy" with the Reconstruction Acts and reclaiming the fruits of victory. Now, in line with national policy, under army protection, loyal Louisiana assembled to make a new constitution. They would restore loyal government, return the state to the Union, and much more.

The New Orleans *Tribune* is mainly responsible for the traditional belief that the convention was equally divided between white and Negro delegates. A precise count, however, reveals that there were fifty black members and forty-eight white. More important, because the black delegates attended the sessions more regularly than their white counterparts, they converted a slight numerical edge of 51 percent into a voting majority that averaged 57 percent and sometimes went as high as 65 percent.[7] Because the staff writers of the *Tribune* were at the scene, the question naturally arises: How could they have made such a mistake? To begin with, the *Tribune* made its delegate count over two weeks before the convention actually met and never revised it. The correspondent of the New York *Times*, by comparison, visited the first session on November 23 and counted forty-four blacks and twenty-five whites.[8] Had the *Tribune* waited, an exact count might

6. Appendix 2, Table 3.
7. On eleven important roll calls, from November to March, the black delegates cast an average 57 percent of the votes; on four of these roll calls the black majority reached 59 percent to 65 percent; the low was 51 percent. Appendix 2, Table 4.
8. New York *Times*, November 24, 1867. In the 1867 edition of Appleton's *Annual Cyclopaedia* it was also observed that the convention "was composed largely of colored delegates."

still have been difficult, because all the members were never on the
floor at one time. Even if they had been, many Louisiana blacks were
so light and many Louisiana whites so dark that, unless a reporter talked
with a delegate personally, he might easily mistake his race. Even then
doubt might remain. In 1869 the following exchange occurred between
J. B. Esnard, a convention delegate, and a congressman:

> QUESTION: Are you colored?
> ANSWER: I cannot answer that; I do not know exactly whether I am or
> not.
> QUESTION: Do you rank and acknowledge yourself as a colored man?
> ANSWER: I do.
> QUESTION: But if you have any colored blood you don't know it?
> ANSWER: No, sir.
> QUESTION: It is charged and you don't deny it?
> ANSWER: Yes, Sir.[9]

The best explanation, though, is that the *Tribune* deliberately mis-
counted. The editors followed Northern events closely, and in turn the
pages of the *Tribune*, the official organ of the state Republican party,
were an important source of information for Northerners interested in
Louisiana affairs. (The newspaper was routinely sent to members of
Congress and major Northern newspapers.)[10] As the convention approached, the *Tribune* grew increasingly alarmed at the Negro-rule-in-
the-South propaganda of the Northern Democratic press. In October
the journal believed that whites comprised a slight majority of the
delegates; relieved, it declared that the "absurd accusation of Africanization is thus set at rest." The white majority proved "that no selfish
design, no exclusive view guided the colored masses." Weeks later, its
count now more accurate, the newspaper still ridiculed the "BUGBEAR
OF A BLACK GOVERNMENT," as its headline announced, because the membership was divided equally between forty-nine whites and forty-nine
Negroes, exactly in line with the Republican platform. Louisiana Negroes, it repeated, had shown admirable restraint and liberality.[11] In

9. *House Miscellaneous Documents*, 41st Cong., 2d Sess., No. 154, Pt. 1, pp. 698–99.
   10. Finnian Patrick Leavens, *"L'Union* and the *New Orleans Tribune* and Louisiana
Reconstruction" (M.A. thesis, Louisiana State University, 1966), 58–59.
   11. New Orleans *Tribune*, October 23 and November 7 (see also November 1), 1867.
The *Tribune's* delegate count has been accepted by historians ever since: John Rose Fick-

short, fearing that the "Copperhead press" would diminish Northern support for Radical Reconstruction, the *Tribune* may have deliberately underestimated black strength in the convention.

Several of the Negro delegates—Dennis Burrell, Solomon R. Moses, William R. Meadows, George H. Jackson, and perhaps one or two more—were freedmen, but the great majority—at least 85 percent—had been free men of color. Some, like Auguste Donoto, Jr., represented well-to-do planting families; while others, like P. B. S. Pinchback, William G. Brown, and Dr. Robert I. Cromwell, had lived in the North or in the West Indies before the war. The majority stepped out of the ranks of barbers, grocers, tradesmen, and shop owners of the native free Negro middle class. Of the white delegates, fourteen were Northern carpetbaggers and the remaining thirty-four, Southern whites. The Northerners, mainly ex-army officers engaged in planting cotton, included in their number former generals, commanders of Negro troops, and agents of the Freedmen's Bureau. As a group, they were conservative but not inflexible; only one refused to sign the constitution. Unionism represented the common denominator among the Southern whites; their diverse membership included some of the ablest and most experienced delegates: James G. Taliaferro, Thomas S. Crawford, W. Jasper Blackburn, William H. Cooley, John T. Ludeling, William R. Crane, Simeon Belden, Michel Vidal, and Rufus Waples—a redoubtable company. Neither the blacks nor the Northerners included the mix of Radicalism and conservatism that characterized the native whites. Few men served in the convention who were more radical than Vidal, George M. Wickliffe, Simon Jones, and George W. Reagan; and none were more conservative than Cooley, Crawford, Ludeling, and John L. Barrett.[12]

len, *History of Reconstruction in Louisiana (Through 1868)* (Baltimore, 1910), 193; Ella Lonn, *Reconstruction in Louisiana after 1868* (New York, 1918), 5–6; Roger W. Shugg, *Origins of Class Struggle in Louisiana: A Social History of White Farmers and Laborers During Slavery and After, 1840–1875* (Baton Rouge, 1939), 221; Roger A. Fischer, *The Segregation Struggle in Louisiana, 1862–1877* (Urbana, Ill., 1974), 48; Joe Gray Taylor, *Louisiana Reconstructed, 1863–1877* (Baton Rouge, 1974), 147; and Charles Vincent, *Black Legislators in Louisiana During Reconstruction* (Baton Rouge, 1976), 47.

12. Appendix 2, Table 3. I have identified the antebellum status of thirty-three of the black delegates with these results: free men of color, 29 (88 percent); slaves, 4 (12 percent). The evidence strongly suggests that most of the unidentified delegates had also been free before the war.

When the convention was first organized, the white delegates appeared to wield an influence that belied their minority status. The convention elected the distinguished old Unionist James G. Taliaferro as president, and, indeed, no Negro was even among the five nominees for the office. Of fourteen committee chairmanships, seven went to Southern whites, four to carpetbaggers, and only three to blacks. The convention also rejected Wickliffe's motion that all the minor offices at the disposal of the assembly be divided equally between the races.[13] Offices, however, did not decide roll calls. When the delegates returned to their homes the following March, the brief list of disgruntled men who had opposed adoption of the new constitution would include the names of five committee chairmen, all Southern whites.[14]

Over the winter the delegates devoted much time and energy to problems barely suggested in the end product of their labor—the constitution of 1868. The final document, for instance, fails to mention a state engineer, a board of health for New Orleans, or levee bonds. Yet the delegates discussed all three issues at some length and, at one point, even provided for two of them in the constitution.[15] The simple reference to a tax ordinance hardly explains the long weeks of controversy over the expenses of the convention and its members. Initially, the delegates attempted to finance the convention with a bond issue, but the plan failed when the banks in New Orleans refused to discount the bonds on favorable terms. They then turned to the alternative, a special property tax. The members feared, however, that disloyal officials would refuse to collect the tax, in which case they would be compelled to rely on the army to enforce it. Unfortunately, the term of the convention coincided with the tour of duty of a new commander of the Fifth Military District, Major General Winfield Scott Hancock, a conservative whose hostility to Reconstruction made him the darling of President Johnson and the Louisiana Democratic party. The delegates

13. *Official Journal of the Proceedings of the Convention for Framing a Constitution for the State of Louisiana* (New Orleans, 1868), 4.
14. They were William H. Cooley, committee to draft; Thomas S. Crawford, general provisions; John T. Ludeling, judiciary; John L. Barrett, legislative; John B. Vandergriff, enrollment (he voted against the constitution but did sign it).
15. *Official Journal (1867–1868)*, 192–93, 200; New Orleans *Tribune*, December 1, 3, 7, & 11, 1867.

fretted for weeks before learning that Hancock intended to enforce the tax levy. Another routine matter, the conferral of the printing patronage, turned into a running feud between the supporters of the New Orleans *Tribune* and the New Orleans *Republican*, the latter representing the more conservative views of Louisiana carpetbaggers and white Unionists. In November the delegates chose the *Tribune* as the official printer to the convention by the margin of a single vote. By March the upholders of the *Republican*—including many free blacks—had effectively reversed the decision, a consequence of the *Tribune*'s refusal to support Henry Clay Warmoth, the nominee of the Republican party, for governor.[16]

At the end of three-and-a-half months, the convention produced a document that, in most respects, closely resembled other state constitutions in American history. It established a form of government instantly recognizable by every citizen. It provided for public schools, a state militia, and the collection of taxes; defined the qualifications for voting; and established procedures for impeachment and revising the constitution. But if the general form was familiar, many of the particulars mainly originated in or were unique to the era of the Civil War and Reconstruction. Some of these caused no controversy: for example, the annulment of the ordinance of secession, the repeal of the black laws of 1865, and the cancellation of Confederate debts. Nevertheless, the principal controversies centered around two problems that grew out of the war: the disfranchisement of white Southerners who had aided the Rebellion, and the civil rights of Negroes.

The Louisiana constitution of 1868 was the first in the state's history to include a Bill of Rights. It asserted the equality of all men and guaranteed every citizen (Article 13), irrespective of race or color, "equal rights and privileges" on public transportation and in licensed "places of business, or of public resort." Other controversial sections required all public officials to accept, by oath, "the civil and political

16. New Orleans *Daily Picayune*, December 4, 11, and 12, 1867, January 18 and 23, March 4, 7, and 15, 1868; New Orleans *Tribune*, December 24 and 25, 1867; *Official Journal (1867–1868)*, 8, 286–89. The list of free Negroes alienated from the *Tribune* included James H. Ingraham, P. B. S. Pinchback, Caesar C. Antoine, Samuel Cuney, Thomas Isabelle, P. G. Deslonde, and others (St. Landry *Progress*, April 11, 1868).

equality of all men," enfranchised male citizens (except disfranchised Rebels) over the age of twenty-one, compelled the state to establish public schools open equally to white and black children, and prohibited any segregated state institution of learning.[17]

More than anyone else, James H. Ingraham, chairman of the Bill of Rights committee, was the principal architect of this program. There were, though, other architects: Robert I. Cromwell, P. F. Valfroit, Thomas Isabelle, David Wilson, and the white Radical George M. Wickliffe.[18] P. B. S. Pinchback initially opposed the "public rights" clauses of the Bill of Rights, but he changed his mind and drafted the final version of Article 13. Negro delegates supported these measures almost unanimously; in addition, they received broad support from Southern whites in the southeast—Union Louisiana—who of necessity had worked closely with black leaders in the Republican party since mid-1865. With such support the voting was one-sided: fifty-seven to eleven; sixty to sixteen; fifty-eight to sixteen; forty-nine to nineteen; and sixty-two to twelve. The only close vote occurred on the suffrage article, thirty-five to thirty-one; and here the vote is misleading because many members opposed not Negro suffrage, but the phrase "except those disfranchised by this Constitution."[19]

By a curious irony, the ideas of the conservative minority who opposed civil rights are more fully accessible than those of the Radical majority who supported them. Unlike the convention of 1864, this body did not provide for printed public debates. The local press covered the proceedings inadequately, often merely reprinting the *Official Journal* of the convention. Nettled by their defeats, the conservatives inserted numerous and sometimes lengthy explanations of their ac-

17. *Digest of the Statutes of the State of Louisiana, in Two Volumes* (New Orleans, 1870), I, 113–14, 129–30, 134.

18. Apart from his role as chairman of the Bill of Rights committee, Ingraham introduced the first proposal for racially mixed schools and also the first proposal for an oath requiring public officials to support the equality of all men. Probably most important, though, was that he was the minority leader on the committee to draft the constitution (*Official Journal [1867–1868]*, 16–17, 22, 96). For the contributions of other black members see *ibid.*, 26, 35–37, 44, 60–61, 67–68.

19. *Ibid.*, 114–15, 117–18, 125, 175–76, 184, 200–201. In some instances my figures differ slightly from those in the *Official Journal*. On pp. 200–201, for example, the *Official Journal* records the vote on Article 134 (later 135) as sixty-one to twelve. A count of the names on the vote tally, however, shows that it was sixty-two to twelve.

tions into the record; the victorious Radicals felt this compulsion much less strongly. But if some of the details are vague, the overall picture is fairly clear. Free men of color made up the largest single bloc in the convention, and the civil rights program represented mainly their achievement. A Northerner at one point asked Robert I. Cromwell to explain the concept of "public rights" in the proposed Bill of Rights. The free Negro physician answered that it gave Negroes the same rights as whites in public transportation, hotels, and churches. "Whites who did not approve of these privileges to the colored man," he added, "could leave the country and go to Venezuela or elsewhere." A black delegate who evidently thought these remarks to be intemperate was bluntly warned, "Go way from me; leave me alone!" The wine merchant Arnold Bertonneau declared that "he did not want to force white persons to drink with him, but simply to have the privilege of drinking in the same saloons." Inevitably, the conservatives accused the black majority of legislating social equality. One man of color agreed that that indeed was the goal. More soberly, James H. Ingraham explained that blacks simply wanted the same rights as other Americans. His people wanted no race war, only justice—"justice in the jury-box, in the school-house, etc.; and they never intended to remain content until those rights were granted them."[20]

The constitution (Article 135) not only prohibited segregation in the public schools but required something no previous law or constitution had required: that the state establish at least one school in every parish. A free Negro delegate from Jefferson Parish believed that these provisions would "elevate and enrich" Louisiana, which heretofore had been blighted by ignorance. Another free black declared that the education article "secures to my child and to all children throughout the State [the] education which their forefathers have been deprived of for two hundred and fifty years." Doubtless, the other Negro delegates in the convention—and many whites as well—shared similar sentiments. It remains nonetheless true that Negroes and whites attended school together almost nowhere in the state during Reconstruction except in about a third of the public schools in New Orleans, where free

20. New York *Times*, January 5, 1868; New Orleans *Daily Picayune*, December 28 and 29, 1867, January 3, 1868.

men of color dominated the school board. Considering that 59 percent of Louisiana free blacks lived in the Crescent City before the war, it is entirely probable that the estimated 500 to 1,000 Negro children who attended these desegregated schools in the 1870s belonged mainly to the *gens de couleur*.[21]

The conservatives in the convention were mainly Southern whites and carpetbaggers from Confederate Louisiana, that is, from the central and northern parishes controlled by Confederate armies during the war (see Map 5). Of twenty-six white delegates from this region, only three voted with the Radicals for civil rights. Conversely, of twenty-two white delegates from the Union parishes, only four voted consistently against civil rights. One of the puzzles of the convention concerns the poor attendance of the conservatives. The twenty-six white delegates from the Confederate region compiled a record of missed roll calls unequaled by any other group in the assembly. Only 38 percent, for example, voted on Article 1 of the Bill of Rights, only 54 percent on Article 13, and only 58 percent on Article 135. Considering the strength of the Radicals, their record on these civil rights measures was perhaps understandable. Disfranchisement, on the other hand, did not follow the ideological alignment of civil rights, and two or three votes often meant the difference between victory and defeat. Yet, on five major roll calls, the eighteen Southern whites from upstate voted only fifty-three times. By comparison, the seventeen black delegates from the region voted seventy-three times.[22]

One of the erring whites, the representative from the remote southwestern corner of the state, attended a few early sessions and then simply disappeared. The white delegate from St. Landry Parish fell ill and missed the last two thirds of the convention.[23] The site of the convention in New Orleans goes far to explain what happened to the rest.

---

21. *Official Journal (1867–1868)*, 201, 289; Louis R. Harlan, "Desegregation in New Orleans Public Schools during Reconstruction," *American Historical Review*, LXVII (April, 1962), 663–75. Roger A. Fischer has found a few "rare instances" of desegregated rural schools; however, his general conclusion is that rural desegregation "failed almost universally" (*Segregation Struggle in Louisiana*, 100–101, 109).

22. In addition to the four disfranchisement votes in Appendix 2, Table 4, the vote on Article 96, Majority Report, January 28, 1868, *Official Journal (1867–1868)*, 182.

23. *Ibid.*, 314; St. Landry *Progress*, January 11, 1868.

Map 5

Union and Confederate Louisiana

☐ Confederate Louisiana

■ Union Louisiana, represented by the seventeen parishes
that voted in the Free State election of February 1864

Each delegate had both to attend the convention and to conduct his private and family affairs. Close to home, the members from New Orleans and the southeast usually did both with little conflict. As a group, the black delegates from upstate were less wealthy than their white counterparts. Commitment aside, the $13 per diem more nearly compensated them for lost business or work. Also, because their farms and businesses were small, their wives, fathers, brothers, and sons more easily ran them in their absence. The affairs of the white delegates from Confederate Louisiana (particularly their cotton plantations), however, demanded personal attention. Sitting the entire winter, the convention lasted from the late cotton-picking season until preparations for spring planting. Double the per diem would not compensate the planter who permitted poor management to spoil his crop. Beyond this was the primitive state of transportation in Louisiana. With no rail connections to the interior, a person could travel to Chicago and back more quickly than he could make the round trip to Shreveport. Hence, the delegate who returned home to Sabine Parish or Morehouse Parish, if only for overnight, missed at least five or six sessions.

One way of looking at the conservatives is through the measures that they proposed as alternatives to the articles actually adopted by the Radical majority. For this purpose, the report of the committee to draft the constitution is invaluable. On December 20 the committee issued a divided report. Chairman William H. Cooley; three other conservatives from the Confederate region; and Rufus Waples, one of the most conservative members of the Orleans delegation, wrote the majority report. James H. Ingraham and three other blacks wrote the minority report. Although the *Official Journal* calls them "reports," they are actually complete drafts of the proposed constitution. For the rest of December and until March, the members used the two drafts actually to make the constitution of 1868. On a specific issue—say, whether judges should be appointed or elected—the debate usually started with a motion to adopt either the article of the conservative majority report or that of the Radical minority report. More often than not, the two documents basically agreed, simplifying the procedure. On controversial subjects, such as civil rights, disfranchisement, or an elective judiciary, the final article often differed markedly from either draft. On civil rights, the convention completely rejected the majority report; however, the document shows how the conservatives would have revised the constitution if they had commanded the votes.

The conservative draft also contained a Bill of Rights, but it failed to mention public rights. All persons, regardless of race or color, possessed "the same civil and political rights." Some conservatives sought to go further. W. Jasper Blackburn, for one, proposed an article prohibiting racial discrimination "either in matters of the common rights of all mankind or of constitutional liberty." Some whites believed it an admirable compromise, but not surprisingly, blacks thought it too vague. On the suffrage issue, Chairman Cooley and the conservatives proposed, for the moment, enfranchising all male citizens. However, after 1871 all men would have to read and write and pay their state taxes to qualify for the suffrage. The conservative oath of allegiance merely required officeholders to swear to uphold the laws and constitutions of Louisiana and the United States. Finally, on education, the conservatives directed the state to educate all children "without prejudice or partiality." This, of course, implied segregated schools.[24]

Judge Cooley and the conservatives were neither committed to their own ideas nor opposed to those of the Radicals in equal degrees. The Radical equality oath, for instance, rankled but remained a secondary issue. Nor did any of the conservatives differ with the Radicals so strongly over the suffrage as to oppose the constitution on that basis alone. But public rights, as defined in Article 13, and mixed schools disturbed all of them immensely; in the end, a recalcitrant minority rejected the constitution rather than accept such changes.

To some degree opposition to these measures emanated from racist hysteria. The conservatives warned darkly of "terrible retribution," a "war of races," and racial strife such as would result in "anarchy and the utter subversion of all law and governments." John T. Ludeling and John L. Barrett claimed that "the direct tendency of the Constitution . . . is to establish negro supremacy in the State." Judge Cooley asserted angrily that the Negroes in the convention wanted more rights

24. *Official Journal (1867–1868)*, 84, 92, 94; New Orleans *Daily Picayune*, January 4, 1868.

than the law now accorded to white people. He came to the convention, he declared revealingly, thinking that "the freedmen of the State could be made to understand their best interests. I have been sadly deceived."[25]

No delegate, though, rested his case solely on forebodings of disaster, nor did all the conservatives resort to them. By common agreement they believed that public rights as defined in the constitution violated personal property rights and represented a futile attempt to legislate social equality. In one exchange, Robert I. Cromwell protested that "we do not expect social rights," and John T. Ludeling replied sharply, "I am glad to hear the delegate say so. I tell you if you want such rights you cannot get them by legislation." W. Jasper Blackburn protested the futility in a democratic society of legislating beyond what public opinion would accept. Already the statute books, he argued, are covered "with those worthless and mischievous paper guarantees" that cannot be enforced. Interestingly enough, the member who wrote Article 13, P. B. S. Pinchback, spoke against public rights in the first round of debate in much the same terms. The national Civil Rights Act of 1866, he said, contained the same guarantees as the proposed Louisiana Bill of Rights, and Negroes were neither more nor less discriminated against than before its passage. He had learned in Ohio that race prejudice existed in the North as much as in the South. To assure Negroes of their freedom, he urged that they be given the standard political rights and the future would take care of itself. Pinchback did not intend to chase "the shadow for the substance, like the dog in the fable."[26]

Could the Radicals erase prejudice through "mere legislation?" The conservatives believed not, and the New Orleans *Tribune* came near to agreeing. Urging the convention to concentrate on enforcement of civil rights, the newspaper editorized, "We say that we have enough of bills of rights and declarations of principles." The Declaration of Independence, the Constitution, and the Civil Rights Act of 1866 made

25. New Orleans *Daily Picayune*, December 28, 1867; *Official Journal (1867–1868)*, 277, 290–92.
26. New Orleans *Daily Picayune*, December 28, 1867; *Official Journal (1867–1868)*, 276.

human equality the law of the land, but inequality persisted. "By being given a new edition of the existing laws," the *Tribune* argued, "we
will be given nothing. It is the practical enforcement of the law that
has to be secured." Prejudice must be confronted; "we have to grasp it,
and to crush it for ever." But how the newspaper proposed "to crush"
prejudice remained unclear. Five sessions of the Louisiana legislature,
between 1868 and 1873, would attempt to enforce Article 13 of the
constitution, without any real success.[27]

If anything, the conservatives opposed mixed schools even more
vigorously than they opposed public rights. Article 13 would simply
prove to be unenforceable, but Article 135 might have far-reaching
consequences. It could defeat ratification of the constitution, or it
could cripple the Republican school system at birth. If the state created
mixed schools, critics warned, whites would not send their children
to school with Negroes. Most of the conservatives, like Ludeling and
Barrett, concerned themselves mainly with the consequences for
whites who, they assumed, would pay for the schools but would be
deprived of using them. "Mixed schools," they argued, "will not elevate the negroes, but will debase the whites." W. Jasper Blackburn also
cared about the consequences for blacks. If enforced, he predicted, Article 135 would either destroy the schools or, reversing the logic of
Ludeling and Barrett, bar Negro children from attending them. "I am
a friend of all men," he claimed, "and more especially of all children,
regardless of race or color; but I desire and aim to be so upon a safe and
practicable basis."[28]

Subsequent events justified Blackburn's concern for practicality.
The Republicans enforced Article 135 only partially in New Orleans
and hardly anywhere in the rural parishes during Reconstruction.
South Carolina added a similar clause to its Reconstruction constitution and enforced it even less than Louisiana. Article 135, in other
words, produced many of the consequences its critics feared. Between
1860 and 1870 white school attendance in the state declined by nearly

27. New Orleans *Tribune*, December 25, 1867. Fischer evaluates these attempts and
concludes that "segregation in Louisiana survived the persistent efforts of Negroes and a
few whites to kill it" (*Segregation Struggle in Louisiana*, 85).
28. *Official Journal (1867–1868)*, 201, 290–91.

8,000, while black school attendance climbed from 275 to only 11,076. In the 1870s, in many parts of Louisiana, freedmen complained not about the state's failure to provide unsegregated schools, but about its failure to provide any schools. "For the past eight years," said one, "they would always tell us that the money had run out; and the children never got any schooling, except maybe a month or so in a year." Some blacks deserted the Radical party in 1876, claimed a Baton Rouge lawyer and Democrat, because of the school question: "They stated to me, many of them, that they had not had an opportunity to send their children to school; that they found themselves no better off than . . . when they got out of slavery."[29]

The conservatives in the convention based their arguments against civil rights on their own racial prejudices and a sure knowledge of the attitudes of their friends and neighbors back home. And to some extent they perceived what is clearer in hindsight, that the judicial and administrative tools needed to enforce mixed schools and "public rights" in the Reconstruction South—or North—simply did not exist.[30] The federal government in the post–World War II era, a leviathan compared to the national government of Lincoln's day or to Republican Louisiana, required great effort and considerably more time than history granted to Reconstruction Republicans to force civil rights and desegregation on a reluctant nation. And without the additional pressures of world politics, even that later commitment might have been far less successfully implemented.

During the debates no delegate talked about how civil rights would affect the Republican party. Perhaps this reflects only the fragmentary reportage of local newspapers, but more likely it resulted from the reluctance of public men to openly discuss partisan motives in such a forum. Yet the impact of public rights and mixed schools on the Republican party was surely a vital concern of the members from the Confederate region. In the Union parishes the party had been organized shortly after the war. Unionists had flourished openly under the

29. *House Miscellaneous Documents*, 44th Cong., 2d Sess., No. 34, Pt. 3, pp. 96, 128. Howard N. Rabinowitz has persuasively argued that segregation was a vast improvement over exclusion (*Race Relations in the Urban South 1865–1890* [New York, 1978]).

30. William Gillette, *Retreat from Reconstruction 1869–1879* (Baton Rouge, 1979), 363.

Federal occupation, and from the beginning the party in this region received support from loyal whites. In Confederate Louisiana a very different situation prevailed. Here the Republican party had hardly existed before the Reconstruction Acts; the real work of party building had occurred in the six or seven months before the convention, and that task continued as the convention sat. In the southeast, mostly Unionists and free Negroes had built the party in the rural parishes, but comparatively few free Negroes lived in upstate Louisiana;[31] and, of greater concern to white Republicans, years of Confederate rule had greatly reduced the original Unionist population.

In a sense, the Confederacy occupied central and northern Louisiana much as the Federals occupied the region around New Orleans. But whereas the Federals protected and strengthened the Unionist minority, the Rebels harassed and weakened it. Under pressure, families with Unionist leanings sent fathers and sons to Confederate armies, and in time blood and sacrifice made them embrace a cause that conviction alone could never have done. Wade H. Hough of Caldwell Parish explained to a congressional committee in 1869 that nearly all of the original Unionists in his area had joined the Rebellion. The turnabout of many of these people was quite remarkable. "Some of the worst men whom I knew in persecuting Union men," Hough stated, "were men who had themselves been for the Union at the beginning of the war." He believed that it was virtually impossible to live in the parish and not join the Rebel side. Hough himself had opposed disunion in the secession convention and refused to sign the ordinance of secession. But he, too, eventually wore a Confederate uniform. "I looked upon it in this way," he explained. "Here I have lived all my life, and have made a very nice property indeed. . . . I cannot leave. . . . I must stay here and do enough to keep me from being hung up to

31. In 1860, 14,252 free Negroes lived in the seventeen Union parishes as compared to only 4,395 in the thirty-one Confederate parishes. In both regions this population was unevenly distributed. The seven parishes of St. Landry, Natchitoches, Pointe Coupee, Calcasieu, St. Martin, Rapides, and Lafayette contained 3,783 of the free blacks in Confederate Louisiana; the remaining twenty-four had just 612 (*Eighth Census, 1860, Population,* 194). Nine of the seventeen black delegates from Confederate Louisiana represented the seven parishes with the largest free Negro populations. Three others, John Scott of Winn, Caesar C. Antoine of Caddo, and James H. Ingraham of Caddo, hailed from New Orleans.

a tree." The picture was not this bleak everywhere. In James G. Taliaferro's Catahoula Parish, below Caldwell, the Unïonist population survived the war relatively intact; and in neighboring Rapides Parish, James Madison Wells recruited eight companies of loyal irregulars during General Banks's Red River campaign.[32]

Whatever their postwar numerical strength, these Unionists were crucial to the future of the Republican party in central and northern Louisiana, and as a group they demonstrated a notable lack of sympathy for such "Radical" notions as the civil rights of Negroes. W. Jasper Blackburn believed that emancipation alone had converted many Union men in the region into Rebels. In May 1867 a Unionist organizer named Thomas B. Waters informed James G. Taliaferro's son Robert that the work of building the Republican party in Catahoula Parish proceeded smoothly. "The negroes are all Republicans, and we shall vote them to a man." He also believed that the freedmen would follow the leadership of whites in party politics. Yet, in the same letter, Waters turned an about-face and expressed the fear that "the Republican party is getting along, almost too fast. The Union men are getting apprehensive that they will be thrown overboard by the negroes." If so, he predicted, it "will be a very bad condition of things, for the Republican party . . . in fact that would ruin us." Shortly after the constitutional convention adjourned, a former Louisiana Whig, now a Georgia Unionist, wrote Taliaferro asking for a job if Taliaferro, a candidate for governor, won the election. As an old friend, the Georgian commented on Louisiana's new constitution; while he liked some parts of it, he strongly disapproved of "the attempt to force social equality between the races." This, he believed, violated "the design of nature," and if carried out it would result in a "miserable mongrel population."[33]

---

32. *House Miscellaneous Documents*, 41st Cong., 2d Sess., No. 154, Pt. 1, pp. 706–707; Thomas B. Waters to Robert W. Taliaferro, May 25, [1867], in James G. Taliaferro and Family Papers, Troy H. Middleton Library, Louisiana State University, Baton Rouge; Walter McGeehee Lowrey, "The Political Career of James Madison Wells," *Louisiana Historical Quarterly*, XXXI (October, 1948), 1018.

33. *House Miscellaneous Documents*, 41st Cong., 2d Sess., No. 154, Pt. 1, p. 75; Thomas B. Waters to Robert W. Taliaferro, May 25, [1867], and W. H. Sparks to James G. Taliaferro, April 5, 1868, in Taliaferro and Family Papers.

The Republican party needed Unionists not simply to win elections, although that consideration certainly mattered. The black vote over roughly half of Confederate Louisiana was fully as decisive as in the southeastern parishes, and none in the convention foresaw the massive terror campaigns the Democrats would later wage against the freedmen. More basically, white Republicans needed other white Republicans because the party, like the state, divided along the color line. Negroes and whites acted together as Republicans to build a party, win an election, make a constitution, and provide jobs. They did not, however, attend church together and sit down with their families afterwards for Sunday dinner. Nor did they form business partnerships or oversee marital partnerships between members of their families. Hence, the problem: If too many whites stayed outside the party, those who joined might be too few in number to form a real community and would find themselves alienated from their own color, unable to support one another. In isolation was vulnerability to physical attack, social ostracism, and sheer loneliness of spirit.

Party considerations also influenced the other major controversy in the convention: the disfranchisement of Southern Rebels. The delegates debated disfranchisement for five days in late January. At one point Simon Jones and John T. Ludeling appeared on the verge of a duel. Understandably, Ludeling objected to Jones's insinuation that he, among others, talked treason. When he protested, Jones snapped, "Very well, sir; you can find me any time you wish at my room." "Very well," Ludeling replied. At bottom, the issue lay between the supporters of harsh versus lenient disfranchisement. The advocates of harshness favored adopting either the restraints of Congress—the Reconstruction Acts and the Fourteenth Amendment—or those of a measure known as the Packard Amendment. The Northerner Stephen B. Packard proposed disfranchising all federal, state, and local officials who had aided the Rebellion. The convention rejected both solutions. On the side of leniency, a sizable minority of eight whites and five blacks wanted *no* restrictions placed on disloyal citizens. At one time they came within two votes of persuading the majority to accept this position. A less extreme proposal—Article 96 of the Majority Report—disfranchised the leaders of guerrilla bands, Federal military officers who aided the Rebellion, and, most important, members of the secession convention and high federal and state officials who encouraged disunion *before* June 1, 1861. The plan reflected the classic Unionist belief that a minority of traitors had pushed the loyal majority into rebellion. Thus, it punished those responsible for the treason, not the loyal citizens "driven into rebel armies," as one member put it, "by the most reckless and relentless despotism that appears in the annals of history." On January 28 the convention adopted Article 96 (Majority Report) by a vote of forty-five to thirty-five.[34]

In late February Packard revived his original amendment, and the consensus on the Majority Report broke down. Rufus Waples thereupon proposed a compromise; it disfranchised guerrilla leaders, registered enemies, members of secession conventions, newspaper editors and ministers who had advocated treason, and civil and military officials who had held office for a year under the Confederacy. These proscribed individuals could regain their rights by writing a public confession acknowledging the immorality and illegality of secession. Plainly, this was bitter medicine compared to the Majority Report. Packard smoothed its passage as Article 99 of the constitution by adding a saving amendment that exempted any person who, prior to 1868, supported the Reconstruction Acts and helped loyal citizens restore Louisiana to the Union. Near adjournment, Waples added another mollifying amendment that directed voter registrars to accept, without question, the oath of any individual that he had supported the Reconstruction Acts and aided loyal men in reconstructing the state.[35]

Throughout, a distinct sectional alignment was evident. Confederate Louisiana supported lenient disfranchisement or no disfranchisement at all. On five sample roll calls, its forty-two delegates voted for leniency by a margin of 101 to 52 votes. By a much less decisive edge, New Orleans. On the five test roll calls, they supported strict disfranchisement 87 to 42. The voting of Negroes, Southern whites, and New Orleans. On the five text roll calls, they supported strict disfranchisement 87 to 42. The voting of Negroes, Southern whites, and

34. New Orleans *Daily Picayune*, January 28, 1868; *Official Journal (1867–1868)*, 182–83, 259, 266. 293.
35. *Official Journal (1867–1868)*, 256–59, 282–83.

carpetbaggers all basically conformed to this sectional alignment. Although as a group blacks supported strict disfranchisement, the seventeen Negro delegates from the Confederate region voted against it, 39 to 34. Most carpetbaggers from upstate preferred leniency; those from the southeast opposed it.[36] Overall, Southern whites voted overwhelmingly against strict disfranchisement, but the handful of native Southerners from the Union parishes outside New Orleans supported it by a nearly two-to-one margin.

Some delegates sincerely believed that disfranchisement was wrong. P. B. S. Pinchback and three other Negroes protested Article 99, arguing that universal suffrage was a cardinal principle of the Republican party. W. Jasper Blackburn wanted to punish the authors of the Rebellion to the maximum degree, but "it was impossible to reach them," he declared, "without dragging into punishment many noble and true men who could not resist the force of . . . overpowering circumstances." One carpetbagger preferred "that twenty bad men should go unpunished than that one innocent man should suffer." Some of the measures before the assembly, he stated, would disfranchise "some of the best men" in his area, including his fellow delegate from Avoyelles Parish. Less convincingly, another Northerner appealed to Christian forgiveness, and the member from Union Parish insisted that he would rather see ninety-nine Rebels escape than one innocent person wrongfully punished. On the other hand, Simon Jones and others despaired over the convention's reluctance to mete out punishment to the disloyal.[37]

Whatever the weight of principles, party considerations mattered most. The delegates from upstate could not win converts to the Republican party and make treason odious at the same time. A similar logic influenced the New Orleans delegation; whites outnumbered blacks in the city by about three to one. If some members thereby concluded that the answer lay in permanent disfranchisement, the majority preferred the thinking of their colleagues from the Confederate re-

36. Stephen B. Packard was the only carpetbagger in the New Orleans delegation. He supported strict disfranchisement.

37. *Official Journal (1867–1868)*, 293; New Orleans *Daily Picayune* January 25, 26 and 28, 1868.

gion. Thus, only in the Union parishes outside New Orleans could Republicans safely—or so they believed—punish the disloyal as the disloyal deserved punishing.

Politically, Article 99 was much inferior to the original article of the Majority Report. Many a Whig had gone to war and stayed the duration, all the while cursing the secession Democrats for starting it. By concentrating on the people responsible for the Rebellion, the Majority Report partially mediated between two conflicting ends: the need of loyal Republicans to punish treason and thereby justify their own sacrifices, and the need of the Republican party to mollify Louisiana whites. Article 99 (as amended), on the other hand, provided an escape for any Rebel who chose to take it while, at the same time, it remained needlessly offensive with its demand for public confession; the amendments, moreover, placed a premium on deceit and probably struck many whites as bribes to join the Republican party.[38] Perhaps, though, it made no difference. Even had the convention adopted universal amnesty, there would have yet remained that larger conflict between the party's need for statewide white support and the civil rights program, which the Radical majority saw as the convention's most important work.

On paper, the Radical constitution guaranteed black Louisianians the same rights and privileges as white people. It also protected the property rights of married women, provided pensions for veterans of the War of 1812, and canceled child labor contracts made without parental consent. But it did not measurably help the tens of thousands of freedmen who would keep the Republican party in office to deal with their fundamental economic problems. More than anything else, the ex-slaves needed land, but barring massive confiscation few practical ways existed to help them get it. At one point George M. Wickliffe introduced a measure intended to assist the freedmen in purchasing land. The lawmakers adopted the first half of the proposal, requiring the subdivision of all lands sold by the courts into small 10-to-50-acre

38. William Archibald Dunning described Article 99 as among the severest disfranchisement provisions of any Reconstruction constitution (*Essays on the Civil War and Reconstruction* [New York, 1897], 197); William A. Russ, Jr., agreed ("Disfranchisement in Louisiana [1862–70]," *Louisiana Historical Quarterly*, XVIII [July, 1935], 575–80).

tracts. It rejected, however, the critical second half of the article, which restricted any person or company from buying over 150 acres at a sale. At the time, Negroes accounted for thirty-six of fifty-five delegates on the floor; the black majority voted twenty-five to eleven against the 150-acre restriction.[39] Many of the black members perhaps failed to recognize the implications of their votes; still, their actions revealed a damaging dim-sightedness of the freedmen's interests.

There also exists the question of whether civil rights, as defined in the constitution, really benefited ordinary blacks. Certainly mixed schools did not. As to public rights, the problem of enforcing Article 13 arose repeatedly in the Louisiana legislature during Reconstruction. When it did, the debate always returned to the same familiar ground. In 1869, for example, William Murrell (who had served in the convention) argued with a white lawmaker in the house over whether Lieutenant Governor Oscar J. Dunn and his wife could obtain passage on steamboats "without being insulted." The white representative asserted that Dunn was "too sensible a man to go anywhere he is not wanted." Murrell replied sharply that if the lieutenant governor "cannot go where he pleases, he ought not to be Lieutenant Governor." Another black representative joined the discussion. The colored people, he declared heatedly, did not want social equality, but they wanted their rights under the constitution "because they have been treated but little better than dogs upon these public conveyances." Three years later, in the 1872 session, David Young of Concordia Parish complained that the captain of the *Robert E. Lee* refused to rent him the same stateroom as he rented whites. "Now," Young said, "I do not want to go into anybody's private chamber, but simply to enjoy the same privilege that other people do. I want, when I take my wife on board of that steamer . . . to give her some refreshments, but I do not want to give it to her in the pantry or on the dock." Young also wanted to attend the theater—"although I don't go to such places." He would not "go ragged and dirty, but in a respectable suit of clothes and a clean face. I don't want to be refused, but want to sit down with my white friends and talk over the play."[40]

39. *Official Journal (1867–1868)*, 266.
40. *Louisiana House Debates*, 1869, pp. 254–61; *ibid.*, 1872, 59–60.

Although he was an ex-slave, David Young had emerged as a successful planter-merchant and politician. His desire for equality was justified by humanity and the law of the land. Yet his demands and those of other successful blacks for equal access to theaters, saloons, and steamboats remained remote from the needs and aspirations of the overwhelming majority of ex-slaves who lived hard lives of toil and ceaseless anxiety. The New Orleans *Tribune* acknowledged this fact during the controversy over the civil rights act of 1869. Raise the question of enforcing Article 13, the newspaper observed, and whites imagine "the colored population rushing in solid phalanx into their most aristocratic places of amusement and accommodation." Such fears were groundless. "The poor [Negro] laborer, coming from his hard work, with his soiled clothes, having gained hardly enough to live, will certainly not pretend to come and pay the price charged by the establishments frequented principally by the whites." Only blacks of means and "good social manners" will patronize such places, the newspaper predicted.[41]

In April 1868 Louisiana voted on the new constitution. The previous summer General Philip H. Sheridan had registered 45,000 whites and 83,000 Negroes as voters. He had disfranchised nearly half the white population, the unrepentant Rebel half. The Republican party needed a white base in the state to ensure its survival. To obtain it, it must appeal to those whites whom Sheridan had not disfranchised. The general's electorate ratified the constitution, 66,152 votes to 48,739. But Republicans who scrutinized the returns closely must have done so with some foreboding. In New Orleans, with nearly 30,000 voters, half black and half white, the constitution lost, 14,763 to 14,291. In the forty-seven parishes outside the city, whites opposed the constitution by an incredible margin of 28,213 to 1,452. Only in Winn Parish did more than 100 whites support ratification. Thirty-four parishes counted less than 50 white votes each for the constitution; twenty-two counted less than 25. Outside of New Orleans, moreover, four times as many blacks (5,853) opposed the constitution as whites supported it.[42]

41. New Orleans *Louisianian*, February 20, 1875; New Orleans *Tribune*, January 10, 1869.
42. New Orleans *Daily Picayune*, August 16, 1867; Donald W. Davis, "Ratification of

Even though black politicians dominated the Radical convention, their triumph was deceptive. Carpetbaggers, although they were few in number, rather than Negroes or white Unionists would dominate Radical Reconstruction in the state. In a series of complicated maneuvers dating from the early summer of 1867, a carpetbagger coalition headed by Henry Clay Warmoth undercut the dominant position of native Southerners, black and white, in the Republican party. In January 1868, the very moment when blacks and Unionists demonstrated their dominance as constitution makers, the state nominating convention of the Republican party met in New Orleans. On the first ballot for governor, Francis E. Dumas, a prominent Crescent City free black, led Warmoth 41 to 37, only four votes away from the forty-five needed to win. The tension in the air at this point must have been as palpable as the blue haze of cigar smoke. On the second ballot Dumas gained two votes, but Warmoth picked up eight and won the nomination forty-five to forty-three.[43] Dumas and a minority of his supporters—notably the owners of the New Orleans *Tribune*—then bolted the regular party and supported James G. Taliaferro, a man not distinguished by black skin and more conservative than Warmoth. In fact, most of the 39,000 Louisianians who voted for him in April saw him as the last bulwark of white supremacy against the black Republicans.

---

the Constitution of 1868—Record of Votes," *Louisiana History*, VI (Summer, 1965), 301–305. Unfortunately, the returns for Orleans and De Soto parishes were not differentiated by race. In the case of De Soto, I counted its vote for the constitution as black and its vote against the constitution as white.

43. F. Wayne Binning, "Carpetbaggers' Triumph: The Louisiana State Elections of 1868," *Louisiana History*, XIV (Winter, 1973), 34; Henry Clay Warmoth, *War, Politics and Reconstruction: Stormy Days in Louisiana* (New York, 1930), 54.

7

Architects
of Power

The summer of 1870 witnessed a famous event in the lore of the Mississippi River: the steamboat race from New Orleans to St. Louis between the *Natchez* and the *Robert E. Lee*. The backers of each boat invested liberal sums on the outcome, and an enormous crowd gathered at the wharf in New Orleans for the start of the race. Hundreds of people lined the banks of the Upper Coast as the two vessels steamed upriver; and when night fell the spectators lit bonfires, fired guns, and shouted cheers from the levees. Aboard the *Robert E. Lee* (which incidentally won the race) was a youthful, handsome man named Henry Clay Warmoth. Thousands recognized, if not his face, then his name; he was Louisiana's "carpetbag" governor from Illinois.[1] His presence on the passenger deck of the *Robert E. Lee* resulted neither from coincidence nor simply from an interest in steamboat races. Before his election he had acted as the attorney for the builder and principal owner of the boat, the New Yorker Asa S. Mansfield. Both men had sought their fortune in Civil War and Reconstruction New Orleans, and both had found it.[2]

The ownership of the *Robert E. Lee* was not public knowledge, but had it become so no Southerner ought to have been surprised. It was a matter of public record in antebellum New Orleans, commented on in the press, that most of the city's leading banks, mercantile houses,

1. As here defined, a carpetbagger was a white man who came to Louisiana, after 1861, from any non-Confederate state in the Union (or foreign country) and supported the Republican party and congressional Reconstruction. This definition is in general agreement with Richard N. Current, "Carpetbaggers Reconsidered," David H. Pinkney and Theodore Ropp, eds., *A Festschrift for Frederick B. Artz* (Durham, N.C., 1964), 144; and Richard L. Hume, "Carpetbaggers in the Reconstruction South: A Group Portrait of Outside Whites in the 'Black and Tan' Constitutional Conventions," *Journal of American History*, LXIV (September, 1977), 315.

2. Henry Clay Warmoth, *War, Politics and Reconstruction: Stormy Days in Louisiana* (New York, 1930), 157–60.

insurance firms, transportation companies, and newspapers, not to mention the public schools and Protestant churches, had been either founded or taken over by migrants from the free states. The Pennsylvanian James Robb, to cite an illustrious example, arrived in New Orleans in 1837, "a moneyless and friendless adventurer," as one newspaper later described him, and made a fortune in banking, utilities, and railroads. He also served in the city government and in the state senate. The voters of New Orleans elected two other Northerners as mayors in the 1850s, and the kingpin of Louisiana politics before the war was John Slidell, a New Yorker (his great rival, Pierre Soulé, was a Frenchman).[3]

Henry Clay Warmoth and Asa S. Mansfield, then, represented merely the most recent of a long line of Yankee migrants. As we have seen, combined with Germans and Irishmen, such migrants largely dominated the earlier stages of Reconstruction in the state. The size of the Northern migration in the Civil War era is a matter of some conjecture. John T. Trowbridge in 1866 estimated that 50,000 Northerners had settled in Louisiana since the fall of New Orleans during the war. Two years later a Northern editor in Vicksburg judged that 10,000 Union veterans resided in neighboring Mississippi. More recently, Lawrence N. Powell has surmised that between 20,000 and 50,000 Northerners took up planting in the entire South during and after the war.[4] Such hard evidence that exists suggests that such figures are greatly inflated. According to the census, the Northern-born population of Louisiana grew steadily throughout the antebellum period, and it fell for the first time during the Civil War and Reconstruction. Numbering 14,202 in 1860, it declined to 11,523 in 1870, and by 1880 had dropped to 9,974.[5] Even allowing that many or most Yankees

3. William W. Chenault and Robert C. Reinders, "The Northern-born Community of New Orleans in the 1850s," *Journal of American History*, LI (September, 1964), 232–47; Robert C. Reinders, "New England Influences on the Formation of Public Schools in New Orleans," *Journal of Southern History*, XXX (May, 1964), 181–95.

4. John T. Trowbridge, *The South: A Tour of Its Battle-Fields and Ruined Cities* (Hartford, Conn., 1866), 411; William C. Harris, *Presidential Reconstruction in Mississippi* (Baton Rouge, 1967), 169; Lawrence N. Powell, *New Masters: Northern Planters During the Civil War and Reconstruction* (New Haven, 1980), xii.

5. These figures are extracted from the Nativity Tables of the Eighth, Ninth, and Tenth United States Censuses.

who moved South in the 1860s returned North before the 1870 census, figures in the range of 20,000 or more—even for the entire region—appear excessive. More likely, 1,500 or so Yankees located in Louisiana in the 1860s and perhaps five times that number in the Southern states.

In a United States Senate hearing in 1879, an astonished senator exclaimed, "Do you mean to say that the Democratic party have carpetbaggers?" William Harper, a Negro Republican from Caddo Parish, explained that Northerners were carpetbaggers only "when they are on the Republican side."[6] Although refuted by revisionist historians, to most Americans the word *carpetbagger* still brings to mind the image of an office-seeking adventurer, hastening South after the Civil War to profiteer on a defeated people's misery, with the sum of his worldly goods stuffed in a carpetbag. As an idea, the carpetbagger represented, in part, a synthesis of two older stereotypes: the zealous abolitionist and the avaricious Yankee (a fusion of race and greed). Neither of these stereotypes was limited to the South. Many Northerners equated abolitionists with race fanaticism no less than their countrymen below the Potomac. Likewise, in the antebellum North, stories of money-grubbing, hypocritical New Englanders suggested to young and old alike the excesses of Yankee enterprise and revealed underlying tensions in a society not fully comfortable with its acquisitive values. In the South the image of the mercenary Yankee served other ends. Defenders of slavery found him a useful symbol of Northern civilization. He also offered a convenient explanation of Northern dominance in such vital areas of commerce as banking, marketing, and shipping. Long before any carpetbagger set foot on Southern soil, these distorted visions of Yankee character had become articles of faith in the South.[7]

It is well known that the carpetbaggers' enemies used unflattering imagery to discredit both their persons and their politics during Reconstruction. Less well remembered is that not all their critics had supported the Confederacy. As early as 1863 George S. Denison, a

---

6. *Senate Reports*, 45th Cong., 3d Sess., No. 855, Pt. 1, p. 27.
7. William R. Taylor, *Cavalier and Yankee: The Old South and the American National Character* (New York, 1963); Michael C. C. Adams, *Our Masters the Rebels: A Speculation on Union Military Failure in the East, 1861–1865* (Cambridge, 1978).

Texas Unionist, complained that Union-occupied New Orleans contained more intriguers and speculators than any other place in America. Every steamer, he said, unloads a new crowd of such people, each expecting "to be a millionaire in six months." At the close of the war, Governor Wells nearly turned the state over to the Rebels in an effort to rid it of Yankee influence. When James G. Taliaferro opposed Warmoth for governor three years later, some Unionists alleged that Warmoth and his friends were "mere adventurers" who sought personal profit "upon the ruins of the true people of Louisiana." At times, the Democratic press was hardly more disparaging of the men from the North than the New Orleans *Tribune*. Resenting the carpetbaggers' preeminence over blacks in the Radical party, the *Tribune*, on the eve of Warmoth's nomination for governor, depicted party leaders as "white adventurers" without honesty or integrity. Black Republicans, on occasion, engaged in such name-calling against their own color. "This person, J. Henri Burch," exclaimed an ex-slave on the floor of the house of representatives, "comes down here from New York, goes to Baton Rouge, and is sent down here to represent the people of Louisiana. Now, sir, I want to know what this nigger carpetbagger knows about the people of New Orleans." The reductio absurdum occurred during the intraparty fights of the 1870s when carpetbaggers accused one another of being adventurers.[8] Of course, the greater part of such invective emanated from the enemies of Reconstruction. Nevertheless, the words that expressed the imagery came easily to the lips of native Southerners, white and black, Democratic and Republican.

Understandably, Northerners resented the epithets, whatever the origin. "Lies, unmitigated lies, notorious and malicious lies," charged

8. George S. Denison to Salmon P. Chase, February 12, 1863, in "Diary and Correspondence of Salmon P. Chase," *Annual Report of the American Historical Association for the Year 1902* (Washington, D.C., 1903), II, 359–60; W. H. Sparks to James G. Taliaferro, March 17, 1868, and D. E. Haynes to Taliaferro, March 20, 1868, in James G. Taliaferro and Family Papers, Troy H. Middleton Library, Louisiana State Library, Baton Rouge; quote in *Tribune* from John Rose Ficklen, *History of Reconstruction in Louisiana (Through 1868)* (Baltimore, 1910), 196; *Louisiana House Debates*, 1872, p. 57; Emerson Bentley to H. C. Dibble, July 6, 1871, in Henry Clay Warmoth Papers, Southern Historical Collection, University of North Carolina, Chapel Hill; New Orleans *Republican*, May 10 and June 2, 1872.

Warmoth. He might be a scalawag, he conceded, but he was no carpetbagger. It particularly embittered the newcomers that stories of their misdeeds received such ready acceptance in the North. "It has always seemed strange to me," Marshall Harvey Twitchell wrote sadly, "that the Northern people should so readily have believed their young men the infamous wretches which the South represented them to be." That his countrymen rejected the report of brave soldiers, "lads of superior character, from the best families of the North," and accepted "the testimony of men reared under the demoralizing influence of slavery, traitors . . . gamblers and bar-room loafers," was almost more than the earnest and long-suffering Vermonter could endure.[9]

Twitchell believed that Reconstruction represented a ten-year effort "to substitute the civilization of freedom for that of slavery." Few carpetbaggers would have disagreed. On the other hand, asked to explain their personal motivation for settling in Louisiana, probably no Northerner could honestly have given that as his reason. The great majority of the newcomers were young men in their twenties and early thirties who had served as officers in the Union army. Much better educated than the average soldier in the ranks, their prospects for a business or professional career would be rated much higher. The war captured their enthusiasm at a time when they had just started what Americans of the day called the race of life. Eighteen-year-old Henry Clay Warmoth opened a law office in Missouri the year of Lincoln's election; Francis J. Herron at the time was a Dubuque banker in his mid-twenties; Cyrus Bussey, a young merchant, had only in 1858 won election to the Iowa legislature; Ephraim S. Stoddard completed college in Massachusetts in the spring of 1861 and accepted his first job; Chester B. Darrall graduated from medical school during the war and entered the army as an assistant surgeon; Marshall Harvey Twitchell studied law, taught school, and worked on his father's farm the year he entered the army.[10] The war separated such men from their youth by a

9. Warmoth, *War, Politics and Reconstruction*, vii, 270; "Autobiography of Marshall Harvey Twitchell," preface. A xerox of this manuscript is in the Marshall Harvey Twitchell Papers, Prescott Memorial Library, Louisiana Tech University, Ruston; the original remains in the possession of Dr. Marshall Coleman Twitchell of Burlington, Vermont.

10. "Autobiography of Marshall Harvey Twitchell," preface, in Twitchell Papers,

chasm of years and experience, but it did not daunt their ambition or their faith in themselves or the future of their country. Asked why they located in Louisiana, most would have unabashedly professed personal gain. The South needed rebuilding. Who better than they, brave ex-soldiers imbued with Yankee enterprise, could regenerate its agriculture and construct the railroads, schools, and factories the region desperately needed? "No better class of immigrants ever blessed a country," one of them wrote.[11]

Judging by the numbers who entered the field, few Southerners worshipped more devoutly at the shrine of plantation agriculture than these newcomers. Of the Northerners who served in the Radical constitutional convention, for example, over half worked cotton and sugar plantations. When Warmoth withdrew from the political wars of the 1870s, he retreated only as far as his sugar plantation in Plaquemines Parish. A quarter of a century later he went to Washington as the representative of Louisiana sugar planters, asking for a higher tariff on foreign sugars.[12] Many of these migrant planters—Whitelaw Reid, Frank Blair, and Henry W. Fuller, among others—soon returned to the North, but numerous others remained in the state for years. One of those who stayed, George C. Benham, left an account of his Southern migration, describing how he and his partners dizzily computed their anticipated profits, and how unforeseen expenses and the army-worm returned them to sobriety. Of his state of mind at the time of his

---

1–6; Warmoth, *War, Politics and Reconstruction*, 5–12; Ezra J. Warner, *Generals in Blue: Lives of the Union Commanders* (Baton Rouge, 1964), 58–59, 228–29; "War Experiences of an Enlisted Man," in Ephraim S. Stoddard Papers, Howard-Tilton Memorial Library, Tulane University, New Orleans; *Biographical Directory of the American Congress, 1774–1971* (Washington, D.C., 1971), 826. That these individuals were by no means unusual is indicated by the birth dates of the following carpetbaggers: Emerson Bentley, 1850; O. H. Brewster, 1832; Thomas W. Conway, 1837; Henry C. Dibble, 1845; Henry W. Fuller, 1839; Cyrus Hamlin, 1839; John S. Harris, 1825; Joseph C. Hartzell, 1842; William Wirt Howe, 1833; William Pitt Kellogg, 1831; John Edwards Leonard, 1845; Albert Lindley Lee, 1834; George B. Loud, 1845; James McCleery, 1837; Frank Morey, 1840; Joseph P. Newsham, 1837; John L. Rice, 1840; Lionel A. Sheldon, 1828; George A. Sheridan, 1840; George Luke Smith, 1837; Jacob Hale Sypher, 1837; Joseph Rodman West, 1822; and William Wilson Wharton, 1846. Lawrence N. Powell has found a similar pattern in his study of Yankee planters (*New Masters*, 8–9, 165).

11. [George C. Benham] *A Year of Wreck: A True Story by a Victim* (New York, 1880), 135.

12. Appendix 2, Table 3; Warmoth, *War, Politics and Reconstruction*, 260–62.

departure from the Midwest, Benham afterwards wrote ironically, "See here before you one of the pioneers from the North, taking his life in his hands, and joining that army of adventurous men who are seeking a home in the South." He and his kind would introduce labor-saving machinery, renew the land, and make it prosper as never before. "I am in love with this country, and fully determined to be a cotton planter," an Easterner just out of the army told him. The young man wanted to aid the freedmen too, of course, and help finish the job of reconstructing Southern society. But "money is the main thing," he stated frankly. "I firmly believe there is no part of the country where there is such a future for young men as this. I have my own fortune to make, and right here I intend to make it."[13]

By far the greater part of the carpetbagger migration to Louisiana was over by the spring of 1866. Ex-soldiers had either taken up residence in the state or returned North. Those who intended to plant sugar or cotton had done so or they must wait until the next planting season. Events during the remainder of the year did not encourage newcomers. In July the terrible race riot in New Orleans erupted, and in the fall and winter the armyworm once again ravaged the cotton crop. With the passage of the Reconstruction Acts the following year, however, the climate abruptly changed, and some who had left the state in 1865 were moved to reconsider. In faraway Kansas, Charles W. Lowell noted the trend of events and decided he no longer cared for the cold weather around Leavenworth. "If sufficient inducements were offered," he wrote Warmoth, "I would go back to Shreveport . . . and open a law office, and look after the interests of loyal people in that section." The farsighted ex-brigadier general even knew what inducement he wanted. The post of register of bankruptcy, he said, "might as well be filled by me as any of the old citizens there who are all rebels." In any event, "I would not like to go back unless I could be assured of *some* appointment." Warmoth's answer must have satisfied him, because Lowell returned to Shreveport and in 1868 became speaker of the house of representatives. Another army acquaintance, a

13. [Benham] *Year of Wreck*, 13–14, 21, 232–34. A Republican judge as well as a planter, Benham published his narrative anonymously to avoid the vengeance of his neighbors. His plantation was located in Carroll Parish.

lawyer in Mobile, Alabama, contacted Warmoth the following year. "I suppose there is no doubt," he said, "of your being elected Governor of your State, and if you are I want you to remember old friends." Like Lowell, this man also knew what he wanted. An appointment as recorder of deeds and mortgages in New Orleans, he declared, "would·suit me first rate." In this case, though, Warmoth's reply must have been less pleasing, for the individual informed Warmoth several years later that he intended to settle in New Orleans despite the governor's lack of enthusiasm.[14] Warmoth's attitude toward old army buddies had perhaps soured over the years; so many, like Lowell, had turned into bitter enemies.

In Reconstruction legend, the men from the North were not only corrupt but ubiquitous. For decades historians matter-of-factly discussed "carpetbag rule," which they rarely defined but assumed existed in almost all of the former Confederate states. An important book on South Carolina devoted only a few pages to carpetbaggers yet assured its readers that they "constituted the head and front of the Radical government." Even Texas—a state in which Northerners were notably scarce after the Civil War—was somehow "under" the carpetbaggers.[15] In recent years, some revisionist historians have suggested that the role of carpetbaggers in the postwar South suffers from exaggeration. "Contrary to the myth of Reconstruction," writes Carl N. Degler, "the so-called carpetbaggers, were always too few in number to play a numerically significant role in the exercise of political power." In this view, Southern scalawags who numerically dominated the Reconstruction constitutional conventions and state legislatures were the crucial political figures of the period.[16]

Numbers, however, can be deceptive. Newcomers from the North

14. Charles W. Lowell to Henry Clay Warmoth, April 5, 1867, and Turner (no first name given) to Warmoth, April 6, 1868, and January 23, 1871, all in Warmoth Papers.

15. Francis Butler Simkins and Robert Hilliard Woody, *South Carolina During Reconstruction* (Chapel Hill, 1932), 124; W. C. Nunn, *Texas Under the Carpetbaggers* (Austin, 1962). James Alex Baggett could find only five carpetbaggers who served on the large executive committee of the Texas Republican party during the entire period from 1865 to 1877 ("Origins of Early Texas Republican Party Leadership," *Journal of Southern History*, XL [August, 1974], 441–42 n.).

16. Carl N. Degler, *The Other South: Southern Dissenters in the Nineteenth Century* (New York, 1974), 194.

were indeed a small minority in the constitutional conventions, but as several scholars have observed, they claimed a disproportionate share of vital committee chairmanships in those assemblies. True, six of the former Confederate states never elected a carpetbag governor; on the other hand, the remaining five had two apiece.[17] Moreover, in the six states in which scalawags dominated the governorship, in none of them, excepting North Carolina, did the Radical regime last beyond the end of 1874; most, in fact, collapsed much earlier. By comparison, in the five states in which carpetbaggers dominated the governor's office, in no case did the Radical government fall *before* the end of 1874, and three lasted until 1877.[18]

Nowhere, though, are numbers more misleading than in Louisiana. The Federal occupation attracted more Northerners than in other Southern states and allowed the Yankees to entrench themselves, politically and economically, to an extent impossible in states like Texas, Alabama, and Georgia. Even so, active carpetbaggers probaby numbered no more than 300 individuals at any time. They held only fourteen seats in the state's constitutional convention and never obtained anything like a majority in either house of the legislature. Yet both of Louisiana's Reconstruction governors after 1867 and all three of its Republican United States Senators were Northerners. Between 1868 and 1879 the state chose thirteen Republicans to the United States House

---

17. Jack B. Scroggs, "Carpetbagger Constitutional Reform in the South Atlantic States, 1867–1868," *Journal of Southern History*, XXVII (November, 1961), 476–77; Hume, "Carpetbaggers in the Reconstruction South," 318–19; Richard N. Current, *Three Carpetbag Governors* (Baton Rouge, 1967), 4.

18.
	Years Republicans in Power	Years Governorship Held by Carpetbaggers
Louisiana	9	9
Arkansas	6	4
Mississippi	6	4
Florida	9	8
South Carolina	9	7

Although this is a significant comparison, too much can be made of it. Excepting Arkansas, the states with carpetbag governors were also those in which blacks had the greatest voting strength. Indeed the 1870 census recorded black majorities in Louisiana, Mississippi, and South Carolina. (*Ninth Census, 1870, Population*, I, 4–5); Peter Kolchin, "Scalawags, Carpetbaggers, and Reconstruction: A Quantitative Look at Southern Congressional Politics, 1868–1872," *Journal of Southern History*, XLV (February, 1979), 63–76.

of Representatives: two Southern whites, one black, and ten carpet-baggers.[19] During most of Reconstruction the Speaker of the Louisiana House of Representatives was also a Northerner. Finally, when the Republicans fell from power in 1877, they went down under the banner of a Maine carpetbagger. The dominance of the newcomers in Louisiana Reconstruction was no myth.

The hegemony of the Northerners rested on a number of factors. To begin with, by 1868 scalawags in Louisiana were not significantly more numerous than carpetbaggers; the two groups combined probably numbered no more than 800 or 900 active men; the scalawag-carpetbag vote seldom, if ever, exceeded 2,500 ballots. The real question is why blacks did not play a larger role in the state. P. B. S. Pinchback provided an answer. At one point during the debates on the constitution, when the perennial subject of race war arose, the militant Dr. Cromwell threatened angrily that blacks intended to have their rights, through revolution and blood if necessary: "We will rule until the last one of us goes down forever." Pinchback jumped to his feet and deplored these intemperate remarks. Blacks in America, he stated bluntly, "could get no rights the whites did not see fit to give them"; this talk of race war was "all humbug." Pinchback developed his point more fully in a subsequent encounter. "In this country," he warned, "there are thirty white men to one black man; therefore it ill becomes the colored men to make violent and intemperate demands. Let them ask for justice, and for nothing more. . . . Any one can see the suicidal policy of arraying the black man against the white."[20] That winter when a supporter attempted to nominate Pinchback for governor, he declined, warning against any Negro standing for the office. This attitude explains a good deal about the constitutional convention. It also partly explains Warmoth's victory over the free Negro Dumas for the governor's nomination: Too many black leaders like Pinchback feared that a black governor would fuel the fires of racism North and South. One secret of carpetbag power in Louisiana, in other words, was that blacks expediently deferred to white leadership.

19. Information on the 40th through the 45th Congresses in the *Biographical Directory of the American Congress.*
20. New York *Times,* December 8 and 15, 1867.

The carpetbaggers were and remained amazingly homogenous. In overwhelming degree they represented the dominant middle-class Protestant culture of the free states, a culture whose superiority over everything Southern—including its loyal politicians—they confidently assumed. The war uprooted their lives and molded them into a transcendent common experience, and it further magnified their sense of superiority by instilling in them that condescension over mere civilians that comes easily to victorious veteran soldiers, whether they have crushed wogs or Rebels. They were remarkably free from the divided loyalties of Unionists and the race dilemmas of blacks. Their only natural constituency was themselves, and the very fewness of their number helped preserve that loyalty inviolate. Few words better express their esprit de corps than those Charles W. Lowell wrote Warmoth, asking for the removal of a certain official at Shreveport: "He was an officer in our service but declines to associate with the ex-officers here [and] seeks the society of the lowest people." The positions on the state supreme court, another Yankee judged, should all go to ex-Union officers; "it is well to have a *friend at Court*," he advised Warmoth. When an ex-Vermont soldier settled on the upper Red River, a Vermont veteran who already lived in the area observed that the newcomer "naturally associated with his old friends and army comrades of the North." [21]

The group identity of the Northerners found expression in an organization that W. McKee Evans, writing about North Carolina, has described as "virtually a party within a party": the Grand Army of the Republic. The individual who took the lead in organizing the Louisiana GAR was none other than that ambitious young man from Illinois named Warmoth. It was no coincidence that two days before the Republican party nominated him for governor in 1868, Union veterans elected him grand commander of the state GAR. [22] In time, the carpet-

21. Charles W. Lowell to Henry Clay Warmoth, March 24, 1868; and George P. Deweese to Warmoth, April 25, 1868, in Warmoth Papers; "Autobiography of Marshall Harvey Twitchell," in Twitchell papers, 145.
22. W. McKee Evans, *Ballots and Fence Rails: Reconstruction on the Lower Cape Fear* (Chapel Hill, 1966), 152–53; Diary of Henry Clay Warmoth, February 27, 1867, in Warmoth Papers; Warmoth, *War, Politics and Reconstruction*, 51.

baggers would commence to fight among themselves, but in the early years of Radical Reconstruction they maintained a united front.

The Northerners had cohesiveness, and they also had influence in the nation's capital. Throughout Reconstruction, every Louisiana government depended on support from Washington for the simple reason that none could protect itself from its enemies without the aid of the national government. That power relationship meant that the capital city acted as the final arbiter of local affairs, not only on vital questions affecting the survival of the regime, but time and again on matters that any Northern state would have decided at home. Hence, beginning under General Butler and continuing through Governor William Pitt Kellogg, Washington assumed the reluctant role of an appellate court in which the "outs" in Louisiana challenged the decisions of those in power in New Orleans: proslavery planters who resented "free labor," free Negroes who demanded suffrage, Unionists ousted by General Banks, Unionists ousted by Governor Wells, enemies of General Philip H. Sheridan, enemies of General Winfield Scott Hancock, anti-Warmothites, anti-Kelloggites, and defeated candidates in every Reconstruction election.

Under such conditions, at a time when the bloody shirt emerged as the dominant issue in national politics, the carpetbaggers had natural advantages over their party allies. Before the debacles of the 1870s discredited them, they enjoyed wide prestige in the North as ex-soldier emissaries of Northern culture and the Republican party in the defeated South. The correspondence of Governor Warmoth reveals an extensive and carefully maintained network of contacts between Louisiana carpetbaggers and influential Northern politicians, business leaders, editors, and churchmen.[23] Initially, the Republicans used these contacts for political fund-raising and planning internal improvement projects. They soon learned to use them for other ends. In 1871 an agent in New York informed Warmoth that Henry S. McComb of the

---

23. Although not always as direct correspondents, these included Henry Wilson, William E. Chandler, T. L. Tullock, Oliver P. Morton, Richard Henry Dana, William Claflin, Thomas A. Scott, Oakes Ames, John A. Griswold, Henry S. McComb, Ben Butler, and John P. Newman.

Southern Railroad Association, who was deeply disturbed over the governor's worsening relations with President Grant, had contacted his friend John W. Forney of the Philadelphia *Press*. "Forney soon after went down to Long Branch & spoke to Grant in our behalf." Another ally suggested asking Warmoth's friend, the Reverend John P. Newman, Methodist chaplain of the United States Senate and formerly pastor of Ames Church in New Orleans, to intervene with the president. Newman "is on your side," the informant wrote, and has already made plans to summer with Grant at Long Branch. If handled right, he might serve as "a committee of one with a full report made out as we want."[24] Unfortunately for Warmoth, a rival carpetbagger had the advantage of being the president's brother-in-law, and the governor never redeemed his influence at the White House. The point remains, however, that those best able to influence the high court on the Potomac were the recent migrants from the North, not Southern Unionists and certainly not P. B. S. Pinchback or Oscar J. Dunn.

Finally, carpetbagger dominance resided in control over federal jobs. Nowhere in America was political patronage more important than among Southern Republicans during Reconstruction. The Radicals' enemies controlled the bulk of wealth and property in the South and soon learned the power of economic coercion against the Republican regimes. Democratic planters and employers signed secret pledges not to hire Negroes and whites who so much as voted the Radical ticket. For most Republicans the only jobs available were those obtained through party patronage. In a typical case, a discharged official pleaded with Governor Kellogg to give him back his job. His politics were too well known for him to find another position in New Orleans, he said, and even his relations had "turned their Backs and closed their 'Doors'" on him.[25]

24. H. C. Dibble to Henry Clay Warmoth, September 22, 1871, and Hugh J. Campbell to Warmoth, April 22, 1871, in Warmoth Papers.

25. Evans, *Ballots and Fence Rails*, 155–62; Lawrence N. Powell, "The Politics of Livelihood: Carpetbaggers in the Deep South," in J. Morgan Kousser and James M. McPherson, *Region, Race, and Reconstruction: Essays in Honor of C. Vann Woodward* (New York, 1982), 315–47; E. W. Fostrick to William Pitt Kellogg, January 9, 1875, in William Pitt Kellogg Papers, Troy H. Middleton Library, Louisiana State University, Baton Rouge.

Three principal sources of patronage existed in Louisiana: the city administration of New Orleans, the state government, and the federal bureaucracy. Under Warmoth the Republicans transferred much of the Crescent City's patronage to the state. Thus, judged solely by numbers, the governor's office directly and indirectly distributed more jobs than the federal government. It remains unlikely, however, that either a patrolman's position with the Metropolitan Police or a teacher's job was as politically useful as a federal appointment. In 1871, for example, fifteen members of the state legislature held posts in the New Orleans Custom House.[26] Qualitatively, the federal government was the most important source of patronage in the state.

By the standards of the Reconstruction states, the federal establishment in Louisiana was a colossus. Concentrated in New Orleans, its offices included Internal Revenue, an assistant treasury, the Fifth District Court, a branch mint, a land office, the post office, and the Custom House. At the beginning of Radical Reconstruction, the New Orleans Custom House employed 63 percent of all the customs service personnel in the former Confederate states. Eight years later the New Orleans Post Office employed more clerks and letter carriers than the post offices of Charleston, Atlanta, Memphis, Mobile, Nashville, and Richmond combined. Excluding rural postmasters (few of whom earned over $50 a year), federal officialdom provided nearly 600 jobs.[27] In 1870 a fight over the control of federal patronage finally shattered carpetbagger accord in the state.

Totally politicized, two kinds of Northerners controlled the major posts throughout Reconstruction: those who had settled in Louisiana before 1861 and the newcomers of the war era—the carpetbaggers.[28] From the time that William Pitt Kellogg took over as collector of the port in 1865, the controlling influence lay with the latter. Kellogg used his office to promote himself to the United States Senate and thence to

26. *Acts of the State of Louisiana*, 1868, 3, 85–98, 232–33; *ibid.*, 1869, 61–62, 92–106, 175–76; Warmoth, *War, Politics and Reconstruction*, 108.

27. United States Civil Service Commission, *Official Register of the United States*, 1867 and 1875; in the latter year 179 jobs were in the post office and 281 in the customs service; Warmoth, *War, Politics and Reconstruction*, 89–91.

28. Appendix 3.

the governorship. His successor, the Kentucky carpetbagger James F. Casey, President Grant's brother-in-law, also aspired to elective office but lacked Kellogg's talent for self-promotion. Thus, leadership in the federal establishment—the so-called Custom House faction—passed not to Casey but to the United States marshal, Stephen B. Packard of Maine. In 1876 he ran as the Republican party's unsuccessful candidate for governor.

In the writings of revisionist historians, carpetbaggers have generally been portrayed as advocates of Negro suffrage and black civil rights who sought "to infuse a new spirit of egalitarianism into the postwar South."[29] Louisiana suggests that that reputation is exaggerated. In the constitutional convention, for example, many native whites supported Negro rights much more actively than carpetbaggers. The Republican platform of June 1867 called for an equal division of offices between white and Negro party members. The extent to which carpetbag politicians honored that commitment may be judged by the following: Of the nineteen top positions in the federal bureaucracy, blacks held, on the average, two during the terms of both Governor Warmoth and Governor Kellogg. Nor did blacks claim more than a small share of lower-level federal jobs. Most Negro Republicans were natives of the state; of 393 positions in 1875, native Louisianians held only 115 (and even most of those, we must assume, belonged to whites).[30] The low status of blacks in federal officialdom contradicted the principles to which Republican Louisiana laid claim as its raison d'être. And in the end it was on a series of unbending contradictions that the Radical regime foundered, contradictions the carpetbaggers, for all their assets, could not escape.

29. Hume, "Carpetbaggers in the Reconstruction South," 325, emphasizes the carpetbaggers' role in framing liberal bills of rights in the state constitutional conventions of 1867 and 1868, as does Scroggs, in "Carpetbagger Constitutional Reform," 477, 481–82. Stressing other issues but in general agreement are Current, "Carpetbaggers Reconsidered," 155, and William C. Harris, "The Creed of the Carpetbaggers: The Case of Mississippi," *Journal of Southern History*, XL (May, 1974), 202–203, 214–15. To a notable degree, however, Thomas Holt's *Black over White: Negro Political Leadership in South Carolina During Reconstruction* (Urbana, Ill., 1977), challenges this tradition. In particular, see his discussion of the racial attitudes of carpetbag governor Daniel H. Chamberlain, 193–95.

30. Appendix 3; the figure 393 represents the total of all the federal offices for which the nativity of the occupants is listed. *Official Register of the United States*, 1875.

8

The Contradictions
of Power

Henry Clay Warmoth celebrated his nineteenth birthday less than a
month after the first shots of the Civil War lit up the early morning
darkness of Charleston Harbor. He entered the army as a lieutenant
colonel in the 32d Missouri, served on the staff of General John A.
McClernand, commanded his regiment at Lookout Mountain, and
hastened to the relief of General Banks during the ill-fated Red River
campaign. His attachment to McClernand involved him in the bitter
rivalry between that general and the rising star of the Union army,
Ulysses S. Grant. Wounded at Vicksburg, Warmoth returned home
on leave, which was subsequently extended (or so he believed). During his absence Grant ordered his dishonorable discharge, alleging that
the young officer, absent without leave, had spread exaggerated accounts of Union losses in the North. Only an appeal to President Lincoln saved Warmoth's career. In later years, President Grant and Governor Warmoth probably never spoke of the incident, but neither man
could have forgotten.

In 1864 General Banks appointed Warmoth judge of the provost
court in New Orleans, a position that proved important to his postwar
career. As provost judge, he "became acquainted with all the members
of the Bar and a great many of the residents of the city." He left the
army in early 1865 and joined the small but influential class of Crescent City lawyers specializing in the legal problems of the occupation
regime: courts-martial, military commissions, the federal bureaucracy, and claims against the government. His practice took him to
Washington, and he was in the capital city the night of Lincoln's
assassination.[1]

1. Henry Clay Warmoth, *War, Politics and Reconstruction: Stormy Days in Louisiana*
(New York, 1930), 14–27; the advertisements of these legal specialists appear in the
New Orleans *Times*, January 1, 1865, *passim*.

Unlike most Northern migrants of the war era, Warmoth pursued a political career from the start. Active in the organization of the state Republican party, he went to Washington in late 1865 as Louisiana's unofficial "territorial" delegate. Though his public speeches from this early period were quite ordinary (he stood for universal suffrage, loyal government, the return of General Butler, and the ex-soldier), his contemporaries marked him as a comer. Louisiana abounded with ex-brigadiers and major generals; yet the former lieutenant colonel emerged as the leader of the Grand Army of the Republic. Warmoth easily formed friendships with influential older men of widely varying views and backgrounds: Thomas J. Durant, the Reverend John P. Newman, General McClernand, George S. Denison, his law partner John F. Deane, William L. McMillen, and later Henry S. McComb. A tall, strikingly handsome man, Warmoth's appearance was one of his strongest political assets. Like Banks, he looked the part of the statesman. In fact, Mrs. Banks had informed him at a wartime ball that he spoke and acted like young General Banks. Warmoth blushed and danced with the lady. Several days later, Banks offered him the judgeship of the provost court.[2]

In his autobiography Warmoth described the condition of Louisiana in July 1868, when he took over as governor. New Orleans and the state government were bankrupt. The value of assessed property had fallen from $470 million in 1860 to only $250 million. Taxes were in arrears for every year since 1859. The state's agriculture had been ravaged by war, flood, and infestation. The longest piece of railroad track stretched a mere sixty miles; the only canal extended six miles from New Orleans to Lake Pontchartrain. The levees of the Mississippi and other waterways remained in a deplorable state. Almost no extractive or manufacturing industries marred the landscape. The public roads were little more than mud trails. Epidemics of yellow fever and malaria visited the state yearly. Of New Orleans, whatever romantic images it usually evokes, Warmoth recorded that it had only four paved

2. New Orleans *Tribune*, July 19, September 26 and 28, October 12 and 19, 1865; Richard N. Current, *Three Carpetbag Governors* (Baton Rouge, 1967), 43; useful on Warmoth is F. Wayne Binning, "Henry Clay Warmoth and Louisiana Reconstruction" (Ph.D. dissertation, University of North Carolina, 1969).

streets, and "the slaughter-houses were so located that all of their offal and filth were poured into the Mississippi River, just above the mains that supplied the people with their drinking water." Overrun with gamblers, prostitutes, and thugs; ruled by corrupt and ignorant officials; the Crescent City was "a dirty, impoverished, and hopeless place."[3] In sum, the state foundered in a veritable sea of troubles, but the paramount concern of the new regime was survival.

The response of the white South to the onset of Radical Reconstruction has been aptly described as "Counter Reconstruction." Rejecting the legitimacy of Republican governments based on Negro suffrage, white Southerners organized secretly and massively to destroy them. By the fall of 1868 there existed in Louisiana, as in other Southern states, a vast shadowland of secret paramilitary political clubs and societies: Knights of the White Camellia, Swamp Fox Rangers, Innocents, Seymour Knights, Hancock Guards, and the seldom seen but widely rumored Ku Klux Klan. The Knights of the White Camellia ranked as the largest and most important of these. Led by the "best" citizens and organized statewide, in many parishes its membership claimed half or more of the white males. The veil of secrecy shrouding these organizations concealed a fantasy world, where respectable citizens, like the heroes of a Thomas Dixon novel, guarded the "nest of the White Eagle" against the "black Vulture."[4] In this paranoid realm, Negro uprisings were always imminent, and the carpetbagger and scalawag stereotypes of Reconstruction legend took on a sinister reality. The need to restore white rule justified every means, every sadistic impulse, every enormity.

A few instances of intimidation and fraud marred the April elections of 1868. On the upper Red River and a few other places, whites kept Negroes from the polls, destroyed Republican tickets, and tampered

3. Warmoth, *War, Politics and Reconstruction*, 79–81.
4. John Hope Franklin, *Reconstruction: After the Civil War* (Chicago, 1961), 152–73; *House Miscellaneous Documents*, 41st Cong., 2d Sess., No. 154, Pt. 1, pp. 238–45, 294–306, 541–63, *passim*; Allen W. Trelease, *White Terror: The Ku Klux Klan Conspiracy and Southern Reconstruction* (New York, 1971), 92–98, 127–36; Melinda Meek Hennessey, "Race and Violence in Reconstruction New Orleans: The 1868 Riot," *Louisiana History*, XX (Winter, 1979), 77–91; Knights of the White Camellia documents in Jean P. Breda and Family Papers, Troy H. Middleton Library, Louisiana State University, Baton Rouge.

with the returns.[5] None of this, though, prepared the new regime for the terrible ordeal of the presidential election. Starting in May and continuing through November, gangs of armed whites rode by day and night, spreading terror across the state. Among the first casualties was William R. Meadows, the literate ex-slave who had represented Claiborne Parish in the constitutional convention. Assassins murdered him in his yard. In a neighboring parish whites pulled a black leader from his home, shot him, and cut off his head. In St. Mary Parish disguised whites entered a hotel in the town of Franklin and publicly murdered the sheriff and judge with knives and pistols.[6] A white Republican warned a colleague that unless the "almost daily" murders of Union men in north-central Louisiana could be stopped and stopped soon, "the Republican Party is at an end." Unprecedented murders and outrages in Franklin Parish convinced local Unionists that their enemies intended to drive them out of the country or exterminate them. In an unsuccessful appeal to President Johnson for more Federal troops, Warmoth estimated on August 1 that 150 persons had been killed in Louisiana since the middle of June. Two weeks later an investigator informed him that his estimate erred by half and that "authentic evidence" indicated "double the number of Murders stated by you in your letter to the President."[7]

The violence crested in the fall in a series of bloody massacres. In the Crescent City the first serious clash occurred on September 22 when white Democrats attacked a Republican procession. The last week in October New Orleans resembled a major European city in the throes of violent revolution. By day and night white mobs roamed the city and its suburbs, robbing, beating, and killing Negroes; breaking up

5. J. H. McVean to Henry Clay Warmoth, April 16 & 21, 1868, William R. Meadows to Warmoth, April 18, 1868, W. S. Laruh to Warmoth, April 30, 1868, and H. C. Farquhar to Warmoth, May 10, 1868, all in Henry Clay Warmoth Papers, Southern Historical Collection, University of North Carolina, Chapel Hill.

6. *House Executive Documents*, 44th Cong., 2d Sess., No. 30, pp. 262–67; "Autobiography of Marshall Harvey Twitchell," Marshall Harvey Twitchell Papers, Prescott Memorial Library, Louisiana Tech University, Ruston, 105; Trelease, *White Terror*, 95; Warmoth, *War, Politics and Reconstruction*, 69.

7. John Ray to A. W. Faulkner, May 30, 1868, and John Lynch to Henry Clay Warmoth, August 14, 1868, in Warmoth Papers; Isaac Crawford and others to Henry Clay Warmoth, August 1, 1868, and Henry Clay Warmoth to Andrew Johnson, August 1, 1868, in Andrew Johnson Papers, Library of Congress.

Republican clubs and processions; and ambushing and so intimidating the police that patrolmen feared to leave their station houses. The violence spread to neighboring St. Bernard Parish where a series of clashes over four days left many people dead. Throughout the strife hundreds of Federal troops stood by passively, unable or unwilling to act. Estimates of deaths vary widely; clearly, however, at least sixty people, mostly black Republicans, died violent deaths between September 22 and election day in St. Bernard, Jefferson, and Orleans parishes.[8]

The former Confederate capital of Shreveport was the largest town on the Red River, and nearly 50 percent of its population was black. It was also one of the toughest places in Louisiana, a watering hole of rough traders and frontier bullies from Texas, Arkansas, and the Indian nation. Late in September an intoxicated Arkansas trader stopped at a place called Shady Grove Plantation, seven or eight miles above the town in Bossier Parish. The trader asked if there were any Radical Negroes about, and when a young black boy pointed out an aged freedman, the man drew his pistol and fired two shots at the old man, missing each time. Blacks on the plantation formed a posse, seized the trader several miles up the road, returned him to the scene of the incident, and chained him to a tree, not being overly gentle with his person. What happened néxt is not entirely clear, but it appears that two local whites tried to free the Arkansas man, quarreled with his captors, killed or wounded several of them, and were in turn killed or wounded themselves. Somehow, though, the trader won his release and crossed the state line. The next morning a small army of Arkansas toughs, estimated at about seventy-five men, invaded Louisiana on a mission of vengeance. They shot up a neighboring plantation and then hit Shady Grove in a mass attack, killing blacks indiscriminately. In the meantime, reports of Negro outrages had reached Shreveport, and a second small army of mounted whites now set out for Shady Grove. For-

8. *House Miscellaneous Documents*, 41st Cong., 2d Sess., No. 154, Pt. 1, pp. 28–36, 44–49, 102–112, *passim*; *House Executive Documents*, 44th Cong., 2d Sess., No. 30, p. 297; Trelease, *White Terror*, 132–35; Hennessey, "Race and Violence in Reconstruction New Orleans," 77–91; Joseph G. Dawson III, "General Lovell H. Rousseau and Louisiana Reconstruction," *Louisiana History*, XX (Fall, 1979), 373–91; *Senate Reports*, 42d Cong., 2d Sess., No. 41, Pt. 1, 251–52.

tunately for anyone left alive there, an agent of the Freedmen's Bureau arrived on the scene first. However, the Shreveport mob had already murdered nine blacks on the road as it rode north. All this occurred on October 1, and it was only the beginning. By the morning of the following day hundreds of armed whites scoured the woods and swamps above Shreveport looking for blacks with guns. In the words of one historian, it was "open season on Negroes" in Caddo and Bossier parishes. In the following weeks residents of Shreveport counted 25 to 30 bodies floating past the town on the Red River. Between the first incident at Shady Grove and election day on November 3, at least 150 and perhaps 200 freedmen died violent deaths in the region.[9]

Two days before the Arkansas trader stopped at Shady Grove Plantation, three Seymour Knights entered a crowded schoolroom in the town of Opelousas and severely caned the teacher, Emerson Bentley, for an article that he had written in the St. Landry *Progress*. For Bentley, a young carpetbagger from Ohio, the incident marked the beginning of a harrowing three-week flight, slipping from one house of concealment to another, and finally across the swamps of the Grosse Tête to safety in a skiff. Fearing Bentley murdered, alarmed blacks rushed into Opelousas after his assault, many carrying weapons. To the Knights of the White Camellia, several thousand strong in St. Landry, here at last was the long-awaited Negro revolt. Superbly organized, they took over the town and demanded the weapons of the outnumbered blacks. No one knows who fired the first shot, but someone did and the massacre started. It spread into the countryside and for three days heavily armed whites pursued their victims through the swamps and forests, shooting armed Negroes on sight. One hundred fifty or more black Republicans died.[10]

9. *House Miscellaneous Documents*, 41st Cong., 2d Sess., No. 154, Pt. 1, pp. 125–32, 161–62, 472–80; Trelease, *White Terror*, 130; *House Executive Documents*, 44th Cong., 2d Sess., No. 30, p. 359; *Senate Reports*, 42d Cong., 2d Sess., No. 41, Pt. 1, pp. 251–52.
10. *House Miscellaneous Documents*, 41st Cong., 2d Sess., No. 154, Pt. 1, pp. 406–416; *House Executive Documents*, 44th Cong., 2d Sess., No. 30, pp. 183–84; Trelease, *White Terror*, 128–29; Geraldine Mary McTigue, "Forms of Racial Interaction in Louisiana, 1860–1880" (Ph.D. dissertation, Yale University, 1975), 293–98; Carolyn E. DeLatte, "The St. Landry Riot: A Forgotten Incident of Reconstruction Violence," *Louisiana History*, XVII (Winter, 1976), 41–49; *Senate Reports*, 42d Cong., 2d Sess., No. 41, Pt. 1, pp. 251–52.

State officials reported that the terrorists of 1868 killed 784 people and wounded or mistreated 450 more. A subsequent federal report estimated the dead alone at over a thousand. Election day revealed the full political effect of the violence (see Map 6). Warmoth had received 65,000 votes in April; in November Grant obtained only 33,000. In twenty-four parishes the Republican tally declined by over 27,000; in seven parishes Grant received not a single vote; in nine others he obtained a total of nineteen.[11]

Had the voters that November chosen a state government, Radical Reconstruction in Louisiana would have ended almost before it started. The lesson was not lost on Warmoth and his party. Over the next three years they adopted an extraordinary legislative program. Like Republicans in other Southern states, they organized a state militia. They feared, however, that a militia made up largely of blacks would prove inadequate; the massacres of 1868 had demonstrated all too vividly that nothing inflamed whites more than Negroes with guns.[12] The regime badly needed dependable law officers in those parishes where the sheriffs were unreliable. Hence, they set up a constabulary force in the rural parishes directly under the governor. The constables and their deputies would guard the voting precincts on election day and arrest people who committed violent crimes. In time of trouble, the constabulary could be expanded indefinitely.[13] In subsequent years Republican constables proved extremely effective in solidly Republican parishes, but much less so in Democratic or contested areas.

The Republican organization had taken a severe beating at the local level in 1868. All over the state party leaders had fled to New Orleans, perhaps 200 from St. Landry Parish alone. To break the Democratic hold over the countryside and reestablish their own position, the Republicans created eight new parishes, securing at least temporary dominance through the simple expedient of letting Warmoth appoint

11. *House Miscellaneous Documents*, 41st Cong., 2d Sess., No. 154, Pt. 1, pp. 161–62, Pt. 2, p. 504; *Senate Reports*, 42d Cong., 2d Sess., No. 41, Pt. 1, pp. 251–52; W. Dean Burham, *Presidential Ballots, 1836–1892* (Baltimore, 1955).

12. *Acts of the State of Louisiana*, 1868, 44–46; *ibid.*, 1870, 164–88. Probably for fear of pouring oil on the fire, Warmoth, despite Republican urging, refused to organize the militia against the terrorists in 1868. See Trelease, *White Terror*, 135, and Joe Gray Taylor, *Louisiana Reconstructed, 1863–1877* (Baton Rouge, 1974), 177–78.

13. *Acts of the State of Louisiana*, 1870, pp. 104–106.

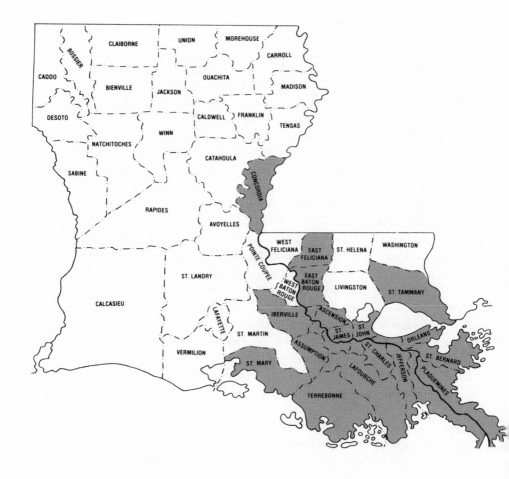

Map 6

Presidential Election of 1868 in Louisiana
(Grant vs. Seymour)

☐ Seymour received majorities

■ Grant received majorities

the new officials who then served until the next general election.[14] This plan proved extremely effective in places. In Red River, for example, Marshall Harvey Twitchell built up such a base that it took the massed power of the White League in the Coushatta Massacre to tear it down. A ninth parish, Lincoln, organized in 1873 under Kellogg, emerged as the bailiwick of the Unionist Allen Greene and his family.[15] Overall, however, parish reorganization did not significantly alter the balance of power in the countryside.

New Orleans ranked high on the Republican agenda. Nearly half the white males in the city belonged to the Knights of the White Camellia and other secret societies. The preelection riots there and in the adjacent parishes of Jefferson and St. Bernard not only cost the Republicans nearly 16,000 votes, they paralyzed the seat of government and mocked the authority of the new regime. The crux of the problem lay with the immense white majority in the Crescent City. Even in an honest election, the Republicans could rarely hope to elect the city government. They could, however, reorganize it, or transfer its powers to the state. In 1869–1870 the legislature gave New Orleans a new charter, joined part of Jefferson Parish to Orleans, and combined the cities of New Orleans and Jefferson. Under this reorganization, Warmoth temporarily appointed the city government. Thus, from 1870 until the 1872 election, for the only time during Reconstruction, the top officials of New Orleans were Republicans. Even more important, the legislature combined Orleans, Jefferson, and St. Bernard parishes into the Metropolitan Police District, administered by a board of commissioners appointed by the governor. It also made the mayor of New Orleans and the sheriffs of all three parishes strictly subservient to the Metropolitan Police in matters of law enforcement. Although normally fixed at 500 patrolmen, the governor could expand the force indefinitely in special circumstances. Much more so than the state

14. McTigue, "Forms of Racial Interaction in Louisiana," 297; Historical Records Survey, *County-Parish Boundaries in Louisiana* (New Orleans, 1939), 79–87; *Acts of the State of Louisiana*, 1868, pp. 151–54; *ibid.*, 1869, pp. 79–81, 83–86; *ibid.*, 1870, pp. 168–69.

15. HRS, *County-Parish Boundaries*, 87; E. R. Hester, "A Thumb Nail Sketch of the Life and Activities of Allen Greene," typed manuscript dated 1959 in Howard-Tilton Memorial Library, Tulane University, New Orleans; *House Miscellaneous Documents*, 41st Cong., 2d Sess., No. 154, Pt. 2, pp. 496–99.

militia or the constabulary, the Metropolitan Police served as the military arm of both Governor Warmoth and Governor Kellogg throughout Reconstruction.[16]

Finally, in the election law of 1870, the legislature gave the governor broad authority over the conduct of elections and, most important, created the state Returning Board. The Returning Board compiled the official results of every election; the law empowered it to discard the polls of any precinct in which violence or intimidation occurred; and the governor, lieutenant governor, and secretary of state served as ex officio members. In the political wars that followed, the Returning Board proved the most feared weapon in the Radical arsenal. The Returning Board cheated the Democrats in 1872, lamented one disgruntled member of that party, and robbed them a second time in 1874, "and we all believed that we would be cheated again in 1876 if the returning board dared to do it."[17]

Considering the provocation, the Republican response was entirely logical. Nonetheless, it entrapped Warmoth and his party in the first of a series of fateful contradictions. The Republicans set out, as they believed, to democratize a land corrupted by the tyranny of slavery and, in fact, created the most democratic government the state had ever seen or would see again for a hundred years. But to protect themselves from those who would destroy them with violence, they constructed a police and election apparatus the internal logic of which subverted democratic government as surely as the tactics of their opponents. What leaders in American history could be trusted with a Returning Board legally authorized to alter election returns at will? Whether they fully realized it or not, the Republicans had created the instruments of one-party rule for the simple, compelling reason that the new implements of power could never be permitted to fall into the hands of the opposition. To lose one election, after all, meant surrendering the po-

16. *House Miscellaneous Documents*, 41st Cong., 2d Sess., No. 154, Pt. 2, pp. 83–84, 339–41; HRS, *County-Parish Boundaries*, 82, 85; *Acts of the State of Louisiana*, 1868, pp. 3, 85–98, 232–33; *ibid*., 1869, pp. 61–62, 92–106; also section 52 of election law, *ibid*., 1870, p. 154; Taylor, *Louisiana Reconstructed*, 177–78.

17. *Acts of the State of Louisiana*, 1870, pp. 145–61; *House Miscellaneous Documents*, 45th Cong., 3rd Sess., No. 31, Pt. 1, p. 898. The election law disqualified any candidate for office from serving on the Returning Board; however, in such case, it allowed those remaining on the board to choose the replacement or replacements.

lice and the Returning Board to Democratic control. Forced to use these powerful tools to remain in power, the Republicans employed them for that purpose in every election after 1870. They then found themselves caught in still another contradiction. Dependent on support from Washington, each time they employed their election apparatus to stave off the Democrats, they lost support in the nation's capital. Weary of the whole Reconstruction question, influential Northerners listened with renewed interest to Southern talk of home rule and the evils of carpetbag government.

At the start, though, all this lay in the future, and Warmoth never attempted to rule by such means alone. His strategy for consolidating Republican strength was twofold: Side by side with the policy of force, he pursued a policy of peace, a conciliatory approach intended to soften white resistance to Republican rule and win white converts to the Republican party. He used his patronage liberally, appointing prominent white conservatives to the bench and other state and local offices. His chief state engineer was a former Confederate general; as adjutant general of the state militia, he chose James A. Longstreet, distinguished corps commander of the Army of Northern Virginia, and he chose Penn Mason, a former officer on Robert E. Lee's staff, as major general. He divided the 5,000-man militia force equally between whites, who were mostly ex-Rebel soldiers, and blacks. Depicting himself as a fiscal conservative, Warmoth obtained a constitutional amendment limiting the state debt to $25,000,000. He vetoed thirty-nine bills, many of them pork barrel projects favored by Republican politicos. The governor also obtained the repeal of Article 99, the disfranchisement clause of the Radical constitution. Campaigning at Shreveport in 1870, the Illinoian boasted that his great-grandfather was a Virginian, his father a Tennessean, and that "every drop" of his own blood was Southern. He claimed that he and President Grant "wanted every old 'Rebel' and every young 'Rebel' to come in and join the Republican Party." He also stressed his efforts to hold down the public debt and promised a railroad to connect the former Confederate capital with New Orleans and Houston; afterwards the band played "Dixie." [18]

18. Warmoth, *War, Politics and Reconstruction*, 88, 98–102, 164–65; Otis A. Singletary, *Negro Militia and Reconstruction* (Austin, 1957), 69–70.

Although they were opportunistic, these actions were not steeped in hypocrisy. Unlike many carpetbaggers, Warmoth, who was a prewar Democrat, remained comparatively free of sectional prejudice. Although outraged by Southern atrocities, he expressed his anger against specific acts committed by specific people. He never concluded, as Ephraim S. Stoddard did, that the South was a "political fungus upon the body politic." Nor does one find him, like Marshall Harvey Twitchell, describing Southern chivalry as a savage and barbaric "remnant of the dark ages." Stoddard and Twitchell, of course, were New Englanders, whereas Warmoth came from southern Illinois and boasted of his Southern blood, probably with genuine pride. The young governor was plainly uncomfortable as the head of a mostly Negro party; whitening the party would have increased his personal self-esteem.[19] Above all he held fast to the hope that expanding the Republican party's support among white voters would gain the respectability and acceptance that would make a repetition of the 1868 terror unthinkable.

Warmoth's policy achieved its most notable success among the state's foreign population. By the 1870 census, 113,486 of Louisiana's 726,915 people had either been born abroad or came from families in which both parents were foreign born. Eighty-two percent of this predominantly German and Irish population was strategically located in New Orleans. The employment rolls of the federal bureaucracy show that the Republicans recruited for members heavily among these people: Of 393 jobholders in 1875 whose nativity is listed, 108 were foreign born.[20] Many other federal employees almost certainly came from immigrant families. If the Republicans could combine enough immigrant votes with black votes, they might challenge Democratic control of the Crescent City.

The Germans of New Orleans revealed divided loyalties during the Civil War and Reconstruction. At least several thousand had entered the Confederate armies; and on the other hand, Governor Michael

19. Ephraim S. Stoddard to H. R. Stoddard, January 12 & 18, 1875, in Ephraim S. Stoddard Papers, Howard-Tilton Memorial Library, Tulane University, New Orleans; "Autobiography of Marshall Harvey Twitchell," in Twitchell Papers, 142; Warmoth, *War, Politics and Reconstruction*, 89, 99.
20. *Ninth Census, 1870, Population*, I, 311; *Official Register of the United States*, 1875.

Hahn, Max F. Bonzano, and other Germans contributed vitally to Free State Louisiana. Both of the German-language newspapers of wartime New Orleans took Unionist stands. One of these, the *German Gazette*, survived through Reconstruction and loyally supported Warmoth, although it broke with Kellogg. German Republican clubs existed in the city at least as early as the spring of 1867, and under Warmoth they were organized in the German sections of the city. The New Orleans *Republican*, the offical mouthpiece of the Warmoth administration, described a club meeting in July 1870. In revival fashion the club's officers appealed for new members: "About eighteen men came forward and signed, . . . making the strength of this club eighty-one members."[21]

Unfortunately, the Republicans proved less successful with the Irish. The Germans were conservative, the Irish even more so. A prominent leader resigned from the Irish Republican Club in 1870, according to the secretary, because the club was "to[o] radical." He departed advising the members "to be more Democratic." The crux of the matter, of course, was race. The New Orleans *Tribune* observed in 1869 that, unlike the Germans, the Irish "have for the most part sided with the Democratic party against us."[22]

Beyond the foreign population, the interim elections of 1870 revealed the Warmoth administration attempting to embrace a broad spectrum of white Louisianians. In the Florida parishes, a predominantly small farming region, the governor asserted that staple of Republican doctrine that held slavery had oppressed "the poor white man" almost as much as the Negro. The Republican party, he therefore concluded, had done as much for Southern whites as for blacks. Too often in the past, he said, yeoman whites had spurned the party of emancipation, but all that had not changed; every day brought new recruits as white Southerners saw the truth. The "old line Whigs" rep-

21. Robert T. Clark, Jr., "The New Orleans German Colony in the Civil War," *Louisiana Historical Quarterly*, XX (October, 1937), 1000–1001, 1011; Robert T. Clark, Jr., "Reconstruction and the New Orleans German Colony," *Louisiana Historical Quarterly*, XXIII (April, 1940), 502–509, 515–21; W. P. Gerard (editor of the *German Gazette*) to Henry Clay Warmoth, July 19, 1872, in Warmoth Papers; New Orleans *Tribune*, May 25, 1867; New Orleans *Republican*, July 10, October 15 and 23, November 5, 1870.

22. New Orleans *Republican*, March 23, 1870; New Orleans *Tribune*, January 29, 1869.

resented another recruitment target; they "are abandoning the ranks of the Democracy and joining the Republican clubs all through the northern portion of the State," asserted the *Republican*. The newspaper also predicted that "scores of the best citizens" in Shreveport and "leading Democratic merchants" in New Orleans intended to vote Republican. The official journal even placed faith in "that large and intelligent class of citizens who vote for the best men without regard to politics." Indeed, wherever the *Republican* looked it discovered unhappy whites deserting the Democratic standard.[23]

The 1870 returns, moreover, seemed to justify optimism. In the freest election of the decade, the Republicans won their most sweeping victory, cementing their hold on the legislature, controlling New Orleans, and sending five carpetbaggers to Congress. In the statewide races for auditor and treasurer, an Irishman, James Graham, and a free man of color, Antoine Dubuclet, rolled up 24,000-vote majorities, sweeping the Crescent City with a 6,000-vote edge, carrying the white-dominated rural parishes, Sabine, Cameron, Tangipahoa, Catahoula and finishing close in others. Warmoth's goal of a Republican party "in which the conservative and honest white people of the State should have a share," appeared on the verge of reality. But the appearance was deceptive. Graham and Dubuclet received only about 300 more votes than Warmoth had obtained in 1868.[24] In other words, Louisiana whites, instead of converting to Radicalism, simply failed to vote.

Despite victory, the Republicans were a troubled party. Many Radicals failed to share the governor's vision of their future; more fundamentally, the policy of peace, like the policy of force, entrapped Warmoth and his party in damaging contradictions. There was, to begin with, the patronage dilemma. In a patronage-hungry party, every job the governor gave a Democrat took a job away from a Republican, arousing resentment in the Radical party. One disgruntled man asked state superintendent of education Thomas W. Conway, if Warmoth "is

23. New Orleans *Republican*, September 10, 13, and 22, October 9 and 26, 1870.

24. Appleton's *Annual Cyclopaedia (1870)*, 457; *House Miscellaneous Documents*, 45th Cong., 3d Sess., No. 31, Pt. 1 (insert contains elections returns for entire period); Warmoth, *War, Politics, and Reconstruction*, 101–102, 161; Charles Vincent, *Black Legislators in Louisiana During Reconstruction* (Baton Rouge, 1976), 114–15.

the staunch Republican you take him to be, why is it, that he invariably appoints the most ultra democrats to offices of trust & emolument?" In East Feliciana Parish, the man claimed, Warmoth appointed a Confederate colonel who tried "to have me snobbed" by the "leading rebel families." Among those most alarmed was Lieutenant Governor Oscar J. Dunn, who, before his death in November 1871, was among the most influential Negro leaders in the South. Pointing to Warmoth's Democratic appointments, he warned a black leader in Opelousas that "an effort is being made to sell us out to the Democrats . . . and we must nip it right in the bud." In a widely published letter to Horace Greeley, Dunn charged that Warmoth "has shown an itching desire . . . to secure the personal support of the Democracy at the expense of his own party, and an equally manifest craving to obtain a cheap and ignoble white respectability by the sacrifice of . . . the masses of that race who elected him." Warmoth, Dunn alleged, was "the first Ku Klux Governor" of the Republican party.[25]

The patronage controversy climaxed in a vicious fight over the collectorship of the port of New Orleans. Under President Johnson the United States Custom House remained notoriously conservative. For three years Kellogg carefully trimmed his sail to the Johnsonian breeze. When Kellogg resigned the collectorship to enter the United States Senate, a coterie of lame-duck Democratic officials put in motion a clever scheme to ensure their position and influence under a Republican president. The interim collector, Perry Fuller, resigned, and President Johnson then recommended President-elect Grant's brother-in-law James F. Casey, a Kentucky Democrat, as his replacement.[26] Grant walked into the trap. Louisiana Republicans found themselves saddled with a Democratic collector of the port, and they were soon up in arms, demanding that either Casey get rid of the Democrats in the Custom House or that Grant remove him. This movement peaked in the spring of 1870 and appeared on the verge of success when War-

25. John Scollard to Thomas W. Conway, June 6, 1871, in Warmoth Papers; Oscar J. Dunn to John Simms, July 26, 1871, in New Orleans *Daily Picayune*, November 22, 1871; Oscar J. Dunn to Horace Greeley, August 31, 1871, in Louisiana Scrapbooks, Howard-Tilton Memorial Library, Tulane University, New Orleans, vol. 17, pp. 33–38.
26. James B. Steedman and Perry Fuller to W. G. Moore, January 15, 1869, in Andrew Johnson Papers, LC.

moth abruptly deserted a united front and swung over to the collector's support. He probably hoped to bring Casey and the Custom House into alliance with himself, at the same time cementing his relations with the president, who was plainly reluctant to fire his wife's brother. He saved Casey, but Kellogg, Packard, and a legion of powerful Republicans never forgave him. And, prophetically, a carpetbagger friend warned him that Casey was faithless to his word: "He will not stand by you one week unless for his interest." [27] Sure enough, the following year Casey abandoned Warmoth and went over to Kellogg and Packard. Warmoth now found the whole of federal officialdom arrayed against him and his once cordial relations with Grant suddenly grown cold.

To blacks, conciliation was not simply a matter of jobs; jobs involved race, and race emerged as the central contradiction in Warmoth's policy. Few words revealed the conflict more fully than those the *German Gazette* wrote about the new editor of the New Orleans *Republican*, Michael Hahn, in 1869. Under Hahn, a German and a Southerner, the *Gazette* observed approvingly, the *Republican* had abandoned its ultra-Radical, anti-Southern bias. Most important, the new editor was not addicted to the "nigger-question." He believed that the Negro had received his due, and the country should now turn to other matters; nothing would be gained by abasing white Southerners for the benefit of Africa. [28]

Warmoth and the official press strove to subordinate the race issue in the 1870 election. At Shreveport the governor stressed that he had not pressed the Negro question on white Louisiana. The party supported the political equality of all men, said the *Republican*, but "we have denounced social equality, for that is neither beneficent nor practical." The official journal looked forward to the day when "the grave of caste and color will be sealed up irrevocably, and our only issues will be as to good men and correct principles." A parish newspaper argued that the Republican party "has got to rise superior to a white man's

27. New Orleans *Republican*, March 26, 1870; William Pitt Kellogg to Henry Clay Warmoth, December 22, 1869, J. Hale Sypher to Warmoth, January 12, 1870, and Lionel A. Sheldon to Warmoth, March 10, 1870, all in Warmoth Papers; Warmoth, *War, Politics and Reconstruction*, 89–91.
28. The New Orleans *Tribune*, January 26, 1869.

party or a black man's party." The Negro, it claimed, had to resist being "the tool of men who would make him . . . vote as a black man and not as a Republican." Another rural Republican paper asserted that promoting individuals to public office merely because they were black "is not the principle of the Republican party." Intelligence and integrity, it argued, ought to be the qualifications for office, regardless of color.[29]

The conflicts in Warmoth's policy showed up most clearly in the long controversy over civil rights in Louisiana Reconstruction. As set forth in the Radical constitution, the legal and political equality of all men was the keystone of the new order, Warmoth asserted in his inaugural address. Yet he recognized that a significant portion of the population, "not wanting in intelligence and virtue," resisted this doctrine. "Let our course," then, "while resolute and manly, be also moderate and discreet." Better, he added, that our laws should lag behind popular opinion than outrun it. Two months later the legislature gave him a chance to demonstrate this manly discretion; it adopted a bill to enforce Article 13 of the constitution, making it a criminal offense for steamboats, railroads, and places of public resort to discriminate against Negroes. Warmoth resolutely vetoed it. Public opinion, he maintained, was not ready for such measures, and "we can not hope by legislation to control questions of personal association." He also observed that the eve of the 1868 election was notably bad timing for "what is practically class legislation." The bill's author, Robert H. Isabelle, a free man of color, and other black legislators fumed.[30]

When the legislature convened again a few months later, P. B. S. Pinchback sponsored a second bill to enforce Article 13. The election was past, and Pinchback, after Dunn, ranked as the most powerful black leader in the state. During his entire governorship Warmoth worked to keep him on his side. In 1871, for example, the New Orleans, Mobile and Chattanooga Railroad denied Pinchback sleeping

29. Warmoth, *War, Politics and Reconstruction*, 100; New Orleans *Republican*, September 28 and October 26, 1870; Grant *Pioneer* in *ibid.*, August 14, 1870; Lafourche *Republican* in *ibid.*, August 16, 1870.

30. *Inaugural Address of Governor H. C. Warmoth and Remarks of Lieut. Governor Dunn* (New Orleans, 1868); *Louisiana House Journal*, 1868, pp. 174, 246–47; Roger A. Fischer, *Segregation Struggle in Louisiana, 1862–1877* (Urbana, Ill., 1974), 66–67.

car accommodations, resulting in a $25,000 lawsuit by the Negro senator. Behind the scenes, Warmoth tried to get the railroad's policy reversed. "Just tell your ticket agents," he advised Henry S. McComb, "to give tickets to those who apply without regard to color and it will be soon forgotten entirely that whites and negroes had not been sleeping together always (as indeed they have in this country)." When Dunn died, Warmoth secured Pinchback's election in his place, or, probably more accurately, Pinchback, controlling the balance of power in the senate between rival factions of the Republican party and the Democrats, secured his own election. Pinchback the realist perceived what Dunn never did: that Negroes would not attain their rights to any greater degree under Kellogg and Packard than under Warmoth.[31] In any event, Warmoth signed the civil rights act of 1869.

Under the new law segregation in Louisiana remained virtually unchanged. The Negro sheriff of Orleans Parish won a lawsuit against a tavern owner, but apart from that race relations continued as they had before. When Senator William Butler demanded equal accommodations on the steamer *Bannock City*, white passengers clubbed him with an iron bar and threw him out of his cabin onto the deck. It was a measure of black frustration that in 1870 the legislature adopted yet a third bill "forbidding unjust discrimination" in places of public accommodation "on account of race or color."[32] It was passed in the last five days of the session, and under Louisiana law Warmoth had until the next legislature met to sign or reject it. It was an election year, and Warmoth waited, his delay coinciding exactly with his turnabout in the Casey controversy. When the annual state convention of the Republican party met in August, a coalition of indignant carpetbaggers and blacks skillfully ambushed him. The convention first nominated both Warmoth and Dunn for president, and then humiliated Warmoth by choosing his lieutenant governor. His enemies then stacked the central executive committee against him and started a heated debate

---

31. Henry Clay Warmoth to Henry S. McComb, July 11, 1871, in Warmoth Papers; Warmoth, *War, Politics and Reconstruction*, 119–20; P. B. S. Pinchback to the New York *Herald*, September 1, 1871, in New Orleans *Republican*, September 8, 1871.

32. Fischer, *Segregation Struggle in Louisiana*, 69–70; *Louisiana Senate Journal*, 1870, 290; *ibid.*, 1871, p. 4.

over the unsigned civil rights bill. Packard and Charles W. Lowell denounced Warmoth as "the great stumbling-block" to Negro rights in the state. Despite the uproar, the governor vetoed the held-over civil rights bill early in 1871.[33]

Warmoth pursued an equally equivocal policy on mixed schools. Under the education act of 1869, Warmoth and Superintendent Conway, a loyal supporter, controlled the state board of education, which in turn controlled the school directors of New Orleans. Thus, the ultimate responsibility for the limited desegregation instituted in New Orleans in 1870 belonged with the governor, who probably felt compelled to satisfy the demands of the *gens de couleur* for enforcement of the constitution. On the other hand, Warmoth and Conway made no effort to desegregate rural schools, and it is clear that they cooperated secretly with officials at Louisiana State Seminary in preserving that institution's lily-white policy. The seminary's president, David F. Boyd, talked with Warmoth and Conway soon after they took office. The governor and the state superintendent would leave the seminary alone, he informed friends, "because they are fully impressed with the belief that if they materially interfere with the school, they will *kill* it, which (for *political* reasons, if no other) they are anxious not to do." Warmoth and Conway adhered to this course throughout their term of office.[34]

By mid-1871 the policy of peace had permanently destroyed the unity of the Radical party. And in a moral climate set by the night riders of 1868, Republican tactics against one another increasingly resembled the terrorists' tactics against them. In August, United States

33. New Orleans *Republican*, August 10 and 11, 1870; Warmoth, *War, Politics and Reconstruction*, 94; *House Miscellaneous Documents*, 42d Cong., 2d Sess., No. 211, pp. 298–99. After failing to override Warmoth's veto, the lawmakers passed an innocuous measure, presumably originating with the governor's supporters, stipulating that all suits brought under Article 13 or the civil rights law of 1869 would be tried by the court or, if requested, by jury (*Acts of the State of Louisiana*, 1871, pp. 57–58). In 1873 the legislature adopted and Kellogg signed yet another civil rights law (Fischer, *Segregation Struggle in Louisiana*, 78–80).

34. *Acts of the State of Louisiana*, 1869, pp. 175–76; David F. Boyd to James M. Boydley, August 22, 1868, in David F. Boyd Letter Books, I, Troy H. Middleton Library, Louisiana State University, Baton Rouge; David F. Boyd to W. L. Sanford, December 23, 1871, in Walter L. Fleming Collection, Troy H. Middleton Library, Louisiana State University, Baton Rouge.

Marshal Packard used the army and federal deputy marshals to control the Republican state convention. Five months later the warring Republicans turned the streets of New Orleans into a scene reminiscent of 1868. On January 4, Packard's deputies arrested Warmoth, Pinchback, and seventeen members of the legislature. The governor obtained bail, proclaimed a conspiracy existed to overthrow the government, and seized the State House with militia and Metropolitan Police. Only the presence of federal troops prevented a pitched battle. These episodes made headlines all over the nation and had far-reaching repercussions. In New York and "everywhere through the north, there is but one feeling," an ally informed Warmoth. "They know little & care less about our fight among ourselves but they won't stand bayonets." [35]

The crisis came to a head in the 1872 election. The party became divided into three separate factions led by Warmoth, Kellogg-Packard, and Pinchback. The Kellogg-Packard and Pinchback groups eventually united, while, as a Liberal Republican, Warmoth tried to lead a fusion party of conservative Republicans, Democrats, and "Reformers." Privy to the inner councils of the Democratic party, David F. Boyd explained what happened to William T. Sherman. Numerous Democrats, he claimed, saw in Warmoth and "*his Republican influence* their only chance . . . for freeing our State from Carpet-bag and negro rule. I was one of them, and . . . wished to run him for Governor." The Democratic majority, however, "said *no*" to Warmoth leading the ticket and resolved instead to "get '*his influence*,' with the understanding that we send him to the U.S. Senate! This policy prevailed. Warmoth was left off the ticket, but still *his influence* was counted upon, with his election law . . . as the *mainspring* of the Liberal and Democratic movement." [36] Warmoth accepted the bargain because he could not again be elected Republican governor of Louisiana; even if he had won the nomination, which was a doubtful proposition, the Kellogg-Packard forces would have run against him, dividing the party and ensuring a Democratic victory.

35. Warmoth, *War, Politics and Reconstruction*, 115–18, 126–40; H. C. Dibble to Henry Clay Warmoth, August 24, 1871, in Warmoth Papers.

36. David F. Boyd to William T. Sherman, December 27, 1872, in Fleming Collection.

Both the Fusionists and the Republicans defrauded one another, although there was no repetition of the horrors of 1868. The Fusionists had more to work with and probably won, but the actual returns mattered little, for this was an extraordinary affair, even by the standards of Reconstruction. For weeks after the election Warmoth and his enemies maneuvered like wild men in some bizarre political theater of the absurd. In a development that its creators never foresaw, the state Returning Board split into two different panels: One proclaimed victory for Kellogg (though it never looked at the returns), the other declared victory for the Fusionist-Democratic candidate John D. McEnery. The house impeached Warmoth in December, and, although he was never convicted, Pinchback acted as governor for the few weeks that remained in his term. The evening before his impeachment, the governor attempted to strike some desperate bargain with his lieutenant governor. "I have slept on the proposition you made to me last night," Pinchback replied, "and have resolutely determined to do my duty to my state, party, and race, by declining. . . . I am truly sorry for you but cannot help you."[37]

On January 14, 1873, William Pitt Kellogg took the oath of office as governor of Louisiana. On the same hour of the same day John D. McEnery swore the same oath at Lafayette Square. That winter and spring rival governors, legislatures, and, in many places, parish officials claimed power in Louisiana. A reign of violence descended on the state. On March 5 the Metropolitan Police, supported by federal troops, bloodily repulsed white mobs that attacked police stations in the Crescent City. The Metropolitans struck back the next day, seizing Odd Fellows Hall and arresting the members of the McEnery legislature, who were inside. In April a conflict between rival officials in Grant parish resulted in the bloody Colfax Massacre. The disputants carried the controversy to Washington, where with evident distaste for the fruits of Radical Reconstruction in Louisiana, the Republican-dominated Congress adjourned without resolving the conflict. Finally, in May President Grant upheld the Kellogg regime,[38] but it proved a

---

37. The pro-Fusionist board was actually a series of three boards appointed by Warmoth and the senate (Taylor, *Louisiana Reconstructed*, 244); P. B. S. Pinchback to Henry Clay Warmoth, December 9, 1872, in Warmoth Papers.

38. Appleton's *Annual Cyclopaedia (1873)*, 444–51; Taylor, *Louisiana Reconstructed*,

costly and barren victory. Kellogg would rule the corpse of Republican Louisiana.

The debacle of the Warmoth years resulted from a failure to resolve a crisis of legitimacy. Louisiana Republicans, as did their counterparts elsewhere in the South, confronted enemies who challenged not only Radical policies but the very existence of the Radical regime, enemies who held Warmoth and all his party to be criminal usurpers. The Warmoth administration met the threat with a twofold strategy: the policy of force and the policy of peace. The strategy failed. The policy of force helped protect the regime, but at an unacceptable cost. The Republican election apparatus was so patently undemocratic that it made Northern voters as well as Southerners question the legitimacy of the Republican government. By the end of 1872 the crisis of legitimacy was fast emerging as a national, not just a regional, problem. The policy of peace, on the other hand, not only failed, on any significant scale, to conciliate white Louisianians, it destroyed the Republican party from within. The Warmoth strategies were in fact mutually contradictory; they negated each other and demolished his government.

254–55; T. Harry Williams, "The Louisiana Unification Movement of 1873," *Journal of Southern History*, XI (August, 1945), 349–50; James D. Richardson (ed.), *A Compilation of the Messages and Papers of the Presidents, 1789–1897* (Washington, D.C., 1896–1897), VII, 223–24.

9

Showdown on
the Red River

"We own this soil of Louisiana," proclaimed a St. Mary Parish news-paper in August 1874; civilization is the birthright of the white race, "and it is ours, and ours alone. . . . Therefore are we banding together in a White League army . . . acting under Christian and high-principled leaders, and determined to defeat these negroes in their infamous de-sign of depriving us of all we hold sacred and precious on the soil of our nativity. . . . Upon the radical party must rest the whole responsi-bility of this *conflict*, and as sure as there is a just God in heaven, their unnatural, cold-blooded, and revengeful measures of reconstruction in Louisiana *will meet with a terrible retribution*."[1] The Radicals would pay dearly for victory in the disputed election of 1872.

Like Warmoth, Governor Kellogg was an Illinoian (although he was born in Vermont). As a young lawyer in his twenties he had helped organize the Republican party in central Illinois. Lincoln appointed him chief justice of the Nebraska Territory, but when the fighting started he returned home and raised a regiment of cavalry. He resigned his commission in 1863 because of ill health; on the eve of that fatal visit to Ford's Theater, the president appointed him collector of the Port of New Orleans. Kellogg's reputation for being more honest than Warmoth may have to do with the fact that his personal papers have been purged of damaging material; whereas, some of the dirt remains in Warmoth's manuscripts. In any event, Louisiana whites cared neither about his virtues nor his real faults. He was "The Usurper," and they reviled him as they had never reviled Warmoth. "Surely such a miser-able weak, contemptible creature," David F. Boyd confided morosely to his diary, "must go to pieces from his own rottenness." In 1873 he escaped an assassination attempt.[2]

1. *Senate Executive Documents*, 43d Cong., 2d Sess., No. 13, p. 31.
2. *Dictionary of American Biography*, X, 305–306; *Biographical Directory of the American Congress*, 1172–73; David F. Boyd Diary, 1874–1875, Troy H. Middleton Library, Loui-

The great depression of the 1870s further poisoned Kellogg's term. Under Warmoth the state's agriculture and commerce had partially recovered from the devastation of the war, and a mood of cautious optimism prevailed at the start of the decade. In the fall of 1873, the fragile economy of Louisiana collapsed along with the nation's. Hard times now presented another indictment of Radical rule; as the *Picayune* maintained, "Bad government is the sole cause of the universal wretchedness of the people of Louisiana." Throughout the state angry whites concluded that the end of Radical government was a prerequisite for recovery.[3]

Louisiana whites united in believing that the Radicals were corrupt; indeed, as they told the story, no people ever endured more venal rulers. The evidence was prima facie: Tax rates doubled and tripled; the cost of state and local government mounted; the state debt, $10 million before the war, climbed to $25 million by 1873; lawmakers took bribes, padded their expense accounts, and contrived per diem pay between sessions of the legislature. Never mind the dislocations of war and emancipation; the years that taxes remained in arrears; the failure of antebellum Louisiana to provide social services, including education, deemed essential in the North;[4] and the dilemma of politicians whose constituents were land-poor black farmers: They either fed at the public trough or went hungry. Never mind that the Warmoth and Kellogg administrations were probably no more corrupt than past (or later) regimes and that graft acted as a prime lubricant of nineteenth-century politics. Never mind, too, that Louisiana corrupted the Radicals every bit as much as the Radicals corrupted the state. "*I don't pretend to be honest*," Warmoth announced testily in a bank law debate. "I only pretend to be as honest as *anybody in politics.*" Here are the leaders of the banking community in New Orleans, he observed, publicly protesting the venality of their lawmakers while, behind the scenes, attempting to buy their votes. "I tell you these

---

siana State University, Baton Rouge, September 21, 1874; T. Harry Williams, "The Louisiana Unification Movement of 1873," *Journal of Southern History*, XI (August, 1945), 349–50; the Kellogg Papers consist of routine official letters and documents that reveal little about the man or his policies.

3. Joe Gray Taylor, *Louisiana Reconstructed, 1863–1877* (Baton Rouge, 1974), 350–63.
4. There is a good discussion of this in *ibid.*, 202–208, 260–65.

much-abused members of the Louisiana legislature are at all events as
good as the people they represent. Why, damn it, everybody is demoralizing down here. Corruption is the fashion." [5] The scapegoating
of Radicals as thieves, one and all, served an important end, of course:
that of justifying the deeper corruption of violence. The Knights of the
White Camellia, the White League, and their kin crippled democracy
in the state and the region for nearly a century. Armies of thieves could
not have equaled their damage.

For most of the state's history, sectional politics in Louisiana has
pitted the French-Catholic southern parishes against the Anglo-
Protestant northern parishes. The politics of Reconstruction, however, as Maps 7 through 11 show, conformed to a racial sectional pattern. In 1870 the population was divided evenly between 364,210
blacks and 362,065 whites; the distribution, however, was skewed.
New Orleans was 73.6 percent white, but the rest of the state remained
58.6 percent black. [6] The Democrats generally won the Crescent City
and other white areas; the Republicans usually dominated the alluvial
Y. In 1872, excepting the two Baton Rouge parishes, the Radicals carried the heavily black areas along the Mississippi River from the
Arkansas border to the gulf; the Fusionists, however, stripped them of
the Red River Valley, the western arm of the Y. The loss, if permanent, reduced the Republicans to a minority party. In the ensuing years
the Red River Valley emerged as the strategic battleground between
the White League and the Radicals.

The Red River rises seven hundred miles northwest of Louisiana on
the Ilano Estacado, the Staked Plain, where its waters cut the deep
gash in the Texas Panhandle known as the Palo Duro Canyon. When
Warmoth became governor, this region remained the domain of the
Antelope Comanche. For hundreds of miles it marked the boundary
between Texas and unorganized Indian territory, nipping Arkansas,
and entering the northwestern corner of Louisiana, flowing diagonally
across the state. "Its waters are excessively turbid, and of a deep red

---

5. *House Reports*, 43d Cong., 2d Sess., No. 261, Pt. 3, p. 973. Richard N. Current
has written that "if Warmoth was corrupt, it would be nearer the truth to say that Louisiana corrupted *him* than to say that *he* corrupted Louisiana" (*Three Carpetbag Governors*
[Baton Rouge, 1967], 63).
6. *Ninth Census, 1870, Population*, I, 33–34.

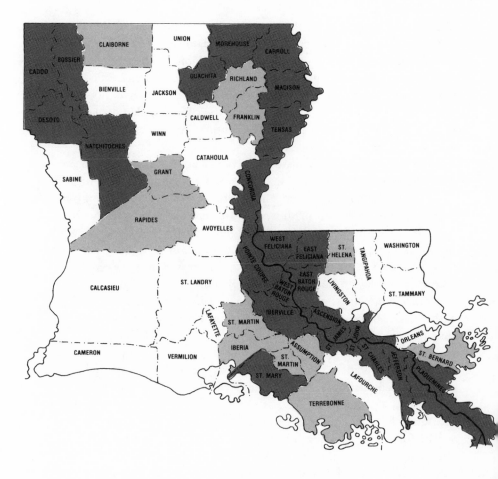

Map 7

Black Population of Louisiana, 1870

60% or more black

50% to 59% black

less than 50% black

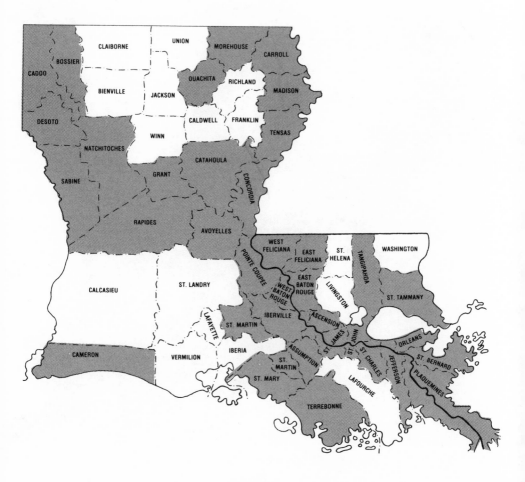

Map 8

Election for State Auditor in Louisiana, 1870
(Graham, Republican, vs. Jumel, Democrat)

☐ Jumel received majorities

▨ Graham received majorities

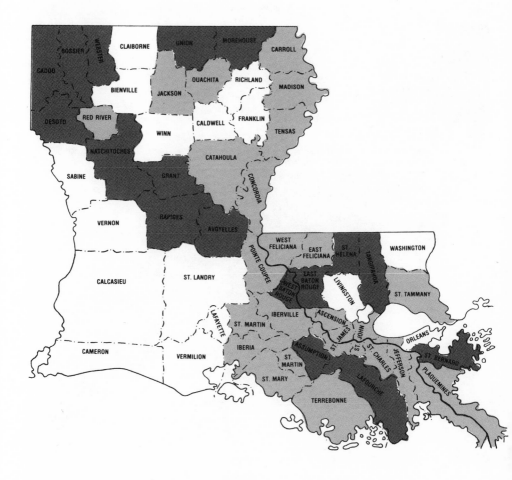

Map 9

Election for Governor in Louisiana, 1872
(Kellogg vs. McEnery)

☐ McEnery received majorities

■ Kellogg received majorities

■ Contested, both candidates claimed majorities

178

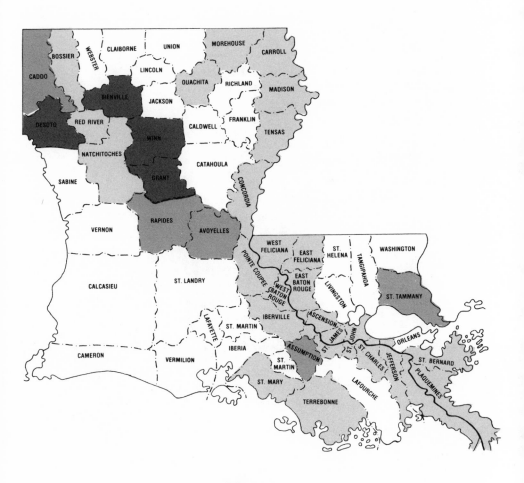

Map 10

Election for State Treasurer in Louisiana, 1874
(Dubuclet, Republican, vs. Moncure, Democrat)

☐ Moncure received majorities

▨ Dubuclet received majorities

▨ Contested, both candidates claimed majorities

■ Vote excluded because of fraud, violence, or other irregularities

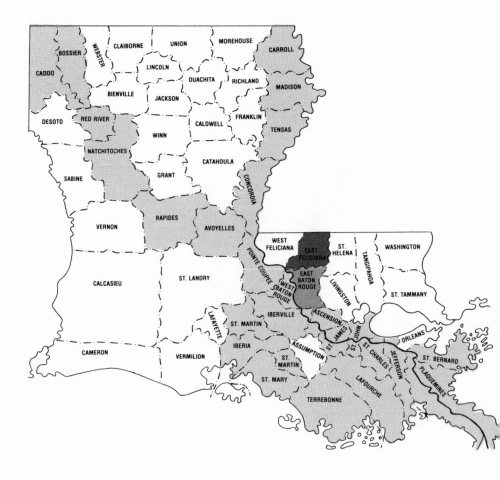

Map 11

Election for Governor in Louisiana, 1876
(Packard, Republican, vs. Nicholls, Democrat)

☐ Nicholls received majorities

☐ Packard received majorities [1]

☐ Contested, both candidates claimed majorities

■ Vote excluded because of fraud, violence, or other irregularities

Source: Based on Democratic compilation and official Republican returns, December 21, 1876.
1. Republican returns give Lafourche to Packard; Democratic returns show vote tied.

color," observed the Louisiana State Seminary surveyor Samuel H. Lockett; "its current is swift; its banks are constantly washing away at one point and building up at another; cut-offs . . . islands, old rivers, and abandoned channels are numerous." Where it joins the Mississippi, its width exceeds a mile, but upriver, above the rapids at Alexandria, navigation grows difficult "on account of its narrowness and extreme crookedness. . . . Eighteen miles above Shreveport, the Great Raft offers an insuperable obstacle to navigation in the main channel." The raft, acting like a huge dam, backs up the waters and forms a connecting series of lakes, bayous, and canals. In October 1865 an agent of the Freedmen's Bureau named Marshall Harvey Twitchell received his orders in New Orleans, and the passage of a few days found him aboard a small stern-wheeler headed up the Red River, his destination the village of Sparta in Bienville Parish. At Alexandria he saw a workman nod his head at him and overheard the comment: "There goes one of our bosses."[7]

Twitchell's parents were Vermont farm people and antislavery Congregationalists. He attended the common schools, graduated valedictorian of Leland Seminary in the small town of Townshend, taught school, and studied law. He joined the army (the 4th Vermont) after First Bull Run at the age of twenty-one and fought in most of the major campaigns of the eastern theater: the Peninsula battles, Antietam, Fredericksburg, Chancellorsville, Gettysburg, the Wilderness (where he received a severe head wound), the siege of Petersburg, and Appomattox. Army records reveal that he had sandy-colored hair, fair skin, hazel eyes, and stood five feet seven inches tall. He remained a sergeant for most of the war, and when another noncom received a lieutenancy ahead of him, he asked for a commission in the United States Colored Troops. At Petersburg Captain Twitchell commanded a company of the 109th Colored Infantry. After Appomattox the 109th went to Indianola, Texas. That August Twitchell requested reassignment with the Freedmen's Bureau in Louisiana.[8]

---

7. Samuel H. Lockett, *Louisiana as It Is: A Geographical and Topographical Description of the State*, ed. Lauren C. Post (Baton Rouge, 1970), 122–23; "Autobiography of Marshall Harvey Twitchell," Marshall Harvey Twitchell Papers, Prescott Memorial Library, Louisiana Tech University, Ruston, 79–80.

8. "Autobiography of Marshall Harvey Twitchell," in Twitchell Papers, 1–79; Civil

Late in the year the Vermonter rode into Sparta with a small detachment of black soldiers and took over the duties of provost·marshal and agent of the Freedmen's Bureau. No telegraph linked the community with the outside world. The former Confederate capital of Shreveport, now the occupation army's undermanned headquarters in northwestern Louisiana, lay forty miles away across swamp and Lake Bistineau. New Orleans was at least a three-day journey. Hundreds of ex-Rebel soldiers lived in the area, and few if any bore any love for the government that Twitchell represented. He wrote years later that had he known what awaited him, he would "have remained with [his] regiment."[9]

The task, as he understood it, was to inform the people of the region, black and white, of the new order: Former master and ex-slave were now employer and employee. As the agent of the government, he represented the arbiter of the free labor system; if landowner and laborer could not agree on wages, he "would fix the pay of the ex-slave" and compel obedience from both parties. Corporal punishment was a relic of the past; labor conflicts and punishment now came under the purview of the Freedmen's Bureau. Upon arrival, Twitchell inspected the jail and freed a young mulatto girl. A brief investigation had revealed the girl's crime: The wife of the town's most prominent citizen believed that she was the illegitimate daughter of her absent husband.[10]

Schooled on the gospel of free labor, the young Northerner's observations of his alien surroundings were invariably critical. Illiteracy characterized both races; the grandeur of the local aristocracy revealed itself in a few oversized log cabins; mulattos traced their origins to the elite of white society (not, as he had presumed, to the bottom rung);

War Pension Files, Record Group 15, National Archives. Students of Reconstruction are indebted to the late Jimmy G. Shoalmire, who discovered the Twitchell Papers, in the possession of Dr. Marshall Coleman Twitchell of Burlington, Vermont, and is responsible for their present availability in Prescott Memorial Library. Shoalmire's "Carpetbagger Extraordinary: Marshall Harvey Twitchell, 1840–1905" (Ph.D. dissertation, Mississippi State University, 1969), remains a valuable work.

9. "Autobiography of Marshall Harvey Twitchell," in Twitchell Papers, 79–80.

10. *Ibid.*, 81–82. Twitchell's autobiography and other papers are very brief on his Freedmen's Bureau experience, and, unfortunately, the National Archives have failed to locate his correspondence in Bureau of Refugees, Freedmen, and Abandoned Lands, Record Group 105.

the Methodist minister and his wife smoked tobacco; the landlady swore like a soldier. He had always wondered how a minority of slave-owners had manipulated the white masses; a few years hence he helped conduct the federal census and "discovered enough ignorance to explain the question." On occasion his critical comments were tinged with admiration. Despite their ignorance and the primitive ritual of foot-washing, Twitchell respected the Hard-shell Baptists of the region "for their honesty, industry and general law-abiding character"; because they had not owned slaves, they were freer from the corruption of slavery than other whites. In all, Bienville Parish confirmed a profound sense of New England superiority.[11]

In mid-1866 the Freedmen's Bureau routinely relieved the Sparta agent and ordered him to New Orleans for mustering out of the army. That Twitchell did not at that point return to his native Vermont owed to a courtship and marriage worthy of a novel by John W. De Forest. Adele Coleman was a young music teacher at Sparta Academy, a high-spirited belle, and the daughter of one of the parish's first families. To the acute dismay of family and friends, Adele decided that the only man worthy of her hand was the hated Yankee captain of the Freedmen's Bureau. The result was melodrama. One evening while walking, for instance, Adele turned to Marshall and calmly asked for his army pistol, which he cautiously handed over. The young woman whirled and fired into the shrubbery of a nearby fence, flushing from hiding an embarrassed rival. The New Englander later concluded that had Adele hit the man, the community would have pronounced the shooting accidental. A young gentleman from one of the best families "could not have been so dishonorable as to have been eavesdropping, while she could not have intentionally shot him. A certain kind of pride and honor were of more importance than life to them." On a later occasion, Twitchell's orderly appeared at the door late one night with the news that a mysterious rider who refused to dismount wanted to see the captain outside. The mystery rider proved to be Adele in disguise, who had come to warn her beau that her brother Gus was gunning for him. The lovers spent the night riding in the moonlight. The

11. "Autobiography of Marshall Harvey Twitchell," in Twitchell Papers, 85–89, 99, 118–19.

Coleman family attempted to send their daughter to South Carolina, but the headstrong Adele refused to go. The family finally resigned itself to the match, and Twitchell married Adele that July.[12]

The Colemans soon rejoiced at their daughter's choice. For one thing, Isaac Coleman, Adele's father, and Marshall discovered that they liked one another. Even more important, the new son-in-law had capital and a head for business that was lacking among the Coleman men. Twitchell and Isaac Coleman purchased adjoining plantations on Lake Bistineau. The year 1867 proved to be a bad one, and Coleman was unable to pay his debts. "You Yankees are said to be awful cute," Mrs. Coleman chided; "[it] seems to me you might take Mr. Coleman's business and straighten it out." The Northerner accepted the challenge and took over the management of the Coleman estates, with notable success. "Thank the Lord the plantation is paid for 'every cent' and there will be no trouble about the balance that Pa owes," Adele wrote proudly to her sister in early 1868. Marshall "has paid off all the land notes and $100 on the stock notes, besides taking up an old note of Barrett's against Pa." In addition, with the help of her brother Gus, he had cleared up her father's debts in Ringgold. "Pa says he don't know what in the world he would have done without his *Yankee* son in law."[13] The alliance also benefited Twitchell, according him respectability and acceptance in the community, and he, too, profited financially.

Only one thing now disturbed the conservative Louisiana family about Adele's husband: He was a Radical. Twitchell entertained few doubts about the leading role that he and other Northerners took in Reconstruction politics. The ex-slaves were too ignorant to govern effectively, the native Unionists too few in number; both groups looked to the ex-Federal soldiers who, though young and politically inexperienced, had learned the lessons of organization in the Union army, or so the young carpetbagger assumed. Twitchell helped organize the

12. *Ibid.*, 91–97; Civil War Pension Files.
13. Twitchell's father died late in the war, and shortly after his marriage, he made an emergency trip to Vermont to settle property matters. The family was not well-to-do, but even a modest inheritance would have gone a long way in the Bienville Parish of 1866. "Autobiography of Marshall Harvey Twitchell," in Twitchell Papers, 72, 98, 100–101, 109, 115; Adele Twitchell to her sister Lou, January 8, 1868, in Twitchell Papers.

Republican party on the upper Red River; he became a member of the constitutional convention, parish judge, justice of the peace, president of the police jury, assistant marshall, president of the school board, state senator, and United States commissioner. He formed a lasting alliance with Edward W. Deweese, a young New Yorker who had succeeded him as the Freedmen's Bureau agent at Sparta. When the two men first met outside Assistant Commissioner Thomas W. Conway's office in the fall of 1865, neither foresaw the perilous events that would bind them together like brothers.[14]

The danger started soon enough. In May 1868 night riders on the upper Red River started the reign of terror that climaxed on the eve of the presidential election. Masked men invaded the home of a black leader named Moses Langhorne, shot him, and cut off his head. Twitchell's young mulatto messenger disappeared without a trace; rumor drifted back that he had been thrown into Lake Bistineau with his hands tied. Mounted men blasted a neighboring carpetbagger with shotguns one evening, luring him from his house by claiming they had a letter for him. They tried the same trick on Twitchell. The wily Vermonter sent a young Negro girl for the letter while he ducked out the back door with his pistol and rifle and circled around to the front. The riders grew uneasy and rode off. For the first time since their marriage, Marshall and Adele endured social ostracism. One Sunday morning at church the minister preached an entire sermon against the young wife for marrying an outsider. Twitchell avoided road ambushes that fall through a combination of luck and caution: He rode only in open country and never went near the woods. Once he read his obituary in the New Orleans *Republican*. As the election grew near, the danger was so great that he advised blacks to stay away from the polls. Recklessly disregarding his own counsel, he cast the only vote that Ulysses S. Grant received in Bienville Parish. The man was fiercely proud. Southern bullies would not intimidate Captain Marshall Harvey Twitchell.[15]

The political fury subsided after the election, and life on the upper

14. "Autobiography of Marshall Harvey Twitchell," in Twitchell Papers, 79–80, 102–106; *Official Register of the United States*, 1867.

15. "Autobiography of Marshall Harvey Twitchell," in Twitchell Papers, 105–113; *House Miscellaneous Documents*, 41st Cong., 2d Sess., No. 154, Pt. 1, pp. 62–66.

Red River resumed its routine. Twitchell's younger brother Homer and his brother-in-law George A. King joined him from Vermont. The carpetbagger now devoted much of his considerable energy to business. For $21,000 he purchased Starlight Plantation, 620 acres of the best land in De Soto Parish on the west bank of the Red River. He invested in steam-powered machinery and put up, under King's management, Starlight Mills, which was a cotton gin, saw mill, and grist mill complex. He constructed a school and new houses for his black employees, scattering the new quarters over the entire plantation instead of putting them in a single cluster as had been done during the slavery period. With the Colemans he obtained a state contract and cleared the debris-clogged Lake Bistineau for navigation. The industrious Yankee also purchased valuable lots in the village of Coushatta, three miles below Starlight on the Bienville side of the Red River.[16]

In 1870 the rest of Twitchell's family moved from Vermont: his widowed mother, his sister Belle (Mrs. George A. King), and his sisters Helen and Kate and their husbands, M. C. Willis and Clark Holland. In the meantime, Deweese's younger brother Robert joined him. The New Yorkers purchased a half-interest in Starlight, and the two brothers joined the Vermonters in De Soto Parish. Other Northerners, Frank S. Edgerton, J. W. Harrison, and Henry A. Scott, settled nearby, creating a regular community. In the space of a few years the Yankee colony infused tens of thousands of dollars of capital into the short stretch of the Red River Valley that bordered De Soto and Bienville parishes. Most of it went into plantations, mills, and other properties that returned a profit, but substantial sums also went for levees, schools, public buildings, and churches. "There has not been a church or public building . . . in that part of the country," Twitchell stated, "that I have not donated money for." He pointed to the town of Coushatta, which when he first arrived had been an insignificant river landing with two houses and in the early 1870s emerged as one of the most prosperous towns on the Red River. Samuel H. Lockett, no admirer of the Radicals, confirmed that boast. Coushatta, he observed in

---

16. "Autobiography of Marshall Harvey Twitchell," 115–18; *Gillespie* vs. *Twitchell*, *Louisiana Annual Reports*, vol. 34, pp. 288–300; *House Reports*, 43d Cong., 2d Sess., No. 261, Pt. 3, p. 385; Shoalmire, "Carpetbagger Extraordinary," 93, 105.

his 1872 topographical survey, "has but recently sprung into existence, but it is one of the prettiest and most enterprising small towns in the state." [17]

Red River Parish, created in 1871, consolidated the political power of Twitchell's Yankee clan. Incorporating parts of De Soto, Bienville, Caddo, Bossier, and Natchitoches parishes, it straddled a twenty-five-mile span of the upper Red River Valley. Its economic and political center of gravity ran northwest to southeast following the alluvial bottomlands through Starlight Plantation and Coushatta, the parish seat. Every member of Twitchell's family held a political office. Deweese was a state representative and member of the police jury. Scalawags and blacks, although they were not excluded, danced to the tune of "Yankee Doodle Dandy." Even so, as events showed, Twitchell achieved what the Radicals in Louisiana rarely achieved: white support for the Republican party, which was probably at least a fourth and possibly two fifths of the white voters. [18]

Red River Parish was nearly 70 percent black. No equalitarian, Twitchell was a paternalist who assumed that blacks "wanted a Northern man for their leader." He referred to blacks as Negroes or colored men, never "niggers" (at least not in any surviving document), and on one occasion he referred to a black Republican as "Mister." In exchange for votes, he secured minor offices such as justice of the peace, recorder, coroner, or alderman for black leaders. Starlight Mills and the Northern-run plantations provided employment to several hundred Negroes on both a wage and a share basis; Twitchell also sold land to blacks. In Red River the authorities treated violent crime against freedmen as serious business; indeed, the carpetbagger claimed that for a time they drove the Negro-baiting element out of the parish. Twitchell made no effort to establish desegregated schools, but he did

17. *House Reports*, 43d Cong., 2d Sess., No. 261, Pt. 3, pp. 385–87; "Autobiography of Marshall Harvey Twitchell," in Twitchell Papers, 120, 124–25; Twitchell Interrogatories, court records relating to *Stafford* vs. *Twitchell*, in Twitchell Papers; Lockett, *Louisiana as It Is*, 67. Twitchell estimated that the Yankees' real estate holdings alone were worth $100,000.
18. "Autobiography of Marshall Harvey Twitchell," in Twitchell Papers, 119–23; *House Reports*, 44th Cong., 1st Sess., No. 816, pp. 649–53, 699, 707; *House Executive Documents*, 44th Cong., 2d Sess., No. 30, pp. 250–52; *House Reports*, 43d Cong., 2d Sess., No. 261, Pt. 3, pp. 386–87, 394–95.

establish schools, two in each ward, one for blacks and one for whites. Initially whites assumed that the black schools would fail for lack of attendance, but when Negro enrollment climbed, rumors abounded that the colored schools would be destroyed. Twitchell announced that if any black school was busted up, tax money would be withdrawn from the white school in that district. That ended the matter. Blacks on the upper Red River voted with their feet too; they "came from Sabine and other parishes," the Yankee boss boasted, "until we did not lack labor at all—we had [an] abundance of it."[19]

Whites alleged every manner of crime against Twitchell, from dictatorship to embezzlement of school funds. He was not a dictator but a political boss who ruled through essentially democratic means. He made most of his fortune before consolidating his political power, and the charges of corruption were never substantiated. In truth, as the commander of the Upper Red River district, Major Lewis Merrill, explained, it made not a particle of difference to whites whether Twitchell and other Radicals were honest or not. No Republican, the major claimed, "whatever his actual character may be . . . could have the reputation of being honest in this state."[20]

Twitchell's real crime was that he made Radical Reconstruction work at the parish level. As late as 1874 most parts of the Red River Valley had no rail or telegraph connections with the outside world. To the people in these communities, black and white, the police jury, the sheriff, the tax collector, and the school board were of more immediate concern than the State House in New Orleans. In 1872 many whites in the region had been willing to concede Governor Warmoth the top spot on the Fusion ticket in order to free parish government from Radical rule. At a state convention in June 1872, one earnest Warmoth

19. *Senate Reports*, 45th Cong., 3d Sess., No. 855, Pt. 1, p. 566; "Autobiography of Marshall Harvey Twitchell," in Twitchell Papers, 105, 109, 117, 123–25, 181; *House Reports*, 43d Cong., 2d Sess., No. 261, Pt. 3, p. 385; *House Reports*, 44th Cong., 1st Sess., No. 816, pp. 709–710, 719–21; Marshall Harvey Twitchell to Thomas W. Conway, May 25, 1870, in Historical Records Survey, State Department of Education Records, Louisiana State Archives, Baton Rouge; Shoalmire, "Carpetbagger Extraordinary," 107–114.

20. *House Reports*, 43d Cong., 2d Sess., No. 261, Pt. 3, pp. 179–80. Shoalmire gives the corruption charges somewhat more credence than I do, but he too concludes that most of the charges were exaggerated or based on misinformation (Shoalmire, "Carpetbagger Extraordinary," 118–32).

supporter urged whites in New Orleans to consider the plight of the river parishes:

> Go to the upper border of this state, and come down the Mississippi river; go to the Red, Ouachita and the Teche rivers, and what do you behold? Immense negro majorities in every parish. . . . Now, I ask the delegates from these parishes if they can elect a single police juror or constable in all of these parishes put together?

> [G]entleman of the City of New Orleans, are we to insist that all of these parishes shall be consigned to negro rule, with negro judges, sheriffs, constables[?][21]

Against the Democratic-Fusion parties, Twitchell's stronghold was the only part of the Red River Valley that remained solid for Kellogg. Elsewhere, along the entire length of the Red River, dual Kellogg and McEnery governments existed throughout the spring of 1873. One of these disputed areas was Grant Parish, directly southeast of Coushatta, which was created in 1869 and named in honor of Ulysses S. Grant. Colfax, the parish seat, named after the vice-president, was not really a town but a collection of old plantation buildings atop the steep east bank of the Red River. The stable, a one-story brick rectangle about seventy-five feet long, served as the courthouse. Three quarters of a mile upriver lived a small community of blacks at Smithfield Quarters. About March 25, some white Republicans broke into the courthouse, which had been locked by the McEneryites, and claimed possession of the parish seat. On the last day of the month, fearing retaliation by the Fusionists, the Radical sheriff deputized some blacks to defend the town. Two days later black deputies and whites exchanged gunfire at long range, but no one was hurt. By this time, blacks in the countryside, fearful of remaining in their cabins, started to gather at Colfax for protection. Their fears proved justified; on April 5, three miles from the town, armed whites came upon a black farmer named Jesse McKinney, who was engaged in building a fence. One of the whites killed the unarmed man with a shot through his head.[22]

21. New Orleans *Daily Picayune*, June 7, 1872.
22. United States District Attorney J. R. Beckwith, a Unionist-Scalawag, prosecuted the Colfax defendants in the federal courts and probably learned more about the mas-

At least 150 black farmers now camped at Colfax with their families. A white force of at least equal size lurked nearby. Most of the blacks were armed with shotguns; the whites carried rifles and were unencumbered with women and children. For about a week the two mini-armies faced one another in an apparent stalemate. The day before Easter the blacks put up low earthworks around the courthouse. By this time most of the white Republicans who had helped initiate the conflict and who now sensed Armageddon, had slipped away. When Easter Sunday dawned on April 13 at Colfax courthouse, Negroes in Grant Parish fended for themselves.

In the late morning Levin Allen, a leader of the blacks, met Columbus C. Nash, a white spokesman, under a flag of truce at Smithfield Quarters. Nash demanded that the Negroes lay down their weapons and surrender the courthouse. Allen, remembering the fate of Jesse McKinney, refused. Nash gave him thirty minutes to get the women and children to safety. It was almost noon.[23]

The attack commenced on schedule. The McEneryites formed a skirmish line that was several hundred yards from the black entrenchments and beyond shotgun range, and they opened fire. The Negroes fought back with their ineffective shotguns and about a dozen Enfield rifles. The whites had taken a small artillery piece from a steamer, mounted it on a wagon, and cut two-inch pieces of iron for missiles. Early in the battle they maneuvered it along the riverbank to a position where it enfiladed the blacks behind their earthworks. A few blasts of iron shot directly in their midst "created consternation and panic among the negroes, and they broke and ran, a portion of them starting down the river, the only portion of the town not environed or besieged, and about sixty . . . retreated into the court-house. . . . The white forces that were mounted immediately pursued the fugitives going down the river and slaughtered all within their reach but

---

sacre than anyone else. The account that follows is based mainly on his testimony in *House Reports*, 43d Cong., 2d Sess., No. 261, Pt. 3, pp. 409–421. The quoted material is all from Beckwith, whose account agrees in every major detail with Judge W. B. Woods' charge to the jury (*Ibid.*, 856–65). See also Manie White Johnson, "The Colfax Riot of April, 1873," *Louisiana Historical Quarterly*, XIII (July, 1930), 391–427.

23. *House Reports*, 43d Cong., 2d Sess., No. 261, Pt. 3, pp. 409–413, 858–59.

one . . . some of them got into the woods, and some of them escaped after they were wounded." [24]

The old stable proved to be a death trap. Promising to spare his life, the whites forced a captured Negro named Pinckney Chambers to crawl across the battlefield with a torch and fire the roof of the court-house. "The negroes in the building then found themselves in this situation; with the walls of the court-house and every opening, a target for a very rapid fire of small-arms, and the court-house on fire over their heads. They made an effort to extinguish the fire by knocking off the shingles on that portion of the roof that was burning, but a fire of bullets was then opened upon that portion of the roof which drove them away." The desperate blacks improvised two white flags from a torn shirt and a page ripped from a book.

> The firing ceased then, and some of the white people came up and shouted to the negroes that if they would lay down their arms and come out they would not hurt them. A condition of panic . . . existed inside the building, and the door was opened at once, and the negroes, unarmed, rushed out, to be met with a volley the moment they made their appearance. In that volley several of them were killed. The negroes that were not in the immediate vicinity of the door rushed back and waited a moment, and then made another rush out, and all, excepting some who were secreted under the floor, got out. Again there were some of them killed, and some taken prisoners: the prisoners, as fast as they were taken, were taken out near a cottonwood tree, in a cotton field, and put under guard.

A handful of the trapped men never came out, choosing the fire over the whites outside. "At about three o'clock in the afternoon . . . the last particle of resistence . . . had ceased, and the condition was, then, a burnt or burning court-house, the ground strewn with dead negroes, and a number of negroes, prisoners and under guard, out in the cotton-field." [25]

The prisoners numbered at least thirty-seven and perhaps as many as forty-seven. They remained under guard in the cotton field for about seven hours. That night at about ten o'clock their captors called them out by name in pairs of two and marched them down the road

24. *Ibid.*
25. *Ibid.*

past the burned-out courthouse in the direction of a cotton gin about a mile away, creating a procession of marching prisoners and guards. Gunfire could be heard from the head of the column. An old black man named Benjamin Brimm, who was marching in the middle of the column, asked the nearest guard if the captives were being killed. The unreassuring reply was that "they were only killing the wounded." The shooting advanced down the column. Brimm "heard a pistol cocked, and as he turned around to beg for his life, the man behind him shot him. The bullet passed in under his left eye and through the nasal passages and out under the angle of his jaw." The old man collapsed, feigning death, while the bloodletting continued. Blood coagulated in his nose and he struggled to breathe. The noise attracted attention: "This nigger is not dead yet," a horseman cried, and shot the suffering man in the back, barely missing the spinal cord. Miraculously, Brimm refused to die. Hours later he crawled away to a ditch, covered himself with brush, and lay concealed all the next day while whites milled about; some looting the dead. Monday night he dragged himself away. The elderly freedman lived to tell his story to a grand jury.[26]

Two days after the massacre a United States commissioner and a deputy marshal arrived at the scene. The dead still littered the landscape. With the help of some freedmen, they buried fifty-nine bodies in a ditch. Their count of the dead did not include the charred remains found beneath the burned-out stable, the bodies that had been carried away by mourning families, or the estimated 15-to-20 bodies that had been lost in the river. Nor could the two officials count those who escaped but later died of their wounds. A subsequent and very thorough investigation by Lieutenant Edward L. Godfrey of the Seventh Cavalry documented the deaths of "*at least*" 105 blacks and 3 whites. Two of the dead whites, leaders of the McEneryites, were probably shot by overeager attackers rather than by black defenders. The massacre at Colfax courthouse ranks as the worst single day of carnage in the history of Reconstruction, exceeding in violence the massacres at New Orleans (1866), Memphis (1866), and Meridian, Mississippi (1871).[27]

26. *Ibid.*
27. *Ibid.*; *House Executive Documents*, 44th Cong., 2d Sess., No. 30, pp. 436–38; on the Meridian Massacre see the accounts of Vernon Lane Wharton, *The Negro in Missis-*

The Colfax Massacre affected the fate of Republicans throughout the South. Federal authorities indicted ninety-eight persons under the Force Act of 1870 and brought nine of them to trial. The first effort resulted in a mistrial, but in the second a jury convicted three of the murderers for violating the civil rights of Negroes. The case went to the United States Supreme Court, which, in the *United States* v. *Cruikshank* (1876), ruled in favor of the defendants. "The fourteenth amendment," stated Chief Justice Morrison R. Waite, "prohibits a State from depriving any person of life, liberty, or property, without due process of law; but this adds nothing to the rights of one citizen as against another."[28] In other words, because a private army and not the State of Louisiana committed the massacre, the federal government was powerless to act. This racist and morally opaque decision reduced the Fourteenth Amendment and the Force Acts to meaningless verbiage as far as the civil rights of Negroes were concerned.

A week after the massacre, Marshall Harvey Twitchell received a warning from an anonymous source who claimed, "I was in the fite at Colfax and if the lord will forgive me for that I wil never be guilty of such a thing agane." The informer stated that a lawyer and a deputy sheriff from Red River Parish had participated in the slaughter and now intrigued with the assassins to overrun Coushatta: "They intend to kill all the yankees and Nigger officers [and] you had better make your escape." Local Democrats verified the threat but assured Twitchell that if he and his family remained indoors, only troublemaking Negroes would be killed. The Vermonter, however, was made of tougher leather than the white Republicans in Grant Parish. He posted the roads from the southeast and put out word that if the Colfax desperadoes entered Red River they would meet fierce resistance. Black couriers rode through the countryside telling the freedmen to keep their powder dry and remain in readiness to assemble in Coushatta at a moment's notice.[29] The invaders never came.

In March 1874 a trio of ex-Confederate soldiers in the lower Red

sippi 1865–1890 (Chapel Hill, 1947); and William C. Harris, *The Day of the Carpetbagger: Republican Reconstruction in Mississippi* (Baton Rouge, 1979).

28. *United States* v. *Cruikshank et al.*, *United States Reports, Supreme Court*, vol. 92, p. 554.

29. "A True Friend" to Marshall Harvey Twitchell, April 16, 1873, in Twitchell Papers; "Autobiography of Marshall Harvey Twitchell," *ibid.*, 127–28.

River town of Alexandria established a newspaper called the *Caucasian*. The history of Louisiana since 1867, the journal charged in its first issue, was a record of "crime, venality, corruption, misrule, and official debasement." A continuation of Republican rule would witness the Africanization of the state. The newspaper challenged whites to discard the party labels of the past, form a "white man's party," and make the next election a "fair, square fight, Caucasian versus African." The *Caucasian's* appeal ignited the state. In Shreveport the *Times* and the *Comet*, in Opelousas the *Courier* and the *Bulletin*, in Franklin the *Enterprise*, in Natchitoches the *People's Vindicator*, in New Orleans the *Daily Picayune*, the *Morning Star*, and the *Catholic Messenger*—all reiterated the summons to a white man's party. It started in Opelousas in April, and by late summer the White League or the White Man's party had spread throughout the Red River Valley, to New Orleans, and over most of the state.[30]

The appearance of the White League coincided with a melancholy in Twitchell that had no connection with politics. He and Adele had been married seven-and-a-half years; his relations with her family remained strong; in fact, the Colemans had become important scalawags in Bienville Parish. Although Adele had borne him three sons (the youngest of whom died in 1870), she had never been a healthy woman. The threat of tuberculosis had hung over her for years. In February 1874, after a long struggle, she finally succumbed to the disease. A month later, tragedy visited tragedy, and the youngest surviving son, Daniel, died. Little Daniel's death marked the fourth in as many years; Twitchell's sister Belle had died in 1871. In his autobiography Twitchell claims that he resolved to abandon politics and devote himself to business. No reason exists to doubt his sincerity. He was a superb businessman, and although he was successful at getting votes, he lacked the temperament of the professional politician. Still, Red River had become the nerve center of the Radical party in northwestern Louisiana, and Twitchell the indispensable man in Red River. Party leaders in De Soto, Red River, and Bienville parishes pointed to the growing

30. Taylor, *Louisiana Reconstructed*, 281–86; Oscar Lestage, Jr., "The White League in Louisiana and Its Participation in Reconstruction Riots," *Louisiana Historical Quarterly*, XVIII (July, 1935), 637–49; *House Reports*, 43d Cong., 2d Sess., No. 261, Pt. 3, p. 906.

strength of the White League and begged him to continue. Unwilling to abandon his friends and allies in the face of danger, he again accepted the Republican nomination for state senator.[31] In later years, he must have reexamined that decision so many times.

On the eve of the White League revolt, Twitchell recalled, few individuals in north Louisiana stood higher in the esteem of the community than he. As chairman of the senate finance committee, he claimed much of the credit for the Funding Act of 1874 that eventually scaled down the state debt to about $12 million. The social ostracism of earlier years had died away; indeed, the Yankee now found himself eagerly courted by prominent whites. If politics had at times divided the Vermonter and his white neighbors, business had just as often united them. The local Democratic merchants had been just as anxious as the carpetbagger to get the new parish created with Coushatta as the parish seat. They had raised a thousand-dollar slush fund and had appreciated the skill with which their Radical state senator used it to wine and dine politicians in the Crescent City. Twitchell had also come to a new appreciation of his Southern neighbors. That spring of 1874, as often occurred, farmers in the hill country ran short of corn, the main staple of their diet, and most of the local merchants denied them credit. The Yankee had learned in years past to buy corn cheap in the fall, store it through the winter, and sell in the spring when the price rose. He gave the desperate farmers corn on credit, accepting only their word of repayment. Experience had taught him that they would often ignore a legally secured debt but would repay a debt of honor. Many whites had probably learned too that the Radical boss represented less of a political threat than they had at first assumed. In the paternalistic Red River system, blacks voted, held minor offices, and worked in comparative security, mainly for white landowners, while political and economic control remained in white hands.[32]

31. James Brewster to William G. Brown, April 24, 1874, and James Brewster to M. C. Cole, August 27, 1874, in HRS, State Department of Education Records; "Autobiography of Marshall Harvey Twitchell," in Twitchell Papers, 116, 130–31; Twitchell genealogy papers, in the possession of Dr. Marshall Coleman Twitchell, Burlington, Vermont.

32. "Autobiography of Marshall Harvey Twitchell," in Twitchell Papers, 130–31; *House Reports*, 44th Cong., 1st Sess., No. 816, p. 652.

Still, the carpetbagger, as he later realized, exaggerated his acceptance in the community. Undercurrents of fear, resentment, and hatred swirled just beneath the surface, and most whites remained deeply ambivalent about the shrewd, enterprising Yankee in their midst. A prominent Coushatta businessman expressed this schizoid attitude in his testimony before a congressional committee:

Q. Are you acquainted with Mr. Twitchell?
A. I am.
Q. Have you financial confidence in him?
A. I have the utmost.
Q. Have you confidence in him as a politician?
A. Not at all.

Of far greater consequence, however, was that whites outside Red River increasingly saw the Radical boss as a symbol of something far more threatening than Radical corruption, incompetence, and failure: Radical strength, efficiency, and achievement.[33]

The first White League meeting in Coushatta on July 4 attracted about ninety whites, according to Twitchell's spies. To test white Republican strength the Yankee called a Republican meeting the same night on Black Lake, attended by some sixty whites. Despite the initial support, he soon noticed a change of attitude in the country. Men whom he considered to be his friends started to avoid him, and several confessed that they feared to be seen with him. Staunch Republicans moved out of the parish, and many others avowed that, unless the climate changed, they too would leave. Twitchell understood the pressure: "You will have to come out and be a White-Leaguer," he said ruefully to a Democratic friend, "or they will drive you out of the country." By mid-July the White League was organizing throughout the parish.[34]

The mounting crisis on the Red River coincided with plans for the August meeting of the Republican state convention in New Orleans.

33. *House Reports*, 44th Cong., 1st Sess., No. 816, p. 721. W. E. B. Du Bois' idea that conservative whites feared black honesty and achievement much more than they feared black corruption and failure also holds true for carpetbaggers (*Black Reconstruction in America* [New York, 1935], 624–25, 633).

34. *House Reports*, 43d Cong., 2d Sess., No. 261, Pt. 3, pp. 386–94; *House Reports*, 44th Cong., 1st Sess., No. 816, p. 654.

Amid reports of impending White League violence, Twitchell boarded a steamer for New Orleans on July 27. (Deweese traveled separately.) Hours later the vessel docked at Campti, and he learned that on that very day a White League mob had forced the resignations of Republican officials at Natchitoches, some miles downriver. For a few anxious minutes he agonized over whether to continue or turn back to Coushatta. The steamer pulled away from the shore, and he went on to New Orleans.[35]

The decision almost certainly saved his life, but it made sense for other reasons too. Natchitoches had been a bloodless coup, not another Colfax Massacre. If Red River stood next on the White League agenda (as informants reported), the tactic of forced resignations lost much of its effectiveness with both Twitchell and Deweese in New Orleans. In the capital, moreover, the two carpetbaggers could personally appeal for federal troops. That thought must have given the White League pause, because the showdown at Coushatta did not occur until a month after the Natchitoches resignations. Twitchell probably counted on the Coushatta Democrats not to harm his family and friends, unaware that White Leaguers from Coushatta had been present at Natchitoches and had received blunt warning to clean out the Radicals in their midst or have their neighbors do it for them.[36]

The situation at Coushatta, as Twitchell soon learned, was in fact desperate. The local White League is "red hot and on the war path," Sheriff Edgerton informed him. Their words are

> too strong for us to doubt their meaning any longer. It is simply extermination of the Carpetbag & Scalawag element. Nothing more nor less. You know how we are situated here. The negroes will support us to a man, but it is useless for us to involve them in a conflict which would be simply a massacre unless we had ammunition so that we can hold out until reinforced. On the other hand if driven to the wall what whites there is of us could and probably will form ourselves into a band and take [to] the woods and go to bushwhacking. But unless we are going to get some aid from U.S. or State forces we would gain nothing as it would be impossible for us to hold out any length of time. My intentions at pres-

35. "Autobiography of Marshall Harvey Twitchell," in Twitchell Papers, 132, 134, 138.
36. *Ibid.*; *House Reports*, 43d Cong., 2d Sess., No. 261, Pt. 3, p. 386.

ent are to hold out as long as possible and if necessary make them com-
mit *murder* before they make any man resign. It is barely possible we can
keep the crisis off for 10 days and perhaps two weeks. (In the language of
Warmoth) if Kellogg is Governor Show it. Urge upon him the necessity
of action and that prompt and vigorous. We are on the verge of Civil
War. An accident a drunken man, or a crazy fanatic is liable to start it at
any moment.

The sheriff added, "It is generally believed here that you have gone
after troops. It is my firm belief that you can live here only on horse-
back in the woods if you do not get them." [37]

Twitchell's reply could hardly have reassured the beleaguered sheriff: "Have seen the governor and United States Marshall. As soon as
some overt act has been committed, a United States marshall can be
sent up there, and will, doubtless, take United States troops with
him." He advised Edgerton to resign if necessary to save his life. [38]

In point of fact, General William H. Emory had taken almost every
soldier in the state to Holly Springs, Mississippi, to wait out the yellow
fever season. Moreover, the president and the army remained unim-
pressed by the White League and Governor Kellogg's pleas for help.
Twitchell thus found himself in a terrible dilemma: The longer he remained in New Orleans, the more the White League upriver suspected
the soldiers were not coming. Yet if he returned empty-handed, he exposed his own bluff. As parish attorney F. W. Howell warned, "Just as
sure as you return without United States Soldiers the trouble will then
commence." Howell observed darkly, "Strange Ruffians are often in
our town and say that they have come to kill Republicans." [39]

The last weekend in August, exhausted and dispirited by futile appeals for troops, Twitchell and Deweese went to Pass Christian, Mississippi, a small resort on the Mississippi Sound where Deweese had a
house. On Monday morning, August 31, a telegram arrived inform-

37. Two letters of same date, Frank S. Edgerton to Marshall Harvey Twitchell, July
30, 1874, in Twitchell Papers. I have taken the liberty of adding punctuation.
38. Marshall Harvey Twitchell to Frank S. Edgerton, August 4, 1874, in *House Reports*, 43d Cong., 2d Sess., No. 261, Pt. 3, p. 885.
39. According to Joseph G. Dawson III, only 130 bluecoats remained in the state at
Colfax, Baton Rouge, and New Orleans (*Army Generals and Reconstruction: Louisiana,
1862–1877* [Baton Rouge, 1982], 156–58); F. W. Howell to Marshall Harvey Twitchell,
August 17, 1874, in Twitchell Papers.

ing Twitchell that his brother Homer, his brothers-in-law Clark Holland and M. C. Willis, Deweese's brother Robert, Sheriff Edgerton, and parish attorney Howell had been murdered the previous day.[40]

The trouble had started the previous Tuesday at a boat landing about ten miles from Coushatta. Marauding whites murdered two black men, one of whom had the audacity to defend himself and kill one of the attackers with a shotgun. Shouting Negro revolt, White Leaguers descended on Coushatta from every part of the upper Red River Valley, and by Thursday night virtually every Republican leader in the parish was under arrest. On Saturday a White League mob hanged two black Radicals after a mock trial, and the next night they killed another Negro named Eli Allen. Some time before that a white horseman had attempted to run down Allen on the street in Coushatta. The muscular black man had grabbed the horse's bridle and pushed the animal away, causing the rider to fall off and break his leg. "Mr. Allen," Twitchell explained, "was a republican, under any and all circumstances, and it requires a brave colored man to say that in North Louisiana." His killers shot him, broke his arms and legs, and tortured him over a fire before he died.[41]

The white Republicans caught in the dragnet were Sheriff Edgerton, the parish attorney, the four members of the Twitchell and Deweese families, and Henry A. Scott, another Vermonter (some accounts mention an eighth figure). They remained prisoners in Coushatta through the weekend, first in a basement, then on the second floor of the hotel. They were permitted to write to but not to see their families. "Katie you can not come up here and don't think of coming for one moment," Clark Holland warned his wife. "We are all right and perfectly safe. . . . Everything will turn out right." "Darling Husband," she replied, they had passed a terrible night at Starlight. "When *Can* I see you?" Scott reassured his wife, too: "I think they mean to give us a fair show and I think we can convince them that we are not to blame for

---

40. "Autobiography of Marshall Harvey Twitchell," in Twitchell Papers, 139; *House Reports*, 43d Cong., 2d Sess., No. 261, Pt. 3, pp. 902–905; *Senate Executive Documents*, 43d Cong., 2d Sess., No. 17, pp. 16–17.

41. *House Reports*, 43d Cong., 2d Sess., No. 261, Pt. 3, pp. 388–89, 902–905; *Senate Executive Documents*, 43d Cong., 2d Sess., No. 17, pp. 16–17; Lestage, "White League," 671–75.

what has happened. Keep up good cheer and trust in God . . . He will deal justly with us."[42]

The captives resigned their offices on Saturday and swore in writing to leave the state. Some leaders of the local White League probably hoped no harm would come to them, but events were beyond their control; the mob on the street numbered in the hundreds and included men from as far away as Texas, and they were clamoring for blood. On Sunday morning, escorted by over thirty guards of their own choosing, the prisoners (except Scott, who remained behind and was allowed to escape) crossed the Red River and rode up the west bank toward Shreveport, planning to cross to the railhead at Monroe and leave Louisiana. "I think that we will get through without any trouble," Clark Holland had written Kate. "I am glad that I have not got another night to spend in Coushatta. . . . This will be the last time I can write before I go. Goodbye and may God bless you all and hope it will not be long before you can be with us." The captives carried a small fortune in cash and jewelry for the journey.[43]

The party crossed the Red River line into Caddo Parish in midafternoon, about thirty miles below Shreveport. A few miles farther on the leader called a halt, ostensibly to rest men and horses, but in fact to allow a lynch mob led by a notorious man called "Captain Jack" to catch up. Robert Deweese spied the forty-odd horsemen rushing upon them: "Mount and ride for your lives!" The prisoners bolted for their horses, but too late. Gunfire blasted Deweese from his horse before he fully mounted. "Give me a gun, I don't want to die like a dog!" shouted Homer Twitchell, before a bullet struck him in the face. Edgerton flung himself "flat on his horse, escaped the first volley, and made considerable distance before he was finally shot from his horse, answering back to their calls of surrender that he would die first." Holland,

42. Clark Holland to Kate Holland, [August, 1874]; Kate Holland to Clark Holland, [August, 1874]; Henry A. Scott to Emma Scott [August, 1874]; all in the possession of Clark Holland, the great grandson of Twitchell's brother-in-law, Medfield, Massachusetts.

43. *House Reports*, 43d Cong., 2d Sess., No. 261, Pt. 3, pp. 902–905; *Senate Executive Documents*, 43d Cong., 2d Sess., No. 17, pp. 16–17; Clark Holland to Kate Holland, [August, 1874], in the possession of Clark Holland.

Willis, and Howell surrendered. At no point did the guards offer the slightest resistance to the attackers.[44]

"Captain Jack" and his crew escorted the three captives to a place called Ward's Store and passed several hours debating their fate. A planter named Stringfellow offered $1,000 for the life of each man, but as he lacked the money in hand, the cutthroats decided to rob and murder them instead. They formed a makeshift firing squad and executed Howell and Willis. Desiring sport, they offered Holland the chance to make a run for it. "No," he replied, "you have murdered my friends now you may kill me." He asked only that his wife and son be allowed to escape unharmed to the North. He walked forward to the bodies of Willis and Howell and died.[45]

Stringfellow and some of his neighbors buried the six Republicans in two graves about two miles apart. They lay undisturbed for over two months. In mid-November a detachment of the Seventh Cavalry rode down from Shreveport and disinterred the bodies. The lieutenant in charge reported that the victims had been robbed ($800 from Homer Twitchell alone) and mutilated: "One of the bodies (name unknown) was so perforated and gashed with bullets that it was only with great care that it could be moved without falling to pieces, while the private parts of another (name also unknown) were mutilated, shot off."[46]

The massacre shattered Republican morale throughout the state. Radical officials had been murdered before, of course: the sheriff and the judge of St. Mary Parish in 1868, and Judge Thomas S. Crawford and District Attorney A. H. Harris in a Franklin Parish ambush in the fall of 1873. But never had six white Republicans, the officials of an

---

44. "Autobiography of Marshall Harvey Twitchell," in Twitchell Papers, 146–48. Twitchell learned the details of the massacre from eyewitnesses, probably the guards and members of the burial detail who had been at Ward's Store. He never identified his informants because it would have exposed them to certain death (*House Reports*, 43d Cong., 2d Sess., No. 261, Pt. 3, p. 395). While no such account could be completely accurate in every detail, Twitchell's version agrees with all the known facts and is as close to the truth as we are ever likely to get. Incidentally, "Captain Jack's" last name was Coleman, but he was not related to Twitchell's in-laws.

45. *Ibid.*

46. *Senate Executive Documents*, 43d Cong., 2d Sess., No. 17, p. 13.

entire parish, been murdered. The killings struck fear into every car-petbagger and scalawag in Louisiana. Who would the next victims be? The impact was no less dramatic on blacks. White Republicans like Twitchell substituted for the paternalism of the antebellum plantation the paternalism of the local Republican machine. The events at Cou-shatta cracked the foundation of that system. Negroes, Twitchell ex-plained, looked to white Republicans for protection and security; they perceived, however, that "if the White League was strong enough to take their leaders from them, and murder them in cold blood, they were strong enough to reduce them to slavery, or anything else they chose." Major Lewis Merrill reported that all along the upper Red River for many weeks after the massacre, "scarcely a negro, and in no instance a negro who was at all prominent in politics, dared to sleep in his home."[47]

By September the White League had overturned or crippled the Radical governments of at least eight parishes. Inspired by success and by President Grant's failure to send troops, the White League in New Orleans planned an even bigger coup: the forced resignation of Gover-nor Kellogg and the overthrow of the Republican state. Organized into militia companies and well equipped with arms from the North, the White League demanded Kellogg's resignation in the early after-noon of September 14. Three hours later some 3,000 black militia un-der General Longstreet and 500 Metropolitan Police engaged a supe-rior White League force. The result was a rout of the Radical defenders and the temporary overthrow of the state government. For three days the White League ruled supreme in New Orleans. The overthrow of Kellogg inspired the eviction of still more Radical officials in the hinterlands.[48]

The news of the Battle of Canal Street reached Twitchell at Pass Christian. He and Deweese had gone to New Orleans immediately after learning of the Coushatta massacre, but unable to go upriver without troops, they had returned to Mississippi. The day after the

47. *House Reports*, 43d Cong., 2d Sess., No. 261, Pt. 3, pp. 176, 389.
48. Dawson, *Army Generals and Reconstruction*, 167–78; Taylor, *Louisiana Recon-structed*, 291–96; Otis A. Singletary, *Negro Militia and Reconstruction* (Austin, 1957), 74–79; see Stuart Omer Landry, *The Battle of Liberty Place: The Overthrow of Carpet-Bag Rule in New Orleans, September 14, 1874* (New Orleans, 1955).

battle Twitchell caught the New Orleans train, stepped off at the Canal Street Station, and ignoring the triumphant White Leaguers on every street, walked briskly and alone through the heart of the city to the Louisiana Safe-Deposit Company. He removed some securities and carried them to the Custom House, which was crowded with Republicans seeking refuge on federal property, and put them in the safe. The Vermonter then walked alone to the station and took the train back to Pass Christian. Friends and enemies alike who witnessed this strange peregrination gaped in astonishment at the solitary figure. Perhaps he was concerned only for the safety of his investments, but one suspects a deeper motive: that his defiance of the White League was the act of a man tormented by guilt, courting death as absolution.[49]

Nothing on the scale of the insurrection in New Orleans had occurred since the Civil War. Grant now had no choice, and six regiments of federal troops rushed back into Louisiana by the end of September. The District of the Upper Red River was created under the command of Major Lewis Merrill, a veteran of the 1871 Ku Klux uprising in South Carolina. A staunch Republican, he had earned the epithet "Dog Merrill" from South Carolina Democrats. The major established Seventh Cavalry headquarters at Shreveport on the eve of the 1874 election. "This whole community is practically an armed mob," he reported. Believing a virtual state of war exists, the people here recognized "no such thing as the existence of law, or any authority save individual will"; the entire region bordered on anarchy. Terrified blacks slept in the woods at night, and one cavalry troop, entering the Campo Bello precinct of Caddo Parish, reported the astonishing sight of freedmen flinging "themselves on the ground shouting with joy" at the sight of Union soldiers.[50]

With eight undermanned companies the major attempted to restore law and order. He helped reinstate Kellogg officials at Shreveport and Natchitoches and suppressed the most overt forms of White League violence. Yet he could not stop white landowners from routinely

49. "Autobiography of Marshall Harvey Twitchell," in Twitchell Papers, 149–50.
50. Dawson, *Army Generals and Reconstruction*, 173–80, 185–89; *Senate Executive Documents*, 43d Cong., 2d Sess., No. 17, p. 5; *House Reports*, 43d Cong., 2d Sess., No. 261, Pt. 3, p. 175.

cheating black farmers of a year's labor or discharging them for voting Republican. The major estimated that 500 black families in Caddo and De Soto parishes were driven from their homes that fall and winter for political reasons. He perhaps exaggerated; on the other hand, Caddo and De Soto were both over 65 percent black and both went Democratic in 1874. In truth, the Republican position on the Red River lay beyond the skill of a few Union companies to restore, no less than Louisiana lay beyond the skill of a few regiments. As Merrill told a United States House committee, "There is not in Louisiana to-day any such thing as a government at all. . . . A government has among its attributes power to enforce at least some show of obedience to law, and that does not exist to-day in Louisiana. The State government has no power outside of the United States Army, which is here to sustain it—no power at all. The White League is the only power in the State." A pro-Democratic officer who investigated the Louisiana situation that December arrived at an identical conclusion: "The present State government cannot maintain itself in power a single hour without the protection of Federal troops." [51]

Events in New Orleans soon proved the aptness of these judgments. The Kellogg Returning Board countered White League terrorism in the 1874 election by recounting the votes, thereby converting a solid Democratic majority in the lower chamber into a fifty-three-to-fifty-three tie, with five contested seats to be decided by the house itself. When the legislature met in January 1875, enraged Democrat-White Leaguers attempted a forcible takeover of the house. Federal troops entered the State House and thwarted yet another coup (although the Democrats later gained control of the house anyway). General Philip H. Sheridan, on the scene at Grant's order, took command and without mincing words proposed that Congress or the president declare the ringleaders of the White Leagues in Louisiana, Arkansas, and Mississippi "banditti" and then let the army deal with them under martial law. "Little Phil's" actions created a furor North and South. The North's eagerness to disengage itself from Reconstruction may be

51. *Senate Executive Documents*, 43d Cong., 2d Sess., No. 17, pp. 58, 73; *House Reports*, 43d Cong., 2d Sess., No. 261, Pt. 3, p. 179.

measured by this: The controversy above the Potomac centered on Sheridan's actions and not those of the White League conspirators.[52]

Twitchell returned to Coushatta in October 1874 in the company of soldiers. In time he restored a semblance of control over the parish, but all attempts to bring the Coushatta murderers to justice ended in failure. Moreover, he lived in continual fear of his own life, never again residing for any length of time at Starlight. In the summer of 1875 he visited Vermont, purchased a home, and moved his mother and son and two orphaned nephews into it.[53] During the trip he renewed his relationship with Henrietta Day, his sweetheart from seminary days. When he returned to Louisiana, they were engaged to be married.

A letter survives that Marshall wrote Henrietta from New Orleans that October; it reveals a man tortured by guilt and mercilessly hounded by threats against his life: "I am just in from the streets where I have been looking for a danger of which I was warned last night. . . . I received a telegram in cypher from Coushatta telling me to 'load my pistol, refuse all company and stay in my room.' I armed myself and went all over town last night and again this morning looking for the danger of which I was warned. [I] can't find it, but I fear this continual harrassing will make a demon of me." Perhaps from his own guilt, he believed that his sisters blamed him for the deaths of their husbands. He was tempted to put "aside as my enemies do, the laws of God and man, and . . . become an avenger." He had fallen asleep the previous night "thinking of it, and strange for me, commenced dreaming." In the dream he stood in a room before his weeping mother and sisters and frightened son. He had resolved to avenge the murders of his family members. "I turned to go and you stood before me attempting to put your arms around my neck. I attempted to avoid you, but at every turn you were in front of me. I felt if you once had your arms around my neck my resolution would fail." No matter which way he turned, Henrietta blocked the door. "I awoke and was thankful it was only

52. Taylor, *Louisiana Reconstructed*, 304–307; William Gillette, *Retreat From Reconstruction, 1869–1879* (Baton Rouge, 1979), 122–29, 134; Dawson, *Army Generals and Reconstruction*, 199–210; *Senate Executive Documents*, 43d Cong., 2d Sess., No. 13, p. 23.
53. "Autobiography of Marshall Harvey Twitchell," in Twitchell Papers, 164.

a dream." A few weeks later Twitchell received another telegram from Coushatta: His sister Kate Holland had died of yellow fever at Starlight.[54]

In the winter of 1876 the Vermonter attended another crisis session of the Louisiana legislature. In February he played a major part in the one-day impeachment and acquittal of Governor Kellogg. He returned to the upper Red River in late April, intending to remain only a week or two and then escape to the North until after the 1876 election. On May 1, Twitchell observed an unusual number of prominent Democrats in Coushatta, for no apparent reason. Asking the occasion, he received the reply that an issue of long standing was being decided. It later occurred to him that the question under discussion was the fate of Marshall Harvey Twitchell.[55]

The following morning the carpetbagger and his surviving brother-in-law George King left Starlight for a meeting of the police jury in Coushatta. A few miles downriver the two men boarded a ferry-skiff with its Negro operator opposite the town. As the ferry neared the Coushatta shore Twitchell noticed a strangely garbed figure walking on the bank above. Witnesses agreed that the man wore a long rubber or oilcloth coat that nearly touched the ground, a false beard, eye goggles, and a hat pulled low over the face. He had ridden into town that morning and waited at the blacksmith shop until he observed Twitchell and King leave their buggy across the river and board the ferry. As the skiff thudded into the Coushatta bank, Twitchell saw him take a Winchester repeater from his coat. "Down in the boat!" he shouted to King. Twitchell was hit almost immediately. King drew a pistol and fired at least once before the assassin above put a bullet in his head, killing him almost instantly. Wounded in the leg, Twitchell, in his own words, "jumped into the water and went under the boat, holding to the edge of the boat first with one hand and then with the other, until he had broken both [my] arms by shots, shielding my body by remaining under the skiff." Children playing not far off thought the

---

54. Marshall Harvey Twitchell to Henrietta Day, October 12, 1875, in Twitchell Papers; "Autobiography of Marshall Harvey Twitchell," both in Twitchell Papers, 164.
55. "Autobiography of Marshall Harvey Twitchell," in Twitchell Papers, 169–73, 176.

man on the bank was shooting an alligator: "It is an alligator. Let us go and see the alligator." A housewife commenced screaming, believing the man with the rifle was shooting her husband. A man rode up from town to investigate the shooting; the disguised figure turned and leveled the rifle on him, telling him, "God damn you, go back!" The rider quickly retreated.

The assassin emptied his rifle and started shooting a pistol. Mrs. E. J. Merrell appeared on the bank: "I saw a man who looked to be dead in the skiff. I said to the ferryman, 'For God's sake save that drowning man.'" She pleaded with the man in the coat to stop firing. The black ferryman reached down and grabbed the wounded and exhausted Twitchell, but a pistol ball through his hand broke his grip. William L. Mudgett, a carpetbagger and a close friend of Twitchell, appeared on the opposite bank and fired his pistol at the assassin across the wide expanse of the Red River. By now a number of people had gathered at the scene. Coaxed by Twitchell, the ferryman called out that the man in the water was dead. The assassin walked to his horse, mounted, and rode calmly away. Mrs. Merrell's servant asked him as he rode past if it was not an alligator. "Yes," he said, "it is a damned black alligator."[56]

Twitchell drifted free in the current, feigning death. The wounded ferryman maneuvered the skiff alongside and somehow got him aboard. He had been hit six times, twice in each arm, once in the leg, and once in the back of the neck. Northern friends carried him to a cabin on the Starlight side of the river and sent for an army surgeon. For nearly a month he struggled for life, and more than once his sister and the friends who nursed and guarded him gave him up for lost. He lived, but the surgeon amputated both arms, and he never fully recovered the use of his injured leg. The first week in June he was carried on a litter before a United States house committee whose members had journeyed upriver to investigate this most recent "Coushatta Affair." Since the 1874 election, the House of Representatives, like the lower chamber in New Orleans, contained a Democratic majority. The Democratic-controlled committee concluded that the murder of

56. *Ibid.*, 176–80; *House Reports*, 44th Cong., 1st Sess., No. 816, pp. 645–46, 649–51, 657–62.

King and the attempted assassination of Twitchell were "not of a political character."[57]

A few weeks later, carried on a litter, Twitchell left Red River Parish
under military guard, never to return. He and his sister Helen Willis
boarded a North-bound train in New Orleans. Helen, however, never
finished the journey. Mentally and physically exhausted, she fell
gravely ill in Indianapolis and died. Of the nine members of the
Twitchell clan who had settled in Louisiana, only Marshall and his
mother, Elizabeth, now survived. For her brother, Helen's death was
both the most difficult to bear and a catharsis.

> I do not think that I am lacking in affection for my friends and relatives,
> but the manner in which they were taken away, the venom of the South-
> ern press and the fact that so many people of both races were looking to
> me for protection, support and encouragement, dried up the fountain of
> my tears, and every fresh outrage but stimulated me to greater exertions
> for the acquisition of wealth and power for the punishment of the
> wrong-doers. Until I was rendered so helpless by their last attack I
> firmly believed that right would finally prevail and that I would see the
> murderers legally punished for their crimes in the judicial district where
> those crimes were committed. When informed that Helen was dead, that
> the last of my family was gone, the only hands which I could trust to do
> my bidding powerless in death, I fully recognized that justice for the
> murder of my family would never be done and for the first time tears
> came to my relief.[58]

Recovered by that autumn, Twitchell was fitted with artificial limbs
at the Centennial Exposition in Philadelphia. Soon afterward he married Henrietta Day (she would bear him two children, but only one
would survive to adulthood). In January 1877 he returned to New Orleans for what proved the last crisis session of the Radical senate. Most
of his Republican colleagues had not seen him since the loss of his
arms, and many could not keep back the tears when he entered the
senate chamber. The Democratic senator Edward D. White, later an
associate justice of the United States Supreme Court, crossed the aisle
and attempted to greet him, but "his emotions would not allow him to

57. "Autobiography of Marshall Harvey Twitchell," in Twitchell Papers, 176–80;
House Reports, 44th Cong., 2d Sess., No. 816, pp. 648–57.
58. "Autobiography of Marshall Harvey Twitchell," in Twitchell Papers, 200–202.

speak and he returned to his own side of the chamber." In 1878 President Rutherford B. Hayes appointed Twitchell the American consul at Kingston in Ontario, Canada. The location enabled him to travel easily to Vermont.[59]

Like the biblical Job, the carpetbagger's misfortunes seemed never-ending. Sensing trouble, he had transferred the titles of his most valuable Louisiana holdings, Starlight and Briar Bend to his mother. Even though he had purchased both estates legally and paid good money for them, the original owners or their heirs brought suit to regain both properties. Unable to live in or even visit Red River Parish, Twitchell had left his lands under the management of attorney J. W. Harrison, another Vermont carpetbagger. In 1878 Harrison was assassinated. Thereafter, Gus Coleman (the Coleman family remained loyal to the end) and William L. Mudgett looked after Twitchell's interests. The litigation dragged on into the early 1880s, and in every instance the state courts ruled against the Vermonters, and the Louisianians foiled repeated attempts to get the cases into the federal courts. Legal fees consumed the remainder of Twitchell's Louisiana holdings. The fortune he estimated at over $100,000 vanished in the space of a few years. The one-time political boss and wealthy landowner lived the rest of his life as the consul at Kingston. At the turn of the century he gathered his papers and newspaper clippings about him and wrote his autobiography, telling his version of Radical Reconstruction on the upper Red River. He died in 1905 and lies buried at the foot of Twitchell Mountain in Townshend, Vermont.[60]

59. *Ibid.*, 225–27, 229–30; Civil War Pension Files.
60. "Autobiography of Marshall Harvey Twitchell," in Twitchell Papers, 229–30, 233; *Stafford* vs. *Twitchell, Louisiana Annual Reports,* vol. 33, pp. 520–32; *Gillespie* vs. *Twitchell,* 288–300; L. Watkins (attorney) to Marshall Harvey Twitchell, September 24, 1878, and A. F. (Gus) Coleman to Marshall Harvey Twitchell, January 25 and April 14, 1880, all in Twitchell Papers; Twitchell Interrogatories, in Twitchell Papers; Shoalmire, "Carpetbagger Extraordinary," 229–37.

Epilogue

Stephen B. Packard, observed the *Daily Picayune* on April 18, 1877, sits in the St. Louis Hotel and watches "every branch of his government falling to pieces." For three and a half months the situation in New Orleans had resembled a revival of 1873, with Packard playing the part invented by Kellogg, and Francis T. Nicholls taking McEnery's role. This time, however, as most Republicans realized, the ending had been rewritten. Over a week had passed since the news flashed across the wires that President Hayes had withdrawn federal troops from South Carolina. P. B. S. Pinchback had foreseen the denouement from the start; on January 13 he and another black senator had taken their seats in the Nicholls legislature (a few others had taken the cue). Understandably, many Republicans remained bitter against President Hayes; one carpetbagger predicted that four years hence Hayes would be returned to private life, his name reviled throughout the land. In the meantime, the newspapers reported that ex-Governor Kellogg, now in the United States Senate, had purchased a house in Washington and had no intention of returning to Louisiana. Ex-Governor Warmoth and his longtime friend and ally William L. McMillen, no admirers of Packard, remained in New Orleans holding the despairing Radicals together. On April 21 the long-dreaded news arrived: Hayes had ordered the soldiers guarding the State House back to their barracks. A black leader from Morehouse Parish expressed the Republican consensus: he had "stood by the Republican ship as long as it was in sight," but it had now vanished from view. Three days later Packard yielded his claim to the governor's office. Louisiana, he observed ruefully, the first state reconstructed, fittingly became the last to fall. In a parting shot, he predicted that Radicalism would rise again.[1]

1. Appleton's *Annual Cyclopaedia (1877)*, 458–65; New Orleans *Daily Picayune*, April 10, 15, 18, 19, 20, 22, 1877.

In the end, the accomplishments of Radical Louisiana were few. Its civil rights laws and constitution represented both a noble effort on behalf of human equality and a testament to the granite rigidity of Southern race traditions. One Northerner had declared in the constitutional convention of 1864, "I tell you, sir, if the South had had a system of free general education the same as the North, this rebellion would have never occurred." To the Republicans' lasting credit, a decade and a half later 34,642 Negroes received the rudiments of an education. Yet white school attendance actually declined slightly between 1860 and 1880, and nearly half the state's people remained illiterate. Republicans hoped to infect Louisiana with the germ of Yankee enterprise; judged by the railroad charters and subsidies approved by the Radical legislature, Louisiana in 1877 was traversed by track and every country town was a thriving entrepôt. But the Republican railroads remained, for the most part, paper projects that the Redeemers completed after their downfall. Of the most important economic development of the period, the evolution of the crop-lien system, it may be said that the Radical government influenced it not at all.[2] In their own defense, the Republicans might have noted the difficulty of building schools and railroads while dodging bullets.

In the 1879 classic, *A Fool's Errand: By One of the Fools*, the North Carolina carpetbagger Albion W. Tourgée explained how the Wise Men of the North entrusted the fate of Southern republics to a handful of carpetbaggers and scalawags and a black race whose members were politically unskilled, wretchedly poor, and largely illiterate. Against this fragile alliance was "pitted the wealth, the intelligence, the organizing skill, the pride, and the hate of a people whom it had taken four years to conquer in open fight when their enemies outnumbered them three to one." Given the North's reluctance to intervene and its "Root, hog, or die!" attitude, the outcome was inevitable. A century of his-

---

2. *Debates in the Convention* (1864), 494–95; *Ninth Census, 1870, Population*, I, 394–95; *Compendium of the Tenth Census, 1880*, Pt. 2, pp. 1641, 1645; Edwin Dale Odom, "Louisiana Railroads, 1830–1888: A Study of State and Local Aid" (Ph.D. dissertation, Tulane University, 1961); economic historians generally discuss the rise of the crop-lien system as if the Republican regimes had never existed; see, for example, Roger L. Ransom and Richard Sutch, *One Kind of Freedom: The Economic Consequences of Emancipation* (Cambridge, Eng., 1977).

torical writing has not significantly altered Tourgée's analysis. "Given prevailing attitudes," concludes a recent writer, "both popular and elite—toward race relations and the role of government, it is difficult to imagine that Southern Republicanism could have been followed by anything other than the Democratic restoration." The ink had barely dried on the Reconstruction Acts before the North began having second thoughts, writes another scholar; Reconstruction ended almost before it started.[3]

This mind-set (of which the present work is admittedly no exception) easily ignores the Republicans' real assets, especially in Louisiana. Outside the Crescent City, the state was nearly 60 percent black, and most black leaders were not impoverished ex-slaves but literate free men of color. The black masses may have been unlettered, but they lacked neither common sense nor bravery. In the 1876 election, despite massive intimidation, every parish on the Red River gave majorities to Packard and Hayes; in fact, the Radicals' hold on the alluvial Y remained unbroken, eloquent testimony to the courage of tens of thousands of anonymous men.[4] We easily forget, too, that while Confederate veterans were legion, some 25,000 Louisiana blacks, scalawags, and carpetbaggers had fought in the Union armies. Governors Warmoth and Kellogg, as well as most of their top aides, were ex-soldiers. The commander of the state militia, James A. Longstreet, ranked as one of the finest corps commanders of the Civil War. At the Battle of Canal Street the White League had the edge in numbers, but the Radicals had a battery of artillery and two Gatling guns. The Civil

3. Albion W. Tourgée, *A Fool's Errand,* ed. John Hope Franklin (Cambridge, 1961), 136–37; Morton Keller, *Affairs of State: Public Life in Late Nineteenth Century America* (Cambridge, 1977), 229; William Gillette, *Retreat from Reconstruction, 1869–1879* (Baton Rouge, 1979), 363–67; see Joe Gray Taylor's "Louisiana: An Impossible Task," in Otto H. Olsen (ed.), *Reconstruction and Redemption in the South* (Baton Rouge, 1980), 202–35.

4. The Democratic returns show Nicholls beating Packard 84,487 to 76,477. The official Republican returns, before the returning board worked its magic act, have Nicholls winning by a much narrower margin, 81,502 to 76,067. The Republican returns probably come closer to expressing the true sentiment of the state (*Senate Reports,* 44th Cong., 2d Sess., No. 701, III, 3002–3003, 3006–3007). Some years ago as a young graduate student I argued that Republican claims of intimidation in the 1876 election were greatly exaggerated ("The Negro, the Republican Party, and the Election of 1876 in Louisiana," *Louisiana History,* VII [Spring, 1966], 101–116). I was clearly wrong.

War had demonstrated many times that mere numbers were no substitute for discipline and firepower; Longstreet had taught that bloody lesson to Union generals on repeated occasions. The failure of the regime in New Orleans was less a failure of resources than a failure of will. The White League embodied an extraordinary consensus that white supremacy was worth fighting for; no such consensus sustained the Radicals.

Nor were white Republicans entirely to blame. During the rioting in New Orleans in 1868, for example, blacks repeatedly sought Lieutenant Governor Dunn's counsel. A revealing exchange on the subject occurred between Dunn and a Congressman:

> *Question.* When [Negroes] were in trouble they would naturally come to you as a leader among them for advice?
> *Answer.* Yes, sir; and when they asked me, I did not like to advise them . . . so I just told them I had no advice to give them, they must use their own judgement.

He confessed that he avoided his people as much as possible during the crisis. Senator Pinchback, for once, reacted differently. Black people "have nearly reached the end of their string," he shouted on the senate floor. "The next outrage . . . will be the signal for the dawn of retribution . . . a signal that will cause ten thousand torches to be applied to this city; for patience will then have ceased to be a virtue, and this city will be reduced to ashes."[5] Events proved, however, that Pinchback's angry words were just rhetoric, and as long as they remained so, whites flogged and murdered Republicans without fear of retribution.

This softness at the core not only crippled the Republicans at home, it badly damaged them in the North. "The Louisiana troubles are doing our party more harm than anything that has occurred in a long time," observed future Republican president James A. Garfield during the "banditti" crisis. The problem, however, lay much deeper than the current controversy. As Garfield noted, "It seems to me there is really no Government in Louisiana." The crisis made a similar impact on General William T. Sherman. "I have always thought it wrong," he

5. *House Miscellaneous Documents*, 41st Cong., 2d Sess., No. 154, Pt. 1, p. 178; New York *Times*, September 6, 1868.

confided to his eminent brother, "to bolster up weak State govern-ments by our troops." He professed embarrassment at "the plain, pal-pable fact, that the Union whites" in New Orleans "are cowardly, and allow the Rebel element that loves to fight, to cow them. Until the Union whites, and negroes too, *fight* for their own rights they will be trodden down." Such views were widespread. The events of Septem-ber 1874, Samuel S. Cox recalled, revealed the complete helplessness of the Kellogg government, "a humiliating confession of incapacity to govern."[6] Many Northerners retreated from Reconstruction, in other words, less because they were racists than because it seemed futile to go on supporting losers.

By the time Kellogg became governor, the Republican cause proba-bly lay beyond repair. In the early years, when their options remained open, the Radicals simultaneously tried defending themselves against whites while, through conciliation, wooing whites into the Republi-can fold. Unfortunately, the search for white support proved as elusive as the end of the rainbow; it also undercut the strategy of defense, as in the case of the disastrous decision, for example, to divide the state mi-litia between blacks and ex-Rebels. The question naturally arises; Why did the Republicans not see the futility of conciliation earlier and, as General Sherman suggested, fight for their rights? Why not create a disciplined, well-armed, and combat-ready black militia? Why not deal with terrorists under martial law with summary trials and execu-tions? Why not teach whites that when Republicans died in ambushes, the certainty existed that white leaders would meet similar fates?

In September 1874 a Bayou Sara official wrote a revealing letter to United States Marshal Packard, pleading for help against the White League: "We have a large majority over the leaguers here, but if we arm the colored people, they will say at once that it is a 'negro riot.' We are in a 'bad fix,' feeling strong enough to whip the whole party,

6. James A. Garfield to Charles E. Henry, January 8 and 15, 1875, in James D. Norris and Arthur H. Shaffer (eds.), *Politics and Patronage in the Gilded Age: The Correspondence of James A. Garfield and Charles E. Henry* (Madison, 1970), 130–35; William T. Sherman to John Sherman, January 7 and February 3, 1875, in Rachel Sherman Thorndike (ed.), *The Sherman Letters: Correspondence Between General Sherman and Senator Sherman from 1837 to 1891* (New York, 1894), 342–44; Samuel S. Cox, *Three Decades of Federal Legisla-tion, 1855 to 1885* (New York, 1885), 366–68.

but afraid, for the reasons given in the foregoing. The parish is in an open state of rebellion. Nothing but United States troops will save us." In other words, given a choice between arming blacks and defeat, Republican officials in the town chose defeat. This mentality doomed the regime. The explanation for it, I believe, lies partly in the Radicals' ties to the North and their awareness of Reconstruction as a partisan issue in national politics. Armed resistance meant black resistance and would have resulted in pitched battles between blacks and whites, perhaps even in the war of races that whites forever warned against. Republicans instinctively realized, General Sherman notwithstanding, that most Northerners would sympathize with Negroes as victims but not—whatever the provocation—as aggressors against whites. One can imagine scenarios, in fact, in which the federal government intervenes on behalf of the Knights of the White Camellia or the White League. Imagine the probable Northern reaction, for example, if black militia had killed 105 whites at Colfax instead of vice versa.[7]

Plainly, though, there was more. The extent to which white paramilitary groups intimidated Reconstruction Republicans calls to mind Michael C. C. Adams' study of the Virginia theater in the Civil War. Adams suggests that the Army of the Potomac was handicapped from the first day of the war by an inferiority complex; many "Northern soldiers, and civilians . . . doubted their ability to whip the Rebels. They felt inferior to the enemy and hence their actions lacked the flair and the drive that confidence supplies." The cause of this inferiority complex lay in the common belief that whereas commerce and industry had made the North soft and sapped its military spirit, the institution of slavery, the plantation, and the cavalier tradition had molded Southerners into a distinctively martial people skilled in the ways of violence.[8] It requires only a small step of the imagination to see the implication of these ideas for Reconstruction. In fact, the statements by Tourgée and General Sherman quoted earlier express exactly the

7. F. A. Weber to Stephen B. Packard, September 22, 1874, in *House Executive Documents*, 44th Cong., 2d Sess., No. 30, pp. 358–59; Taylor, "Louisiana: An Impossible Task," 221.
8. Michael C. C. Adams, *Our Masters the Rebels: A Speculation on Union Military Failure in the East, 1861–1865* (Cambridge, 1978), vii–viii.

kind of attitudes to which Adams refers. Tourgée describes the Southerners as "a people whom it had taken four years to conquer in open fight when their enemies outnumbered them three to one," and Sherman claimed that "the Union whites . . . allow the Rebel element that loves to fight, to cow them."[9] If Northerners had doubted the ability of their own sons to whip the hard-fighting Rebels, how much more might carpetbag governors, or scalawags, have questioned the ability of Negro militia to fight those same Rebels organized as the White League on anything like equal terms. The specter of race war haunted Reconstruction like a recurring nightmare; no white Republican wanted the responsibility for triggering such a conflict because none of them doubted who the winners would be.

Black Republicans were also intimidated. Unlike some carpetbaggers, they need not have read cavalier novels to know that their exmasters were prone to violence; they had learned that at the source. They knew how long the Yankees had struggled to subdue the South and the respect that Rebel military feats engendered in most Northerners. They had witnessed a succession of terrorist campaigns since the war, campaigns that neither their own Radical government nor the government of the North seemed able to stop. More fundamentally, even if modern historians have exaggerated the paternalistic nature of slavery, the likelihood is that the experience of that institution created a formidable barrier to the kind of broad-scale military resistance that the Republicans needed. Seeing the White Leaguers, who were obviously ready for a fight, advancing across the open river front that sultry September 14 in New Orleans, an armed black man would have been only human were he to experience a sinking depression and heed a voice inside his head that was urging him to flee. In point of fact, no more than ten minutes elapsed before Kellogg's militia broke and ran.[10]

Still, none of this, not anxiety about the North, the ex-Rebels' genuine military prowess, nor any Radical inferiority complex fully ex-

9. Tourgée, *Fool's Errand*, 136; William T. Sherman to John Sherman, February 3, 1875, *Sherman Letters*, 344.
10. Stuart Omer Landry, *The Battle of Liberty Place: The Overthrow of Carpet-Bag Rule in New Orleans, September 14, 1874* (New Orleans, 1955), 99, 106, 121.

plains the Republicans' dismal military performance. Handicaps, after all, can be overcome. If the Army of the Potomac had no psychological handicap at the start of the Civil War, years of uninspiring generalship certainly gave it one, yet in the end it slugged its way into Richmond. The case can be made that Louisiana whites started Reconstruction with greater disadvantages than the Republicans. As a voting minority they challenged not only Warmoth and Kellogg, but the victorious North and the army that had beaten Lee. President Grant ripped victory from their grasp time and again without daunting their spirit. The overthrow of Reconstruction, Kenneth M. Stampp has written, "shows what a people can do against overwhelming odds when their morale is high, when they believe in their cause, and when they are convinced that defeat means catastrophe." [11] High morale, commitment, and the daring to fight against odds were exactly the qualities that were in short supply on the Republican side. More often than not, as Northern critics charged, Kellogg and his party wallowed in helplessness, crying for federal troops. A harsh verdict can scarcely be avoided: Reconstruction failed on the lower Mississippi mainly because Louisiana whites believed more devoutly in white supremacy than the Radicals believed in the rights of man.

Such a conclusion suggests a hidden factor in the Radicals' downfall. To understate the matter, most white Republicans were less than comfortable as the leaders of a mostly black political movement. For their part, blacks endured such mealymouthed spokesmen in the hope of defusing the race war time bomb. Militant Republican resistance against white terrorism would have upset this relationship. The creation of a Spartan black militia, one capable of fighting toe-to-toe with the White League, would likely have resulted in battles that would have made Colfax and September 14 seem like schoolboy roughhousing. Such battles just might have saved the regime, however, and perhaps even inspired Republicans in other states to emulate the example. Putting aside the real potential for federal intervention against the militant blacks, one almost certain result of such a scenario would have been a drastic loss of power by white Republicans. With the race war

11. Kenneth M. Stampp, *The Imperiled Union: Essays on the Background of the Civil War* (New York, 1980), 269.

issue out in the open and the bomb detonated, Negroes would no longer need or tolerate white leaders like Warmoth and Kellogg. If black militia had put down the 1874 White League uprising, P. B. S. Pinchback or someone like him would likely have become governor in the next election. Thereafter white Republicans would have played the kind of second-class role that they had previously assigned to blacks. Whether white leaders thought such matters through is unclear, but they often acted as if they preferred a White League victory to the consequences of successful black resistance.

Appendix I

Louisiana Unionists
1861–1865

The Unionists in Table 1 and Table 2 were identified mainly from these sources: *Proceedings of the Convention of the Friends of Freedom;* mass meeting of Union men reported in the New Orleans *Times,* January 10, 1864; *Debates in the Convention (1864)*; *Louisiana House Debates,* 1864–65 (Free State legislature); *Louisiana Senate Debates,* 1864–65 (Free State legislature); and *House Miscellaneous Documents,* 41st Cong., 2d Sess., No. 154, Pts. 1–2.

The principal sources of information were the United States Census, Manuscript Returns, 1860, Population; *Official Register of the United States,* 1863–1879 (inclusive); *House Miscellaneous Documents,* 41st Cong., 2d Sess., No. 154, Pts. 1–2; and various New Orleans city directories. The criterion for inclusion was overt evidence of Unionism and knowledge of nativity. With some misgivings I have included the names of a few men like Edmund Abell and Thomas Cottman whose Unionism was plainly shaky. Because I was never able to learn their place of birth, I have not included some important figures such as Ezra Heistand and John Henderson. There is no reason to believe that their inclusion would have changed the overall pattern in any way.

Table 1. LOUISIANA UNIONISTS
(Those Living Outside Orleans and Jefferson Parishes)

Name	Residence, 1860	Year and Place of Birth	Occupation, 1860	Property	Slaves
Balch, Joseph H.	Iberville	New York	Assistant Marshal/ Notary Public	$9,000	5
Barlow, J. H. C.	Rapides	Louisiana	Lawyer/Planter		At Least 20
Beauvais, Raphael	St. James	1836, Louisiana	Lawyer	None Listed	0
Belden, Simeon	St. Martin	1830, Massachusetts	Lawyer	None Listed	0
Benson, Robert R.	St. Martin	1820, New Jersey	Hotelkeeper	$15,000	2
Blackburn, W. Jasper	Claiborne	1820, Arkansas	Editor	$6,000	0
Boyce, Charles W.	Rapides	1827, Massachusetts	Printer	$20,000	2
Burbank, Samuel M.	St. John	1825, New York	Planter	$70,000	55
Calhoun, William	Rapides	1834, France	Son of Meridith Calhoun (Pennsylvania)	Father owned $1,129,900	(Father Owned 709)
Cazabat, Anthony	Rapides	1830, France	Lawyer	$10,500	3
Collin, Emile	Ascension	1827, France	Cooper	$600	0
Cooley, William H.	Point Coupee	1832, Louisiana	Lawyer	$12,500	8
Cottman, Dr. Thomas	Ascension	1810, Maryland	Planter/ Veterinarian	$14,000	28
Crawford, Isaac W.	Franklin	1826, Kentucky	Lawyer	$3,400	1
Crawford, Thomas S.	Caldwell	1819, Kentucky	Lawyer	$23,574	1 (35 in trust; wife also owned 1)
Daniels, Victor	Opelousas	1822, France	Surveyor	None Listed	0
Demarest, A. J.	St. Mary	1829, New York	Painter	$1,000	0

Dupay, Joseph	Assumption	1822, France	Lawyer	None Listed	0
Edwards, Henry C.	Avoyelles	1834, Louisiana	Lawyer	None Listed (however, William Edwards, the father, owned $21,000.00 and 16 slaves)	0
Emmons, David	Winn	1840, Mississippi	Farmer	$360	0
Faulkner, A. W.	Caldwell	1823, Ohio	Planter	$85,000	34
Garrett, Isiah	Ouachita	1813, Tennessee	Lawyer/Planter	$194,000	63
George, James H.	St. Helena	1812, Georgia	Physician	$2,200	1
Gorlinski, Joseph	Baton Rouge	1825, Poland	Civil Engineer	$6,000	0
Greene, Allen	Jackson	1818, Georgia	Planter	$67,000	42
Haynes, D. E.	Rapides	1819, Ireland	None Listed	None Listed	0
Heard, H. J.	Baton Rouge	1812, Maryland	Lawyer	$21,000	14
Higginbotham, Thomas	Winn	1820, Alabama	None Listed	$500	0
Hough, Wade H.	Caldwell	1819, South Carolina	Lawyer	$17,750	8
Hudenall, Thomas	Morehouse	1807, Virginia	Worked on Brother's Farm		
Jones, Thomas H.	Bienville	Georgia	Farmer		
Kugler, Peter A.	Baton Rouge	1815, Germany	Butcher	$6,000	0
Laloire, Louis	St. Martin	1828, Louisiana	Merchant	$5,500	0
Lawton, William H.	St. James	1817, Massachusetts	Telegraph Official	$3,600	4
Ludeling, John T.	Ouachita	1827, Louisiana	Lawyer/Planter	$73,000	14
Mace, A. B.	Assumption	1817, Massachusetts	Cooper	$1,300	0
Mailhot, E. E.	Assumption	1820, Canada	Planter	$460,000	62
Mann, William D.	Baton Rouge	1815, Ohio	Ice Merchant	$12,500	1
Marie, Frederick	Lafourche	1826, France	Hotelkeeper	None Listed	0
May, Thomas P.	St. John the Baptist	1842, Louisiana	Planter	$60,000	68

Name	Residence, 1860	Year and Place of Birth	Occupation, 1860	Property	Slaves
Mills, William Reed	Assumption	1829, Vermont	Lawyer	$13,000	2
Montague, Robert V.	Madison	1802, Virginia	Planter	$285,000	116
Newell, John A.	Rapides	1827, Louisiana	None Listed	None Listed	0
Normand, Lucien P.	Avoyelles	1828, Louisiana	Farmer	$2,020	2
O'Conner, John	Baton Rouge	1828, Ireland	Merchant	$7,500	0
Otto, Frederick	Baton Rouge	1833, Germany	Carpenter	$2,900	4
Parker, Ruben	Winn	1821, Alabama	Farmer	$840	0
Peniston, Fergus	East Baton Rouge	1827, Louisiana	Planter	$284,700	151
Phillips, Francis M.	East Baton Rouge	1837, Louisiana	Farmer	$1,300	0
Pintado, E. G.	Assumption	1821, Cuba	Justice of the Peace	$1,500	1
Piquée, Joseph R.	Natchitoches	France	Physician		
Plaisance, Prosper	St. James	1811, France	Storekeeper	$1,400	3
Ray, John	Ouachita	1816, Missouri	Lawyer	$17,000	None Listed
Robinson, N. A.	Natchitoches	1840, Louisiana	Laborer	None Listed	0
Rotgé, John	Assumption	1830, France	Tailor	$2,000	0
Rougelet, Alfred	Terrebonne	1830, France	Language Teacher	$6,000	1
Ryan, Michael	Rapides	1818, Ireland	Lawyer/Planter	$177,300	75
Sarta, Justin	Lafourche	1815, France	Schoolteacher	None Listed	0
Schnurr, Martin	Port Hudson	1831, Germany	Blacksmith	$650	0
Sherman, William T.	Rapides	1820, Ohio	Superintendent		

Name	Location	Nativity	Occupation	Wealth	
Southworth, M. A.	Texas	New York	Physician		
Sullivan, James B.	Rapides	1799, Virginia	Planter	$185,240	121
Taliaferro, James G.	Catahoula	1798, Virginia	Lawyer/Planter	$91,000	27
Taylor, O. L.	Rapides	1824, Massachusetts	Clerk	$1,500	1
Towne, Ezra B.	Madison	1821, Ohio	Planter/Printer	$33,500	22
Wallace, J. W.	St. Mary	1830, Tennessee	Mason	None Listed	0
Waters, Thomas B.	Rapides	1829, Louisiana	Planter	$35,000	14
Wax, Nicholas	Baton Rouge	1832, Germany	Merchant	$5,000	0
Wells, James Madison	Rapides	1808, Louisiana	Planter	$400,400	96
West, George A.	St. Martin	1837, Indiana	Clergyman	$500	0
White, Iona C.	Lafourche	Mississippi			
Wrotnowski, Stanislas	Baton Rouge	1803, Poland	Farmer	None Listed (he was known to own land and sugar refinery)	0
Yerks, Johnson E.	St. Helena	New York	Dentist		

Summary of Nativity

Border Slave States (Missouri, Maryland, Kentucky, and Delaware)	5 (6.6%)
Northern Free States	19 (25%)
Foreign Nations	22 (29%)
	46 (61.3%)
Confederate States	29 (38.6%)

Table 2. LOUISIANA UNIONISTS
(Those Living in Orleans and Jefferson Parishes)

Name	Residence, 1860	Year and Place of Birth	Occupation, 1860	Property	Slaves
Abell, Edmund	New Orleans	Kentucky	Lawyer	$1,000	0
Baker, William	New Orleans	1820, England	Bookstore Owner		9
Barker, Jacob	New Orleans	1779, Maine	Banker	$240,000	1
Barrett, John T.	New Orleans	1816, Vermont	Merchant	$3,000	
Beckwith, J. R.		New York			
Belden, James G.	New Orleans	1822, New York	Physician	$14,000	2
Bonzano, Max F.	New Orleans	1820, Germany	Physician	$9,500	3
Bouligny, John E.	New Orleans	1824, Louisiana	Lawyer/United States Congressman		
Brownlee, John	Algiers	1819, Canada	Custom House	$2,500	0
Bullitt, Cuthbert	New Orleans	Kentucky	Commission Merchant		
Carter, J. B.		Maine			
Christie, Daniel	New Orleans	New Jersey	Carpenter		
Collins, Bartholomew	New Orleans	1825, Ireland	Contractor	$800	
Cook, Terrence		Ireland			
Crane, William R.	New Orleans	1809, District of Columbia	Lawyer	$32,000	4
Crozat, F. M.	New Orleans	1810, Louisiana	Custom House	$1,200	0
Cutler, Rufus King	Jefferson	1822, Virginia	Lawyer	$6,300	3
Dewees, D. S.	New Orleans	1807, Pennsylvania	Merchant	$50,000	6
Dostie, Anthony P.	New Orleans	1821, New York	Dentist	$7,000	0
Duane, James		Ireland			
Durant, Thomas J.	New Orleans	1817, Pennsylvania	Lawyer		4

Name	Location	Birth Year, Birthplace	Occupation	Value	Number
Egan, Michael	New Orleans	1836, Ireland	Coffeehouse Owner	$1,500	0
Ennemoser, Julius	Jefferson	1837, Germany	Druggist	$600	2
Ennis, James	New Orleans	Ireland	Bookstore Owner		
Fellows, J. Q. A.	New Orleans	1825, Vermont	Lawyer	$3,000	2
Fernandez, Anthony	New Orleans	Louisiana	Auctioneer	$11,800	3
Field, Alexander P.	New Orleans	1800, Kentucky	Lawyer	$7,000	
Fish, William R.	New Orleans	1836, New York	Lawyer/School Principal	None Listed	0
Flanders, Benjamin F.	New Orleans	1816, New Hampshire	Secretary-Treasurer of Railroad	$27,000	
Flood, Edmond	New Orleans	1804, Ireland	Carpenter	$9,400	4
Fosdick, George A.	New Orleans	1820, Louisiana	Merchant	$25,000	
Gottschalk, William	New Orleans	1846, Indiana	Son of German Watchmaker		0
Gastinel, Louis	New Orleans	1797, France	Shoe Dealer	$10,600	0
Graham, James	New Orleans	1819, Ireland	Notary Public	$15,000	2
Hahn, Michael	New Orleans	1830, Germany	Lawyer		
Hall, William B.		Maine			
Hart, Edward	New Orleans	Louisiana			
Heath, Edward	New Orleans	1820, Maine	Upholsterer	None Listed	0
Hire, William H.	New Orleans	1819, England	Physician	$1,500	0
Hornor, Charles W.	New Orleans	1813, Pennsylvania	Lawyer	$22,000	
Hunt, William H.	New Orleans	1823, South Carolina	Lawyer	$34,000	1
Jackson, James	New Orleans	New York	Businessman		
Jervis, Alfred	New Orleans	1821, Pennsylvania	Superintendent of Orphan Asylum	$300	0

225

Name	Residence, 1860	Year and Place of Birth	Occupation, 1860	Property	Slaves
Kennedy, Hugh	New Orleans	Ireland	Printer	$4,000	
King, William H. C.	New Orleans	1825, Pennsylvania	Lawyer	$10,000	0
Lacey, George S.	New Orleans	1820, Louisiana	Lawyer	$600	0
Leaumont, Charles	New Orleans	1831, Louisiana	Lawyer/Teacher	None Listed	0
Lynch, Bartholomew L.	Jefferson	1830, Ireland	Tailor	$200	
McWhirter, John	New Orleans	1822, Germany	School Principal		
McNair, John	New Orleans	New York	Physician	$800	
Maas, Benjamin	New Orleans	1821, Germany	Cooper	$6,000	2
Maas, Henry	New Orleans	1808, Germany			
Meeks, Theodore		New York	Tailor	None Listed	
Meeks, W. R.	New Orleans	1816, Louisiana	Mayor of City	$10,000	1
Michel, John T.	Jefferson	1828, Louisiana	Saw Mill Proprietor	$1,500	
Miller, Jacob	Jefferson	1812, Norway	Carpenter	$15,500	
Miller, William R.	New Orleans	1815, Pennsylvania	United States Mint	None Listed	0
Millspaugh, Howard	New Orleans	1814, Virginia	Truck Farmer	$32,000	7
Mithoff, William	Jefferson	1814, Germany	Custom House	$2,500	2
Montamat, John P.	New Orleans	1833, Louisiana	Auctioneer	$5,000	
Montgomery, Robert T.	New Orleans	1825, Kentucky	Merchant	$17,500	1
Morris, Robert	Jefferson	1797, Tennessee	Commission Merchant	$15,000	
Murphy, Edward	New Orleans	1834, Louisiana	Clerk	$1,500	0
Murtagh, Arthur N.	New Orleans	1832, New York	Clothing Merchant	$10,000	0
Mushaway, James	New Orleans	1815, Massachusetts	Auctioneer	$3,000	2
Neville, Julian	New Orleans	1813, Pennsylvania			

Name	City/Parish	Birth	Occupation	Property	
Piper, William	Jefferson	1814, Germany	Grocer	$17,000	
Pitkin, J. R. G.	New Orleans	Louisiana		$5,000	
Pursell, Samuel	Jefferson	1815, Vermont	Country Store Owner		
Ready, James	New Orleans	Tennessee	Physician		
Riddell, Dr. J. L.	New Orleans	1807, Massachusetts	Professor of Chemistry	$145,000	9
Robinson, Boyd	New Orleans	1821, New York	City Court Clerk	$500	
Roselius, Christian	Jefferson	1803, Germany	Lawyer	$180,000	9
Rozier, Joseph Adolph	New Orleans	1817, Missouri	Lawyer		
Schilling, J.	New Orleans	1822, Germany	Shoe Store Owner	$1,200	
Schneider, Nicholas	Jefferson	1815, Germany	Lumber Dealer	$2,600	
Schroeder, J. B.	New Orleans	1810, Germany	Merchant	$3,200	
Shaw, Alfred	New Orleans	1826, Pennsylvania	School Principal	$1,500	1
Spellicy, John A.	New Orleans	1829, Canada	Policeman	None Listed	
Stauffer, Cyrus W.	New Orleans	Pennsylvania			
Stocker, William T.	New Orleans	1830, Kentucky	Lumber Dealer	$3,500	
Straight, Seymour	Ohio/New Orleans	Ohio	Commission Merchant		
Sullivan, John	New Orleans	1807, Ireland	Custom House	$500	0
Summers, Henry M.	New Orleans	1792, New York	Commission Merchant	None Listed	
Terry, J. Randall	New Orleans	New York	Druggist		
Tewell, James E.	New Orleans	District of Columbia			

Name	Residence, 1860	Year and Place of Birth	Occupation, 1860	Property	Slaves
Torrey, Samuel H.	New Orleans	1822, New York	Lawyer	$750	1
Train, Henry	New Orleans	1815, Louisiana	Lawyer	$1,600	0
Walton, John S.	New Orleans	New Jersey	Commercial Firm		
Waples, Rufus	New Orleans	Delaware	Lawyer		
Whitaker, John S.	New Orleans	1825, Massachusetts	Lawyer	$7,000	
White, Edwin	Jefferson	1815, Missouri	Livestock Dealer	$3,000	2
Woolfley, Francis A.		Switzerland			

Summary of Nativity

Border Slave States (Missouri, Maryland, Kentucky, and Delaware)	8 (8%)
Northern Free States	41 (42%)
Foreign Nations	30 (31%)
	79 (81.4%)
Confederate States	18 (18.5%)

Appendix 2

The Constitutional Convention of 1867–1868

The first priority in compiling the biographical lists that follow in Table 3 was the separation of the white from the black delegates. Some delegates identified their race by documents inserted in the *Official Journal* of the convention. The New Orleans *Daily Picayune* and the New York *Times* identified delegates by race in reporting the debates. A document that proved invaluable is the *Extract from the Reconstructed Constitution of the State of Louisiana with Portraits of the Distinguished Members of the Convention & Assembly. A. D. 1868*, as it appears in Vincent's *Black Legislators in Louisiana*. Although used extensively, the United States Census, Manuscript Returns, 1860, Population, proved less useful than expected, mainly because of the geographical mobility of people in the 1860s. Also useful were the St. Landry *Progress*, the Boston *Liberator*, the New Orleans *Tribune*, the New Orleans *Louisianian*, and the letter signed by thirty-two black legislators in Henry Clay Warmoth, *War, Politics and Reconstruction*, 146–47. New Orleans, Mayor's Office, Register of Free Colored Persons Entitled to Remain in the State, 1840–1864, proved a disappointment. Finally, I used the lists compiled by other historians: Vincent, cited above; A. E. Perkins, "Some Negro Officers and Legislators in Louisiana," *Journal of Negro History*, XIV (October, 1929), 523–28; and the excellent work by David C. Rankin, "The Origins of Black Leadership in New Orleans During Reconstruction," *Journal of Southern History*, XL (August, 1974), 436–40.

Direct evidence from the sources identifies forty-seven black delegates; the remaining three are identified by Perkins, "Some Negro Officers and Legislators."

Regarding the white delegates, unless there was direct evidence that a member was a carpetbagger, I classified him as a Southern white.

With the exception of Adolph Bernard, who attended a few early sessions of the convention and then simply disappeared, all of the delegates show up in newspaper and other accounts of Republican party meetings and conventions of the period. The conservatives described in the convention, in other words, were conservative Republicans, not Democrats.

Table 3. DELEGATES
CONSTITUTIONAL CONVENTION OF 1867–1868

Blacks

Name	Legal Status (1860)	Parish Represented	Occupation	Military Service (Native Guards or Corps d'Afrique)
1. Antoine, Caesar C.	FMC	Caddo (Lived in New Orleans Until After War)	Grocer (Barber in 1860)	Captain
2. Bertonneau, Arnold	FMC	New Orleans	Wine Merchant	Captain
3. Blandin, Ovide C.	FMC	New Orleans	Grocer	
4. Bonnefoi, Emile	FMC	West Baton Rouge		
5. Bonseigneur, Henry	FMC	New Orleans	Cigar Store	
6. Brown, William G.	FMC	Iberville (from New Jersey)		
7. Burrell, Dennis	Slave	St. John the Baptist	Blacksmith	
8. Butler, William		St. Helena		
9. Cromwell, Robert I.	FMC	New Orleans (from Wisconsin)	Physician	
10. Cuney, Samuel E.	FMC	Rapides		
11. Deslonde, Pierre G.	FMC	Iberville	Sugar Planter Before War	
12. Donoto, Auguste, Jr.	FMC	St. Landry	Son of Well-to-do FMC Planter and Slaveowner	
13. Dupart, Gustave		St. Tammany		
14. Dupart, Ulger		Terrebonne		
15. Esnard, J. B.	FMC	St. Mary	Son of FMC Slaveowner	

231

Blacks

Name	Legal Status (1860)	Parish Represented	Occupation	Military Service (Native Guards or Corps d'Afrique)
16. Francois, Louis	FMC	East Baton Rouge	Grocer	Sergeant
17. Gair, John	FMC	East Feliciana	Carpenter	
18. Gardner, R. G.		Jefferson		
19. Guichard, Leopold		St. Bernard	Clerk	
20. Ingraham, James H.	FMC	Caddo (lived in New Orleans Until After War)	Former Carpenter	Captain
21. Isabelle, Robert H.	FMC	New Orleans	Clerk, Dyer, Policeman	Captain
22. Isabelle, Thomas	FMC	New Orleans	Sewing Machine Shop	Lieutenant
23. Jackson, George H.	Slave	St. Landry		
24. Kelso, George Y.	FMC	Rapides		
25. Lange, Victor M.	FMC	East Baton Rouge	Ex-Ice Cream Vendor	
26. Leroy, Charles	FMC	Natchitoches	Shoemaker	
27. Lewis, Richard		West Feliciana		
28. Martin, Thomas N.	FMC	Jefferson	Carpenter	
29. Massicot, Jules A.	FMC	New Orleans	Well Educated	
30. Meadows, William R.	Slave	Claiborne	Farmer	
31. Morris, Milton		Ascension		
32. Moses, Solomon R.	Slave	New Orleans		
33. Murrell, William	FMC	Lafourche (from New Jersey)	Minister	
34. Myers, Theophile	FMC	W. Baton Rouge	Planter	
35. Oliver, Joseph C.	FMC	St. James		Captain

Name	Civil War Loyalty	Parish Represented	Place of Birth	Occupation	Slaves (1860)
38. Poindexter, Robert		Assumption		(Riverboat Steward in 1860)	
39. Pollard, Curtis		Madison		Farmer & Baptist Preacher	
40. Riard, Fortune	FMC	Lafayette		Businessman	
41. Riggs, Daniel D.		Washington			
42. Roberts, J. H. A.		Jefferson			
43. Rodriguez, Lazard A.	FMC	New Orleans		Shoemaker	Captain
44. Scott, John	FMC	Winn (Lived in New Orleans Until After War)		Carpenter	
45. Snaer, Sosthene L.		St. Martin			
46. Thibaut, Charles A.		Plaquemines		Clerk	
47. Tinchant, Edward		New Orleans			Soldier
48. Valfroit, P. F.		Ascension			
49. Williams, Henderson		Madison & Franklin			
50. Wilson, David	FMC	New Orleans		Barber	
Southern Whites					
1. Baker, L. W.		Bossier	Vermont	Lawyer	
2. Barrett, John L.	Union	Union			
3. Belden, Simeon		New Orleans	Massachusetts	Lawyer	
4. Bernard, Adolph		Calcasieu & Vermillion			0

Southern Whites

Name	Civil War Loyalty	Parish Represented	Place of Birth	Occupation	Slaves (1860)
5. Blackburn, W. Jasper	Union	Claiborne	Arkansas	Editor	0
6. Cooley, William H.	Union	Pointe Coupee	Louisiana	Lawyer	8
7. Crane, William R.	Union	New Orleans	District of Columbia	Lawyer	4
8. Crawford, Thomas S.	Union	Caldwell	Kentucky	Lawyer	1 & 35 in Trust; Wife 1
9. Dearing, George W., Jr.		Rapides	Mississippi		Father Owned 13
10. Demarest, A. J.	Union	St. Mary	New York	Painter	0
11. Depasseau, Charles		New Orleans			
12. Deslonde, Joseph B.		St. John the Baptist			
13. Douglas, David		New Orleans			
14. Drinkard, John G.	Union	St. Landry	Kentucky	Grocer (In both St. Landry & Rapides)	2
15. Duplessis, C. B. H.	Union	New Orleans	Louisiana	Customs Official Until 1865	
16. Edwards, Fielding		Avoyelles	Kentucky	Planter	16
17. Harrison, Thomas P.		Morehouse	Mississippi	Physician	
18. Heistand, W. H.	Union	Natchitoches			
19. Jones, Simon	Union	New Orleans	Lived in Texas Before War; Colonel in		

21. Ludeling, John T.	Union	Ouachita	Louisiana	Lawyer/Planter	14
22. McLeran, Benjamin		Caddo			
23. Marie, Frederick	Union	Terrebonne	France	Hotelkeeper	0
24. Mushaway, James	Union	New Orleans	Massachusetts	Clothing Merchant	0
25. Reagan, George W.	Union	East Baton Rouge			
26. Schwab, N.	Union	Jefferson		Jeweler	
27. Smith, Charles	Union	New Orleans	Massachusetts	Carpenter in 1860	
28. Snider, G.		De Soto	South Carolina	Mechanic	
29. Taliaferro, James G.	Union	Catahoula	Virginia	Lawyer/Planter	27
30. Underwood, Napoleon		St. James	Louisiana	Painter in 1860	
31. Vandergriff, John B.		St. Martin		Physician	
32. Vidal, Michel	Union	St. Landry	France	Journalist	
33. Waples, Rufus	Union	New Orleans	Delaware	Lawyer	
34. Wickliffe, George M.		New Orleans		Dentist	

Northern Carpetbaggers

Name	Residence (1860–1861)	Parish Represented	Union Military Service	Occupation
Daniels, Nathan W. (Died before convention, replaced by N. Schwab)	North	Jefferson	Colonel, Louisiana Native Guards	
1. Ferguson, George W.	New York	Jackson	None	Sergeant of Police in New Orleans During War
2. Fuller, Henry W.	New Hampshire	Avoyelles	Lieutenant Colonel, 16th New Hampshire; Colonel, 75th U.S. Colored Infantry; Brevet Brigadier	Cotton Planter
3. Gould, Abram N.	North	Tensas	Captain	Cotton Planter
4. Harper, Peter	North	St. John the Baptist	Captain, 99th U.S. Colored Infantry	
5. Harris, John S.	Wisconsin	Concordia	None	Cotton Planter
6. Hempstead, Orlando H.	Connecticut	Assumption	Lt., 2d New Orleans; Freedmen's Bureau	
7. Landers, James H.	New Hampshire	Concordia	Captain, 8th New Hampshire	Cotton Planter

8. Lynch, John	Ohio	Carroll	Major, 114th Ohio	Cotton Planter
9. McMillen, William L.	Ohio	Carroll	Surgeon, 1st Ohio; transferred to line, rose to Brevet Major General	Cotton Planter
10. Newsham, Joseph P.	Illinois	West Feliciana	Staff Officer for Generals Fremont & Smith; 32d Missouri	Lawyer
11. Packard, Stephen B.	Maine	New Orleans	Captain, Maine Regiment	
12. Reese, Daniel H.	North	Lafourche	Lieutenant, 75 U.S. Colored Infantry	
13. Steele, Hiram R.	Vermont	Tensas	Captain, 10th Vermont; Brevet Major	Cotton Planter
14. Twitchell, Marshall Harvey	Vermont	Bienville	Sergeant, 4th Vermont; Captain, 109 U.S. Colored Infantry; Freedmen's Bureau	Cotton Planter

Table 4. ROLL CALLS
Constitutional Convention of 1867–1868

	Total Vote	Black Vote	White Vote	Black % of Total Vote
1. NOVEMBER 25, 1867: Wickliffe proposal to divide convention patronage equally between blacks and whites.	85	45	40	53
2. DECEMBER 20, 1867: Thomas Isabelle amendment to insert "public" in the Bill of Rights.	76	45	31	59
3. JANUARY 3, 1868: Article 13, guaranteeing blacks equal accommodations on public transportation and in public places.	74	44	30	59
4. JANUARY 24, 1868: First part of Waples amendment on suffrage.	64	39	25	61
5. JANUARY 27, 1868: Cooley amendment favoring lenient disfranchisement.	82	42	40	51
6. JANUARY 28, 1868: Packard amendment favoring harsh disfranchisement.	79	41	38	52
7. FEBRUARY 4, 1868: Desegregated schools.	74	42	32	57
8. FEBRUARY 27, 1868: Motion to table Packard disfranchisement amendment.	70	40	30	57
9. FEBRUARY 28, 1868: Waples compromise disfranchisement proposal.	73	40	33	55
10. FEBRUARY 29, 1868: Division of land sold by court decree.	55	36	19	65
11. MARCH 2, 1868: Final vote on adoption of the constitution.	77	44	33	57
TOTALS	809	458	351	57

Appendix 3

Major Officeholders in the Federal Bureaucracy in Louisiana 1867–1875

1867

Name	Office	Birthplace	Arrival in Louisiana
John S. Walton	Assistant Treasurer	New Jersey	Before War
John S. Walton	Director of Mint	New Jersey	Before War
James Ready	Assessor, Internal Revenue, New Orleans	Tennessee	Before War
James B. Steedman	Collector, Internal Revenue, New Orleans	Pennsylvania	After 1861
William P. Kellogg	Collector of Port	Vermont	After 1861
Sydney A. Stockdale	Special Deputy Collector	Missouri	After 1861
Charles H. Shute	Deputy Collector	New Hampshire	
James Jackson	Appraiser, Custom House	New York	Before War
Edgar H. Whitaker	Auditor, Custom House	Massachusetts	
Robert W. Taliaferro	Postmaster	Louisiana	
Frederick J. Knapp	Pension Agent	Maryland	Before War
Edward H. Durell	District Judge	New Hampshire	Before War
Samuel H. Torrey	District Attorney	New York	Before War
Francis J. Herron	United States Marshal	Pennsylvania	After 1861

SOURCE: *Official Register of the United States*, 1867, 1871, and 1875.

1871

Name	Office	Birthplace	Arrival in Louisiana
Charles Clinton	Assistant Treasurer	Massachusetts	
No Listing	Director of Mint		
Blance F. Joubert	Assessor, Internal Revenue, New Orleans	Louisiana	

239

Name	Office	Birthplace	Arrival in Louisiana
Sydney A. Stockdale	Collector, Internal Revenue, New Orleans	Missouri	After 1861
James F. Casey	Collector of Port	Kentucky	After 1861
Philip F. Herwig	Special Deputy Collector	Haiti	Before War
Theodore V. Coupland	Deputy Collector	Alabama	
James Longstreet	Surveyor of Port	South Carolina	After 1861
Charles Dillingham	Naval Officer	Vermont	After 1861
Charles H. Merrett	Auditor, Custom House	New York	
John R. G. Pitkin	Appraiser, Custom House	Louisiana	
Thomas Ong	Appraiser, Custom House	Pennsylvania	After 1861
James Jackson	Appraiser, Custom House	New York	Before War
B. P. Blanchard	Postmaster, New Orleans	No Listing	
Robert H. Isabelle (black)	Pension Agent	Louisiana	
Edward H. Durell	District Judge	New Hampshire	Before War
James R. Beckwith	District Attorney	New York	Before War
Stephen B. Packard	United States Marshal	Maine	After 1861
Everett W. Foster	Surveyor General	Massachusetts	After 1861

1875

Name	Office	Birthplace	Arrival in Louisiana
B. F. Flanders	Assistant Treasurer	New Hampshire	Before War
Max F. Bonzano	Director of Mint	Germany	Before War
John Cockram	Collector, Internal Revenue, New Orleans	New Jersey	
James F. Casey	Collector of Port	Kentucky	After 1861
Philip F. Herwig	Special Deputy Collector	Haiti	Before War
Theodore V. Coupland	Deputy Collector	Alabama	
E. P. Champlin	Deputy Collector	Michigan	

Name	Office	Birthplace	Arrival in Louisiana
Charles Dillingham	Naval Officer	Vermont	After 1861
James M. Wells	Surveyor of Port	Louisiana	
W. M. Aikman	Auditor, Custom House	Indiana	
John R. G. Pitkin	General Appraiser, Custom House	Louisiana	
C. W. Ringgold (black)*	Appraiser, Custom House	Louisiana	
James Jackson	Appraiser, Custom House	New York	Before War
John M. G. Parker	Postmaster, New Orleans	Massachusetts	After 1861
Robert H. Isabelle (black)	Pension Agent	Louisiana	
O. H. Brewster	Surveyor General	New York	After 1861
Edward H. Durell	District Judge	New Hampshire	Before War
J. R. Beckwith	District Attorney	New York	Before War
Stephen B. Packard	United States Marshal	Maine	After 1861

*For a time Ringgold was postmaster of New Orleans, which was the highest federal position held by any Negro during Louisiana Reconstruction.

Select Bibliography

PRIMARY SOURCES

Manuscripts

Historical Society of Pennsylvania, Philadelphia
    Chase, Salmon P. Papers.
Howard-Tilton Memorial Library, Tulane University, New Orleans
    Hester, E. R. "A Thumb Nail Sketch of the Life and Activities of Allen
        Greene," 1959.
    Louisiana Scrapbooks, vol. 17.
    Stoddard, Ephraim S. Papers
Library of Congress, Washington, D.C.
    Banks, Nathaniel P. Papers.
    Chase, Salmon P. Papers.
    Johnson, Andrew. Papers.
    Lincoln, Abraham. Papers.
Louisiana State Archives, Baton Rouge
    Historical Records Survey. State Department of Education Records.
National Archives, Washington, D.C.
    Bureau of Refugees, Freedmen, and Abandoned Lands. Record Group 105.
    Civil War Pension Files. Record Group 15.
    United States Census, Manuscript Returns, 1860. Record Group 29.
New York Historical Society, New York
    Durant, Thomas J. Papers.
Prescott Memorial Library, Louisiana Tech University, Ruston
    Twitchell, Marshall Harvey. Papers.
Private Collections
    "Autobiography of Marshall Harvey Twitchell," and other Papers. In the
        possession of Dr. Marshall Coleman Twitchell, Burlington, Vermont.
    Holland, Clark. Papers. In the possession of Clark Holland, Medfield,
        Massachusetts.
Southern Historical Collection, University of North Carolina, Chapel Hill
    Warmoth, Henry Clay. Papers.
Troy H. Middleton Library, Louisiana State University, Baton Rouge
    Boyd, David F. Diary, 1874–1875.

Boyd, David F. Letter Books.
Breda, Jean P. and Family. Papers.
Fleming, Walter L. Collection.
Grand Army of the Republic. Papers.
Historical Records Survey. Transcriptions of Police Jury Minutes.
Kellogg, William Pitt. Papers.
Koch, Christian D. and Family. Papers.
Moore, Thomas O. Papers.
Taliaferro, James G. and Family. Papers.
University of Rochester Library, Rochester
Seward, William H. Papers.

PUBLIC DOCUMENTS: FEDERAL

UNITED STATES CONGRESS
Serial

1292. "New Orleans Riots," 1866. *House Executive Documents*, 39th Cong., 2d Sess., No. 68.

1304. "New Orleans Riots," 1866. *House Reports*, 39th Cong., 2d Sess., No. 16.

1308. Reconstruction Correspondence, 1867. *Senate Executive Documents*, 40th Cong., 1st Sess., No. 14.

1406. New Orleans Custom House, 1870. *Senate Executive Documents*, 41st Cong., 2d Sess., No. 73.

1435. Election of 1868. *House Miscellaneous Documents*, 41st Cong., 2d Sess., No. 154, Pts. 1–2.

1484. Ku Klux Klan. *Senate Reports*, 42d Cong., 2d Sess., No. 41, Pt. 1.

1527. Republican Feud in Louisiana, 1871. *House Miscellaneous Documents*, 42d Cong., 2d Sess., No. 211.

1629. Louisiana Affairs, 1874–75. *Senate Executive Documents*, 43d Cong., 2d Sess., No. 13.

1629. "Affairs in Louisiana," 1874. *Senate Executive Documents*, 43d Cong., 2d Sess., No. 17.

1657. "Affairs in Louisiana," 1874 Election. *House Reports*, 43d Cong., 2d Sess., No. 101, Pts. 1–2.

1660. Louisiana in 1874. *House Reports*, 43d Cong., 2d Sess., No. 261, Pts. 1–3.

1716. "Federal Officers in Louisiana; 'Coushatta Affair.'" *House Reports*, 44th Cong., 1st Sess., No. 816.

1735–1737. Louisiana in 1876. *Senate Reports*, 44th Cong., 2d Sess., No. 701, 3 vols.

Serial

1755. Army in the South. *House Executive Documents*, 44th Cong., 2d Sess., No. 30.

1765–1767. Presidential Election Investigation, 1876. *House Miscellaneous Documents*, 44th Cong., 2d Sess., No. 34, Pts. 1–6.

1840. "Louisiana and South Carolina in 1878." *Senate Reports*, 45th Cong., 3d Sess., No. 855, Pts. 1–2.

1864–1865. "Presidential Election Investigation," 1876. *House Miscellaneous Documents*, 45th Cong., 3d Sess., No. 31, Pts. 1–4.

1899–1900. "Negro Exodus from Southern States." *Senate Reports*, 46th Cong., 2d Sess., No. 693, Pts. 1–3.

Biographical Directory of the American Congress, 1774–1971. Washington, D.C., 1971.

Negro Population 1790–1915. Washington, D.C., 1918.

Richardson, James D., ed. *A Compilation of the Messages* and *Papers of the Presidents, 1789–1897.* 10 vols. Washington, D.C., 1896–1897.

United States Civil Service Commission. *Official Register of the United States.* Washington, D.C., 1863–1879.

The War of the Rebellion: A Compilation of the Official Records of the Union and Confederate Armies. 128 vols. Washington, D.C., 1880–1901.

PUBLIC DOCUMENTS: STATE

Acts of the State of Louisiana.

Debates in the Convention for the Revision and Amendment of the Constitution of the State of Louisiana. New Orleans, 1864.

Digest of the Statutes of the State of Louisiana, in Two Volumes. New Orleans, 1870.

Inaugural Address of Governor H. C. Warmoth and Remarks of Lieut. Governor Dunn. New Orleans, 1868.

Louisiana House Debates.

Louisiana House Journal.

Louisiana Senate Debates.

Louisiana Senate Journal.

Official Journal of the Proceedings of the Convention for Framing a Constitution for the State of Louisiana. New Orleans, 1868.

Official Journal of the Proceedings of the Convention for the Revision and Amendment of the Constitution of the State of Louisiana. New Orleans, 1864.

NEWSPAPERS

Alexandria *Louisiana Democrat*
Bossier *Banner*
Boston *Liberator*

New Orleans *Black Republican*
New Orleans *Daily Picayune*
New Orleans *Daily True Delta*
New Orleans *Louisianian*
New Orleans *Republican*
New Orleans *Times*
New Orleans *Tribune*
New Orleans *Union*
New York *Times*
St. Landry *Progress*

PUBLISHED DOCUMENTS, CONTEMPORARY ACCOUNTS, MEMOIRS

Appleton's *American Annual Cyclopaedia and Register of Important Events* (1862–1877). New York, 1863–1878.

Basler, Roy P., ed. *The Collected Work of Abraham Lincoln.* 9 vols. New Brunswick, N.J., 1953–1955.

[Benham, George C.] *A Year of Wreck. A True Story, by a Victim.* New York, 1880.

Brown, William Wells. *The Negro in the American Rebellion.* Boston, 1867.

Devol, George H. *Forty Years a Gambler on the Mississippi.* New York, 1887.

"Diary and Correspondence of Salmon P. Chase." *Annual Report of the American Historical Association for the Year 1902.* 2 vols. Washington, D.C., 1903.

Grant, Ulysses S. *Personal Memoirs of U. S. Grant.* 2 vols. New York, 1885.

Hepworth, George H. *The Whip, Hoe, and Sword; or, The Gulf-Department in '63.* Boston, 1864.

Historical Records Survey. *County-Parish Boundaries in Louisiana.* New Orleans, 1939.

Hunt, Thomas. *The Life of William H. Hunt.* Brattleboro, Vt., 1922.

Landry, Stuart Omer. *The Battle of Liberty Place: The Overthrow of Carpet-Bag Rule in New Orleans, September 14, 1874.* New Orleans, 1955.

Lockett, Samuel H. *Louisiana as It Is: A Geographical and Topographical Description of the State.* Edited by Lauren C. Post. Baton Rouge, 1970.

McPherson, James M., ed. *The Negro's Civil War: How American Negroes Felt and Acted during the War for the Union.* New York, 1965.

Parton, James. *General Butler in New Orleans.* New York, 1864.

Proceedings of the Convention of the Friends of Freedom. New Orleans, 1863.

Proceedings of the Convention of the Republican Party of Louisiana. New Orleans, 1865.

Reed, Emily Hazen. *Life of A. P. Dostie; or, The Conflict in New Orleans.* New York, 1868.

Reid, Whitelaw. *After the War: A Tour of the Southern States, 1865–1866.* Edited by C. Vann Woodward. New York, 1965.

Simmons, William J. *Men of Mark; Eminent, Progressive and Rising.* Cleveland, 1887.

Trowbridge, John T. *The South: A Tour of Its Battle-Fields and Ruined Cities.* Hartford, Conn., 1866.

Warmoth, Henry Clay. *War, Politics and Reconstruction: Stormy Days in Louisiana.* New York, 1930.

SECONDARY ACCOUNTS

BOOKS

Adams, Michael C. C. *Our Masters the Rebels: A Speculation on Union Military Failure in the East, 1861–1865.* Cambridge, 1978.

Belz, Herman. *Reconstructing the Union: Theory and Policy During the Civil War.* Ithaca, N.Y., 1969.

Berlin, Ira. *Slaves Without Masters: The Free Negro in the Antebellum South.* New York, 1974.

Blassingame, John W. *Black New Orleans, 1860–1880.* Chicago, 1973.

Capers, Gerald M. *Occupied City: New Orleans Under the Federals, 1862–1865.* Lexington, 1965.

Caskey, Willie Melvin. *Secession and Restoration of Louisiana.* Baton Rouge, 1938.

Cox, LaWanda. *Lincoln and Black Freedom: A Study in Presidential Leadership.* Columbia, S.C., 1981.

Current, Richard N. "Carpetbaggers Reconsidered." In *A Festschrift for Frederick B. Artz,* edited by David H. Pinkney and Theodore Ropp. Durham, N.C., 1964.

———. *Three Carpetbag Governors.* Baton Rouge, 1967.

Dawson, Joseph G. III. *Army Generals and Reconstruction: Louisiana, 1862–1877.* Baton Rouge, 1982.

Degler, Carl N. *The Other South: Southern Dissenters in the Nineteenth Century.* New York, 1974.

DuBois, W. E. Burghardt. *Black Reconstruction in America.* New York, 1935.

Eaton, Clement. *The Freedom-of-Thought Struggle in the Old South.* Revised edition. New York, 1964.

Evans, W. McKee. *Ballots and Fence Rails: Reconstruction on the Lower Cape Fear.* Chapel Hill, 1966.

Ficklen, John Rose. *History of Reconstruction in Louisiana (Through 1868).* Baltimore, 1910.

Fischer, Roger A. *The Segregation Struggle in Louisiana 1862–77.* Urbana, Ill., 1974.

Foner, Eric. *Free Soil, Free Labor, Free Men: The Ideology of the Republican Party before the Civil War.* New York, 1970.

———. *Politics and Ideology in the Age of the Civil War.* New York, 1980.

Foote, Shelby. *The Civil War: A Narrative.* 3 vols. New York, 1958–1974.

Franklin, John Hope. *The Militant South, 1800–1861.* Cambridge, 1956.

————. *Reconstruction: After the Civil War.* Chicago, 1961.

Gerteis, Louis S. *From Contraband to Freedmen: Federal Policy Toward Southern Blacks, 1861–1865.* Westport, Conn., 1973.

Gillette, William. *Retreat from Reconstruction, 1869–1879.* Baton Rouge, 1979.

Harrington, Fred Harvey. *Fighting Politician: Major General N. P. Banks.* Philadelphia, 1948.

Hattaway, Herman, and Jones, Archer. *How the North Won: A Military History of the Civil War.* Urbana, Ill., 1983.

Holt, Thomas. *Black Over White: Negro Political Leadership in South Carolina during Reconstruction.* Urbana, Ill., 1977.

Johnson, Ludwell H. *Red River Campaign: Politics and Cotton in the Civil War.* Baltimore, 1958.

Jordan, Winthrop D. *White over Black: American Attitudes Toward the Negro, 1550–1812.* Chapel Hill, 1968.

Keller, Morton. *Affairs of State: Public Life in Late Nineteenth Century America.* Cambridge, 1977.

Kousser, J. Morgan, and McPherson, James M., eds. *Region, Race, and Reconstruction: Essays in Honor of C. Vann Woodward.* New York, 1982.

Litwack, Leon F. *Been in the Storm So Long: The Aftermath of Slavery.* New York, 1979.

Lonn, Ella. *Reconstruction in Louisiana after 1868.* New York, 1918.

Macdonald, Robert R., Kemp, John R., and Hass, Edward F., eds. *Louisiana's Black Heritage.* New Orleans, 1979.

McConnell, Roland C. *Negro Troops of Antebellum Louisiana: A History of the Battalion of Free Men of Color.* Baton Rouge, 1968.

McCrary, Peyton. *Abraham Lincoln and Reconstruction: The Louisiana Experiment.* Princeton, 1978.

McKitrick, Eric L. *Andrew Johnson and Reconstruction.* Chicago, 1960.

McPherson, James M. *Ordeal By Fire: The Civil War and Reconstruction.* New York, 1982.

————. *The Struggle for Equality: Abolitionists and the Negro in the Civil War and Reconstruction.* Princeton, 1964.

Messner, William F. *Freedmen and the Ideology of Free Labor: Louisiana 1862–1865.* Lafayette, La., 1978.

Mills, Gary B. *The Forgotten People: Cane River's Creoles of Color.* Baton Rouge, 1977.

Nevins, Allan. *The Emergence of Lincoln.* 2 vols. New York, 1950.

Olsen, Otto H., ed. *Reconstruction and Redemption in the South.* Baton Rouge, 1980.

Overy, David H. *Wisconsin Carpetbaggers in Dixie.* Madison, 1961.

David Potter. *The Impending Crisis, 1848–1861*. New York, 1976.

Powell, Lawrence N. *New Masters: Northern Planters During the Civil War and Reconstruction*. New Haven, 1980.

Ripley, C. Peter. *Slaves and Freedmen in Civil War Louisiana*. Baton Rouge, 1976.

Roussève, Charles Barthelemy. *The Negro in Louisiana: Aspects of His History and His Literature*. New Orleans, 1937.

Sansing, David G., ed. *What Was Freedom's Price?* Jackson, Miss., 1978.

Shugg, Roger W. *Origins of Class Struggle in Louisiana: A Social History of White Farmers and Laborers during Slavery and After, 1840–1875*. Baton Rouge, 1939.

Singletary, Otis A. *Negro Militia and Reconstruction*. Austin, 1957.

Sitterson, J. Carlyle. *Sugar Country: The Cane Sugar Industry in the South, 1753–1950*. Lexington, 1953.

Stampp, Kenneth M. *The Era of Reconstruction, 1865–1877*. New York, 1965.

———. *The Imperiled Union: Essays on the Background of the Civil War*. New York, 1980.

Taylor, Joe Gray. *Louisiana Reconstructed, 1863–1877*. Baton Rouge, 1974.

Taylor, William R. *Cavalier and Yankee: The Old South and American National Character*. New York, 1963.

Thomas, Emory M. *The Confederate Nation: 1861–1865*. New York, 1979.

Trelease, Allen W. *White Terror: The Ku Klux Klan Conspiracy and Southern Reconstruction*. New York, 1971.

Vincent, Charles. *Black Legislators in Louisiana During Reconstruction*. Baton Rouge, 1976.

Warner, Ezra J. *Generals in Blue: Lives of the Union Commanders*. Baton Rouge, 1964.

White, Howard A. *The Freedman's Bureau in Louisiana*. Baton Rouge, 1970.

Winters, John D. *The Civil War in Louisiana*. Baton Rouge, 1963.

Woodman, Harold D. *King Cotton and His Retainers: Financing & Marketing the Cotton Crop of the South, 1800–1925*. Lexington, 1968.

Wooster, Ralph A. *The Secession Conventions of the South*. Princeton, 1962.

ARTICLES

Baggett, James Alex. "Origins of Early Texas Republican Party Leadership." *Journal of Southern History*, XL (August, 1974), 441–54.

Berlin, Ira. "The Structure of the Free Negro Caste in the Antebellum United States." *Journal of Social History*, IX (Spring, 1976), 297–318.

Berry, Mary F. "Negro Troops in Blue and Gray: The Louisiana Native Guards, 1861–1863." *Louisiana History*, VIII (Spring, 1967), 165–90.

Binning, F. Wayne. "Carpetbaggers' Triumph: The Louisiana State Elections of 1868." *Louisiana History*, XIV (Winter, 1973), 21–39.

Burton, Vernon. "Race and Reconstruction: Edgefield County, South Carolina." *Journal of Social History*, XII (Fall, 1978), 31–56.

Chenault, William W., and Reinders, Robert C. "The Northern-born Community of New Orleans in the 1850s." *Journal of American History*, LI (September, 1964), 232–47.

Christian, Marcus B. "The Theory of the Poisoning of Oscar J. Dunn." *Phylon*, VI (Fall, 1945), 254–66.

Clark, Robert T., Jr. "The New Orleans German Colony in the Civil War." *Louisiana Historical Quarterly*, XX (October, 1937), 990–1015.

———. "Reconstruction and the New Orleans German Colony." *Louisiana Historical Quarterly*, XXIII (April, 1940), 501–24.

Connor, William P. "Reconstruction Rebels: The *New Orleans Tribune* in Post-War Louisiana." *Louisiana History*, XXI (Spring, 1980), 159–81.

Davis, Donald W. "Ratification of the Constitution of 1868: Record of Votes." *Louisiana History*, VI (Summer, 1965), 301–305.

Delatte, Carolyn E. "The St. Landry Riot: A Forgotten Incident of Reconstruction Violence." *Louisiana History*, XVII (Winter, 1976), 41–49.

De Verges, Edwin X. "Honorable John T. Monroe: The Confederate Mayor of New Orleans." *Louisiana Historical Quarterly*, XXXIV (January, 1951), 25–34.

Dew, Charles B. "The Long Lost Returns: The Candidates and Their Totals in Louisiana's Secession Election." *Louisiana History* X (Fall, 1969), 353–69.

———. "Who Won the Secession Election in Louisiana?" *Journal of Southern History*, XXXVI (February, 1970), 18–32.

Everett, Donald E. "Ben Butler and the Louisiana Native Guards, 1861–1862." *Journal of Southern History*, XXIV (May, 1958), 202–17.

———. "Demands of the New Orleans Free Colored Population for Political Equality, 1862–1865." *Louisiana Historical Quarterly*, XXXVIII (April, 1955), 43–64.

Grosz, Agnes Smith. "The Political Career of Pinckney Benton Stewart Pinchback." *Louisiana Historical Quarterly*, XXVII (April, 1944), 527–612.

Harlan, Louis R. "Desegregation in New Orleans Public Schools during Reconstruction." *American Historical Review*, LXVII (April, 1962), 663–75.

Harris, William C. "The Creed of the Carpetbaggers: The Case of Mississippi." *Journal of Southern History*, XL (May, 1974), 199–224.

Hennessey, Melinda Meek. "Race and Violence in Reconstruction New Orleans: The 1868 Riot." *Louisiana History*, XX (Winter, 1979), 77–91.

Hume, Richard L. "Carpetbaggers in the Reconstruction South: A Group Portrait of Outside Whites in the 'Black and Tan' Constitutional Conventions." *Journal of American History*, LXIV (September, 1977), 313–30.

Johnson, Manie White. "The Colfax Riot of April, 1873." *Louisiana Historical Quarterly*, XIII (July, 1930), 391–427.

Kolchin, Peter. "Scalawags, Carpetbaggers, and Reconstruction: A Quantitative Look at Southern Congressional Politics, 1868–1872." *Journal of Southern History*, XLV (February, 1979), 61–76.

Lestage, Oscar H., Jr. "The White League in Louisiana and Its Participation in Reconstruction Riots." *Louisiana Historical Quarterly*, XVIII (July, 1935), 615–95.

Lowrey, Walter McGeehee. "The Political Career of James Madison Wells." *Louisiana Historical Quarterly*, XXXI (October, 1948), 995–1123.

McLure, Mary Lilla. "The Elections of 1860 in Louisiana." *Louisiana Historical Quarterly*, IX (October, 1926), 601–702.

Perkins, A. E. "Oscar James Dunn." *Phylon*, IV (Spring, 1943), 105–21.

———. "Some Negro Officers and Legislators in Louisiana." *Journal of Negro History*, XIV (October, 1929), 523–28.

Price, John Milton. "Slavery in Winn Parish." *Louisiana History*, VIII (Spring, 1967), 137–48.

Rankin, David C. "The Impact of the Civil War on the Free Colored Community of New Orleans." *Perspectives in American History*, XI (1977–1978), 379–416.

———. "The Origins of Black Leadership in New Orleans During Reconstruction." *Journal of Southern History*, XL (August, 1974), 417–40.

Reinders, Robert C. "The Churches and the Negro in New Orleans, 1850–1860." *Phylon*, XXII (Spring, 1961), 241–48.

———. "The Decline of the New Orleans Free Negro in the Decade Before the Civil War." *Journal of Mississippi History*, XXIV (April, 1962), 88–98.

———. "The Free Negro in the New Orleans Economy, 1850–1860." *Louisiana History*, VI (Summer, 1965), 273–85.

———. "New England Influences on the Formation of Public Schools in New Orleans." *Journal of Southern History*, XXX (May, 1964), 181–95.

Reynolds, Donald E. "The New Orleans Riot of 1866, Reconsidered." *Louisiana History*, V (Winter, 1964), 5–27.

Russ, William A., Jr. "Disfranchisement in Louisiana (1862–70)." *Louisiana Historical Quarterly*, XVIII (July, 1935), 555–80.

Scroggs, Jack B. "Carpetbagger Constitutional Reform in the South Atlantic States, 1867–1868." *Journal of Southern History*, XXVII (November, 1961), 473–93.

Shugg, Roger A. "A Suppressed Co-operationist Protest Against Secession." *Louisiana Historical Quarterly*, XIX (January, 1936), 199–203.

Simpson, Amos E., and Baker, Vaughan. "Michael Hahn: Steady Patriot." *Louisiana History*, XIII (Summer, 1972), 229–52.

Tregle, Joseph G., Jr. "Thomas J. Durant, Utopian Socialism, and the Failure of Presidential Reconstruction in Louisiana." *Journal of Southern History*, XLV (November, 1979), 485–512.

Tunnell, Ted. "Free Negroes and the Freedmen: Black Politics in New Orleans During the Civil War." *Southern Studies*, XIX (Spring, 1980), 5–28.

———. "The Negro, the Republican Party, and the Election of 1876 in Louisiana." *Louisiana History*, VII (Spring, 1966), 101–16.

Vandal, Gilles. "The Origins of the New Orleans Riot of 1866, Revisited." *Louisiana History*, XXII (Spring, 1981), 135–65.

Williams, T. Harry. "The Louisiana Unification Movement of 1873." *Journal of Southern History*, XI (August, 1945), 349–69.

Unpublished Theses and Dissertations

Binning, Francis Wayne. "Henry Clay Warmoth and Louisiana Reconstruction." Ph.D. dissertation, University of North Carolina, 1969.

Campbell, Clara L. "The Political Life of Louisiana Negroes, 1865–1890." Ph.D. dissertation, Tulane University, 1971.

Everett, Donald Edward. "Free Persons of Color in New Orleans, 1803–1865." Ph.D. dissertation, Tulane University, 1952.

Jones, James Howard. "The Members of the Louisiana Legislature of 1868: Images of 'Radical Reconstruction' in the Deep South." Ph.D. dissertation, Washington State University, 1975.

Leavens, Finnian Patrick. "*L'Union* and the *New Orleans Tribune* and Louisiana Reconstruction." M.A. thesis, Louisiana State University, 1966.

McTigue, Geraldine Mary. "Forms of Racial Interaction in Louisiana, 1860–1880." Ph.D. dissertation, Yale University, 1975.

Mills, Wynona Gillmore. "James Govan Taliaferro (1798–1876): Louisiana Unionist and Scalawag." M.A. thesis, Louisiana State University, 1968.

Odom, Edwin Dale. "Louisiana Railroads, 1830–1880: A Study of State and Local Aid." Ph.D. dissertation, Tulane University, 1961.

Shoalmire, Jimmy G. "Carpetbagger Extraordinary: Marshall Harvey Twitchell, 1840–1905." Ph.D. dissertation, Mississippi State University, 1969.

Wetta, Frank Joseph. "The Louisiana Scalawags." Ph.D. dissertation, Louisiana State University, 1978.

Index